The Emergence of
a Binational Israel

The Emergence of a Binational Israel

The Second Republic in the Making

EDITED BY

Ilan Peleg and Ofira Seliktar

Westview Press
BOULDER, SAN FRANCISCO, & LONDON

Westview Special Studies on the Middle East

This Westview softcover edition is printed on acid-free paper and bound in softcovers that carry the highest rating of the National Association of State Textbook Administrators, in consultation with the Association of American Publishers and the Book Manufacturers' Institute.

Published in 1989 in the United States of America by Westview Press, Inc., 5500 Central Avenue, Boulder, Colorado 80301, and in the United Kingdom by Westview Press, Inc., 13 Brunswick Centre, London WC1N 1AF, England

Library of Congress Cataloging-in-Publication Data
The Emergence of a binational Israel: the second republic in the making
/edited by Ilan Peleg and Ofira Seliktar.
    p.   cm.—(Westview special studies on the Middle East)
Includes index.
ISBN 0-8133-7528-2
1. Israel—Politics and government.   2. Palestinian Arabs—Israel—
Politics and government.   3. Jewish-Arab relations—1973-   .
I. Peleg, Ilan, 1944–   . II. Seliktar, Ofira. III. Title:
Binational Israel.   IV. Series.
DS126.5.E48   1989
320.95694—dc19   88-38580
                                                                                  CIP

Printed and bound in the United States of America

10   9   8   7   6   5   4   3   2   1

To the next generation:

Gil and Talia Peleg
Dror and Yaron Seliktar

Contents

PART 3
INTERNATIONAL IMPLICATIONS OF A
BINATIONAL ISRAEL

Preface

This book deals with the State of Israel as a binational political entity. The book's eleven chapters analyze different dimensions of the increasingly binational reality of Israel, but most importantly, the authors attempt to offer a new conceptual framework for the analysis of Israel's central political dilemma. Binationalism is approached as a complicated political reality, a psycho-attitudinal state of mind, and as a legal condition. The various authors offer analyses of binationalism in the past, in Eretz Israel/Palestine of the mandatory era, and in other periods and places; they spend even more time on the uneasy binationalist reality of the present and examine in some detail future binational scenarios. Above all, this book is trying to shed light on the dynamics of an *emerging* binational polity.

Most of the chapters in this volume—all of which were prepared as original contributions especially for the book—focus on patterns of political behavior in Israel today in an atmosphere of continuing crisis, growing fragmentation and polarization, and important changes in the country's domestic and international environment. Special attention is given by the authors to the actual involvement of Israeli Arabs in the political process as well as to the subjective, perceptual dimension of this central aspect of Israeli politics. Other chapters dwell in great detail on the changing role of the Israeli army in meeting the state's challenges as defined by those who are at the helm of power and on the economy of the binational Israel; projections are offered regarding potential developments in the future.

The last part of this volume deals with the international implications of Israeli binationalism, with specific focus on its impact on the neighboring Arab states and on the future relations between the United States and Israel. The impact of the Arab uprising in the West Bank and the Gaza Strip on the future of Israel is touched upon by many of the contributors as well.

A number of individuals assisted us in preparing this volume. Susan McEachern of Westview was an efficient, conscientious editor. Ilan Peleg was assisted by Keith Abouchar and Mark Basurto and Ofira Seliktar by Lisa Moore. These individuals carried out their tasks over and above the call of duty, as did Ruth Panovec, Julia McDonald, and Rose Miller, who typed the manuscript's many versions. Dr. Paul Schlueter read some of the chapters and offered useful comments. Professor Lewis W. Snider offered us valuable comments that also improved the quality of this volume.

These are not easy times for the people living between the Mediterranean Sea and the Jordan River in a country called by some Eretz Israel and by others Palestine. We hope that this book may contribute in at least a modest manner to the solution of the area's enormous problems. It is with this hope that the editors dedicate this volume to the next generation, their children Gil and Talia Peleg, and Dror and Yaron Seliktar. May they grow up to witness a holy land more in peace with itself and with its neighbors.

Ilan Peleg
Ofira Seliktar

PART 1

Binationalism as a Concept and as a History

1

Conceptualizing Binationalism: State of Mind, Political Reality, or Legal Entity?

Ofira Seliktar

In February 1896, the first edition of Theodor Herzl's book *Der Judenstaat* (The Jewish State) appeared in Vienna. The creation of Israel some fifty years later made Herzl's dream a reality. Yet four wars and forty years since its founding the national character of Israel is increasingly being debated.

At the core of the debate is the balance between the group and the territorial membership of Israel. The traditional socialist Zionist ideology has always emphasized the supremacy of a Jewish uninational state over any territorial consideration. The rival New Zionist belief system, composed of neo-revisionist and national-religious ideologies, has advocated the territorial integrity of Eretz Israel.[1] When Likud came to power in 1977, New Zionism became the ideological standard bearer of the Second Republic. Subsequent efforts to implement the vision of Greater Israel galvanized the Israelis into awareness that eventually a large Palestinian population in the occupied territories would turn Israel into a binational state. This was coupled with the realization that the increase in the number of Israeli Arabs was bound to have an important effect on the Jewish state, irrespective of the fate of the territories.

In fact, the discussion on a uninational as opposed to a binational state has rapidly emerged as the most important legitimization debate in Israeli society. An understanding of the extreme complexity of this discourse requires a theoretical discussion of the legitimization process of nationalism. Broadly conceived, a debate on the national character of the state will focus on the question of who are the members and what is the territory. The criteria for group membership are based on such factors as kinship, language, culture, or religion. These traits form the basis of the "admission policy" of a group and are used to grant membership. The criteria for claiming territorial expanses can range from the very instrumental to the sentimental-normative. The former is based on perception of the territorial tract as property, resource, or military asset, whereas in the latter the expanse is perceived as the center of the moral-religious order of the group. In between is the most common perception of the territory as the ancestral home of the group.[2] Sovereignty in this context refers to the exclusive rights of members to legitimize the criteria used to define the membership and territorial boundary of the group.

Focusing on these two major dimensions of state legitimacy serves to illustrate the extremely complex and dynamic process through which more primordial groups evolve into a nation state. In ideal situations, in which a fairly homogeneous group is settled in a relatively stable ancestral territory, tension can nevertheless be produced over principles of inclusion and exclusion of new members. Wars, foreign conquest or internal upheaval can open new questions of national or territorial membership. Irredentism, border wars and tensions between ethnic groups unable to agree upon a common national definition of their state are all expressions of difficulties and failure in the legitimization debate.

Even in cases in which a national state has evolved, the presence of ethnic challenge groups may belie its uninational character. When such a challenge is successful a national state must transform itself into a binational one or breakup. Unfortunately, the vast literature on binationalism does not offer a clear perspective on how a binational state is defined and who should define it. One complex question is the difference between a uninational state with an ethnic minority and a binational state, which requires identifying those threshold conditions which transform an ethnic minority into a nation. While the literature offers many perspectives—historical, legal, and political—it is quite clear that at a very basic level the conversion of an ethnic group into a nation hinges upon the psychological dimension of self-identity. National self-identification is essentially a private, individual thought and value which must be translated into political reality. Political processes and institutions render this act of psychological preference collectively meaningful. While not strictly sequential, political reality, i.e. structure and process, is a complementary dimension of binationalism because it reflects the actual power struggle between the superordinate majority and the challenge group over the ultimate definition of the state. Moreover, the outcome of this struggle will determine the legal framework of the coexistence of the two national groups. Only when this conflict is amicably settled, does political binationality become a legal entity. In this sense, legal binationalism is the final dimension in the long process of transforming a state from a unitary entity into a statutory binational state. When it is not amicably settled, the challenge group would strive to create a separate state.

This chapter will analyze the three pertinent dimensions of binationalism—pyschological self identification, political reality and the legal structure as they apply to Israel.

Binationalism as a State of Mind

There are numerous factors which can trigger the conversion of a group's self-identity into nationhood. In one common pattern a tribal society would evolve toward nationhood by consolidating control over territory and establishing a central authority system—both necessary state prerequisites. In less clear-cut cases, ethnic minorities whose link with their historical nation lay in either the distant or the near past have been known to embark upon the psychological process of self-definition as a nation. In still some other instances, ethnic groups which were members of an extant nation but were never defined as a national group, proceeded to evolve a national self identity. In the last case, the existence of a separate language, culture, history or religion can facilitate the process of self definition but is not entirely necessary for an act of psychological self-assertion. In one of the more famous and rapid cases of nationalist assertion, the Moslems of India opted to become the separate nation of Pakistan, promoting one observer to remark that "the case of Pakistan came close to sustaining the theory that a nation is whatever can get away with establishing its claim to being one."[3]

Applied to Israel, this psychological dimension shows some interesting patterns. Herzl's greatest contribution to Zionism was to legitimize the claim that the Jews are not merely an ethnic group but a nation. Acting upon this new self identity, Jews emigrated to Palestine in order to claim statehood for their group. Since the Jews had been a historical nation and had a religious and ethnic culture which preserved national symbols throughout the ages, it was relatively easy to progress from merely ethnic to national self-perception. Years of semi-autonomy under the Mandate, as well as the clash, somtimes violent, with the Arab inhabitants ensured that when the state was formally established in 1948, this national self-identity had become already firmly entrenched.

The case of the Palestinians was more complex. The Arabs who lived in mandatory Palestine had never constituted a nation which could claim historical statehood in Western terms. Likewise, the territorial boundaries of the Palestinian groups had never been defined. The Pan Arab ideology, quite prevalent toward the end of the Ottoman Empire, has further detracted from the crystallization of a Palestinian self-identity. These handicaps notwithstanding, the mass Jewish immigration to Palestine acted as an important external stimulus toward generating a new Palestinian identity among the mandatory Arabs. This process was severely disrupted by the outcome of the 1948 war, but it resumed after the Israeli occupation of the territories in the Six Day War.

There were a number of reasons for the rapid evolution of Palestinian self-perceptions of nationhood. First, by 1967, the traditional foci of self-identity such as the hamullah, tribe or Arab nationalism had either eroded or lost their credibility. Second, the daily conflicts with the occupying force of Israel had stimulated a new national self-awareness. Third and most important, there was a growing number of Palestinian elites sharing the common experience of exile or refugees camps who could legitimize the national claim and interject it into the main legitimizing discourse of society. The earliest and best known is the PLO elite, but the mayors and the university intellectuals have subsequently emerged as powerful representatives of the claim to nationhood.

The Six Day War also affected the group perception of the Israeli Arabs. Abundant research in psychological self-identification has demonstrated that whereas prior to 1967 their national identity was blurred and fragmented, a decade after the war the label Palestinian was being chosen by most of the Israeli Arabs to describe their national identity. Moreover, already in 1976, a group of Arab mayors suggested that they should be regarded as a nation and not merely as a minority; accordingly, Israel should be perceived as a binational state rather than a Jewish state.

Although the psychological processes which help generate a new national identity among the members of a group do not depend on any one set of legitimizing factors, three considerations are normally important. The first one is the *demographic balance between the host population and the group which aspires to nation statehood.* The larger the size of the aspiring group as a percentage of the total population, the easier it is for individual group members to adopt the national claim as part of their self-identity. The large numbers contribute to the probability of success should the group decide to act upon its desire to achieve a legal recognition of the national claim. Conversely, small groups claiming historical national ancestry may feel more inhibited in defining themselves in national terms because of the doubts about the probability of success.

In the Israeli case, there is no doubt that the demographic factors were a major catalyst in the current psychology of Palestinian national self-identification. The most recent and comprehensive study found that the number of Palestinians in the West Bank and Gaza had reached 1,363,000 in 1985, in addition to the 749,000 Israeli Arabs. The number of Jews stands at 3,500,000. Proportionally, the Jews constitute 62.5 percent of the total population of Eretz Israel as opposed to 37.5 percent for the Palestinian Arabs. A longitudinal analysis of population growth trends reveals a greater dynamic of the Palestinian demographic mass. Given a continuation of present population trends (fertility rates, mortality rates, immigration and emigration levels) the Palestinian population is projected to increase by the year 2000 to between 1.9 to 2.5 million and the number of Israeli Arabs is expected to rise to 1.2 million. The number of Jews would reach 4.2 to 4.3 million. At a 45:55 ratio parity would nearly be reached, bolstering the national claim of the Palestinians.[4]

Analysis of these trends indicates that the population growth rate of Israeli Arabs is much higher than that of Israeli Jews. Although the growth rate of Israeli Arabs has declined from an average of 44.9 in the years 1965-1969, in 1984 it was 32.3 as opposed to the comparable Jewish rate of 14.3. Again, assuming continuity, the ratio of Jews to Arabs within the Green Line will stand at 78:22 by 2020 and may reach parity in some 100 years. Even if all the occupied territories were returned, the demographic mass of Israeli Arabs would become important in articulating claims of binationality.

The second factor which facilitates national self-definition is geographical cohesion. Obviously, a group which enjoys geographical proximity finds it easier to articulate a claim to nationhood than a group whose members are territorially dispersed. The geographical proximity of the Palestinian settlements in the territories is historically continuous. In spite of twenty years of Jewish settlement, 92 percent of the inhabitants in Judea and Samaria are Arabs, in the Gaza Strip 98 percent of them are non-Jews and in the Golan Heights there is a Druze majority of 66 percent.

The geographical proximity of the Israeli Arabs has, by and large, been preserved. The vast majority of them live in the Galilee and the Triangle; central Galilee has an 80 percent Arab majority. Both the Galilee and the Triangle support large metropolitan centers which can nourish a separate economic and cultural Arab Israeli entity. Moreover, the Israeli Arabs have actually managed to broaden their territorial base by expanding into adjacent Jewish areas, both agricultural and urban. One of the newest trends is the tendency of Israeli Arabs to spread into territories which have not been previously settled by either the Arabs or the Jews, such as the Kabri-Yagur highway in the North, Vadi Arah in central Israel or Siagh region in the Negev.[5]

This geographical homogeneity has been countered by the Israeli policy of intermingling, that is, locating Jewish settlements in densely populated Arab areas. Such a policy had been used in the past by a number of binational states including Ireland in order to create a quilt-like pattern of ethnic settlements, thus avoiding partition. The emphasis here is on the number of settlements rather than on the number of inhabitants. Thus, for instance, the Israeli authorities have created some 240 Jewish settlements in Judea and Samaria between 1974 and 1986. The policy of Jewish settlements in the Galilee, over the years, has produced some notable achievements like the town of Carmiel and a dozen smaller centers. However, it is not clear whether intermingling without altering the demographic balance can detract from the psychological process of national self definition of a group.

The third element which plays an important part in the process of national self-identification of an ethnic group is *the amount of commonality it shares with the superordinate society*. Among the indices of commonality are ethnic homogeneity, language, religion, history, culture and the type and degree of economic development. When the minority group shares with the superordinated majority such commonalities as language, religion, history and culture, the claim to nationhood would be impeded. Homogeneity in type and degree of economic development would normally act to dampen any separate national description. For instance, ethnic Irish in Britain who happen to be economically well-integrated Protestants are not likely to articulate claims for separate nationhood. The Sikh case in India, though, is a notable exception to this norm. On the other hand, an ethnic group which differs on all or most of the indices would find it psychologically easier to legitimize its claim to separate nationhood.

The extremely low level of commonality between the Jews and the Arabs is well known. The Palestinians and the Israeli Jews do not share any of the common characteristics which can work for integration. Despite forty years of coexistence, the two groups have made only small inroads into a fusion of identities, retaining most of their separate ethnic and religious characteristics. Whether by design or default, geographical isolation and patterns of economic development have actually enhanced the potential for nationhood claims. This argument is in line with the theories of ethnic pluralism which predict that in the absence of cross cutting cleavages, ethno/national identity will come to dominate other forms of labelling.

The psychological dimension of binationalism whereby two or more ethnic groups define themselves as nations does not lead to an immediate political or legal transformation of a state into a binational or multinational entity or breaking up of state. The most obvious reason impeding such a transformation pertains to the fact that claims to national legitimacy are normally articulated amidst intense conflict between the superordinate and subordinate groups. Most of the conflict is taken up by efforts of one group to delegitimize the claims of the rival group.

Since the Jews were the first to articulate a claim to nationhood in Palestine, they were also forced to define their perception of the status of the Palestinians. Historical research shows that the Jews were neither unanimous nor consistent in their attempts to define who the Palestinian Arabs were. When the debate reopened in 1967, a somewhat similar pattern emerged. Initially, the official Israeli position was that the West Bank and Gaza Palestinians were not a legitimate national group, but rather a part of a fairly amorphous Pan-Arab nation. This position was apparently reflected in the often-cited question of Golda Meir, "who are the Palestinians?"

However, as the perception of Palestinian nationality has increased, Israeli society has begun to redefine its position. Interestingly enough, this process of reformulation has not reproduced the pre-1948 political lines of thinking. Instead, the new Israeli right has supported the claim that the Palestinians are a legitimate nation whose right to a separate state should be realized within the territorial boundaries of Jordan. The logical corollary of this argument is obvious. Jordan does not have a legitimate right to statehood, because, according to the Israeli right, the Jordanians have never constituted a legitimate national group. Rather, the state and its ruling monarch are an arbitrary creation of the British. This stand was summed up in the dictum 'Jordan is Palestine' and was based on the statistical reality of Jordan, where the Palestinians are already a dominant demographic majority.

The small Israeli left, like the right, recognized that the Palestinians are a legitimate national group entitled to a separate state. Yet the left wing advocacy took a diametrically opposed stand on the territorial issue. Accordingly, the Palestinian state should coincide with the boundaries of the West Bank and Gaza Strip. Significantly, the group completely abandoned the historical proposals of some leftist movements such as *Brit Shalom* and *Hashomer Hatzair* to establish a Jewish Palestinian Federation.

Perhaps the most interesting change took place in the policy of the moderate Socialist Zionist camp represented by the Labor's followers. The current Labor elite moved closer to both the left- and the right-wing advocacies by recognizing that the Palestinians are a legitimate national group within the limits of historic Palestine. On the question of territory, though, Labor seems considerably closer to the right-wing. The party refused to recognize the right of the Palestinians to establish a second Arab state within the limits of historical Palestine. In the past four or five years, Labor adopted the 'Jordan is Palestine' theory which has also become the official policy of the Israeli government.

Jewish recognition of the Palestinians as a national group has never been extended to Israeli Arabs. The 1976 suggestion by several Arab mayors that Israel should be considered a binational rather than a uninational Jewish state was unanimously rebuffed. A *Jerusalem Post* editorial emphasized that the Arabs in Israel should be given rights as individual citizens but would never be recognized as a national group.[6] Subsequent efforts to argue in terms of demography, i.e., that one of every six Israelis is an Arab, have not changed the official Israeli view. There is a virtual Jewish consensus that the status of the Green Line Arabs does not necessitate a change from a Jewish to a binational state.

Palestinian delegitimization of the Jewish national group has been more comprehensive. Ever since the arrival of the first Jewish immigrants in Palestine at the turn of the century, they were regarded as individual settlers. The subsequent PLO advocacy does not regard the Jews as a national group but as individuals of a particular religious faith. As such, they do not have any national rights of any kind in any part of Palestine.

This delegitimizing philosophy is reflected in the model of settler colonialism popular in PLO circles. According to this model, Jews, like other Europeans, have settled in Asia because of the then prevalent colonial norms rather than legitimate national rights. Consistent with this line of reasoning, the advocacy has denied all Jews who came to Palestine since the turn of century and their native-born descendants the right to stay in Palestine. Indeed, one of PLO's earlier conditions for conflict resolution was to demand that all Israelis who originated in the immigration waves should return to their countries of origin. Moreover, as far as the PLO was concerned, the creation of the state of Israel was null and void. Up until now, in the official parlance of the organization, Israel was not a state but a Zionist entity.

Although the settler colonialism model has never been officially abandoned, more moderate Palestinians are inclined to accept the legitimacy of the Jews as a national group entitled to some state rights in historical Palestine. Ironically, compared to the totally exclusionary implication of the settler colonialism model, the more recent "Zionism is racism" thinking is an indicator that the Palestinians have come to recognize the Jews as a native, albeit racist national group. There has also been some change in the moderate elite's perception of the legitimate borders of the Jewish state. Whereas previous demands involved the 1947 Proposed Partition border, the more recent advocacy assumes that the Green Line is a more realistic proposition.

The Israeli Arabs, through normally identified with the Palestinian cause, have always differed on the issue of Jewish legitimacy. Whether forced to accept Israel as an immutable reality or convinced because of their citizenship, Green Line Arabs have been fairly consistent in accepting the legitimacy of the Jewish state. This acceptance has been demonstrated in numerous surveys spanning some three decades. For instance, a comprehensive study by Smooha did not find support for the expectation that the Six Day War would cause the Israeli Arabs to delegitimize the Israeli state and support the advocacy of a Greater Palestinian state. On the contrary, the data suggests quite conclusively that the Israeli Arabs view themselves as Palestinians only in the broadest ethnic sense of the term with little consequence for their current status as citizen of the Jewish state.[7]

The mutual process of forming claims of acceptance or delegitimization cannot be fully understood without considering the impact of the international system. Both the status quo and the challenge group try to enlist the support of the international order in enhancing legitimacy claims and delegitimizing the opponents. Normally, the status quo group enjoys an advantage over challengers because of extant recognition enjoyed through diplomatic ties and membership in the United Nations and other international organizations. Yet national challenge groups can make inroads into this pool of legitimacy. Sometimes they obtain a status equivalent to that of the host society or even manage to induce members of the international society to delegitimize the superordinate group. In some extreme cases such as South Africa, the regime is totally rejected by the international system.

Both the Jews and the Palestinians have relied very heavily on outside legitimizing support. The Jews achieved some success when they were recognized as a national entity though the Balfour Declaration. The subsequent UN Partition Plan acknowledges their right to a state as well. The Palestinians, who have enjoyed considerable recognition as a national group, forfeited the international acknowledgement accorded by the UN Partition Plan but have rebounded after the 1967 war. At the height of Palestinian popularity in the 1970s, the PLO attained the status of an observer in the UN as well as semi-diplomatic recognition by a large number of countries. In the comparable period, many Communist and Third World countries delegitimized Israel by breaking off diplomatic relations with the Jewish state. Overall, the international system has facilitated the articulation of Palestinian legitimization claims.

International input has not readily extended to the periodic attempts of the Israeli Arabs to move Israel in a binational direction. This reflects considerable reluctance of the international system to interfere in the domestic affairs of its states. Since ethnic conflict is prevalent in many countries, the interational system is constantly innundated with claims of ethnic groups for autonomy or even secession. This reluctance exists even when ethnic demands result in an exceptionally long or brutal struggle such as in the case of Northern Ireland, the Basques in Spain or Biafra's quest to leave Nigeria. Needless to say, low key challenge groups such as Israeli Arabs attract much less attention internationally. At the same time, a dramatic change in the demographic balance of the Jews and Arabs may alter this historical reticence and provoke an active demand of the international system to create a binational state in Israel.

Whatever the actual inputs from concrete factors like demography or international support, they do not detract from the broad analytical argument that binationalism is first of all a state of mind. Psychological definition is a necessary condition for any binational reality to emerge, for if nondominant ethnic groups were willing either to completely assimilate into the identity of the superordinate group or were content with individual/civic rights, the concept of a national state would never be challenged. In this sense then, Israel within the Green Line has been a binational state since 1968; the presence of the Palestinians since 1967 has only amplified the psychological dimension of binationalism.

Israel and the Political Reality of Binationalism

In spite of the psychological binationalism of the Israeli Arabs, the political reality of Israel prior to 1967 cannot be considered binational. One reason for the lack of political manifestation of binational sentiments was the simple arithmetic of democracy. Even in the most just democratic system, under normal majority rule, political outcomes are inevitably a majority alternative. In other words, the statistical majority defines the rules of the national game. Under these circumstances, the most Israeli Arabs could have had hoped for was equal treatment as individuals. Challenging the Jewish character of the state was beyond the democratic means of the minority, unless they could claim group rights.

The second reason pertains to the more complex reality of what Lustick has called the systems of controls under which the minority lived. Partially designed by Israel and partially generated by the cultural, religious and ethnic characteristics of the Israeli Arabs, the system of controls explains how a superordinate group can dominate a subordinate group through a mixture of inducive and coercive means. The system of controls consists of segmentation, dependence and cooptation. Segmentation refers to efforts to isolate and fragment the subordinate group, dependence describes the enforced reliance of subordinate group on political and economic goods provided by the dominant group and cooptation implies the use of side payments to the subordinate elite for the purpose of internal policing and surveillance The policy of controls prevented the Arabs from articulating ethnic/national preferences and at the same time blocked any effort to create political mechanisms which could promote a more binational definition of the state. The Military Administration was created in 1950 in order to implement the system of control.[8]

As long as the survival and security concerns of the new state dominated public opinion, internal Israeli criticism of the Military Administration was marginal. But as the security imperatives began to recede, the Administration was modified and finally abolished in 1965. Although Jewish patrimonial rights were still considerable, the dissolution of the military government bolstered the civic realm of the state where Jews and Arabs would share rights as citizens. The mixture of patrimonial and civic rights constitutes the basis of Israel's sectoral democracy. Unlike the Herrenvolk democracy of South Africa, *sectoral democracy* extends full civic rights to the minority but reserves other rights only to the patrimonial majority. The disbursement of still other rights is based on service. For instance, the Israeli Arabs have a right to vote, but only the Jews are entitled to immigration. Many other rights and privileges are based on military service and thus are restricted to Jews and Druze Arabs.

As a result of the 1967 war Israeli Arabs have turned into a national challenge group. Such a transformation took place because *Arab ethnicity became an increasing source of political choice for the group members*. It is important to emphasize the logic and consequences of this change. In a uninational democratic state, the rules of the "authoritative allocation of values" and, ultimately, the resources of a society are dictated by the majority. A minority member can best prosper politically by fitting into this allocative scheme which obviously entails that he abstain from framing his choices in ethnic terms. However, at a certain point minority members become convinced that ethnically defined choices would benefit them more by leading to change in the extant rules for allocating values. At such a juncture the primordial community becomes a terminal community, that is, it commands the ultimate loyalty of the members and dictates their political choices. Thus, whereas previously an Arab citizen would choose to collaborate with the Israeli authorities as the best way to secure his interest, in the new scheme of things fighting for national rights has become an acceptable and even more profitable alternative.

Once political choices were framed in national/ethnic terms, Israeli Arabs proceeded to evolve the organizational means for challenging the uninationality of the Israeli state. The most important effort in this strategy has been the establishment of purely Arab or Arab-dominated political parties. Following the failed attempt to incorporate the El Ard party, the Arab elite has focused on the Communist Rakah party as well as on the newer Progressive List for Peace. The thinking behind this strategy is that binationalism can be realized through the relatively straight-forward use of the democratic system in Israel. The democratic calculus of the Israeli Arabs is highly justifiable, given the nature of Israel's simple proportional representation and coalition government. Under certain coalition outcomes, the Arab vote would be amplified beyond its actual numerical strength. For instance, in a Likud-Labor stalemate, one side might strike a deal with Arab oriented parties. Alternatively, the Jewish parties may become increasingly solicitous of the Arab vote.

Another important organizational tool for articulating binational demand is various pressure group organizations. Modeled on the Committee for the Defense of Arab Lands, formed in 1975, interest groups have been increasingly successful in challenging primordial Jewish criteria for value allocation and resource distribution. Among the most active interest groups have been the various student organizations whose national board has spearheaded the struggle for rights to Arabs as a national group rather than as individuals. Other groups such as the radical Ibn-el-Bilad have actually gone beyond the binational state idea by demanding the right of sovereign self determination for Israeli Arabs. Although this advocacy does not enjoy a broad support, the Ibn-el-Bilad activities have helped to sharpen the scope of the national demands of the community within the framework of a potential binational state in Israel.

Increased organization of Israel's Arabs is an outcome of a more sophisticated understanding of the modes of political struggle possible in the Israeli democratic system. The primary focus is on electoral, pressure and protest activity, but there is also a major effort to challenge the system through the country's legal system. The use of confrontational violence and terrorism advocated by the radical fringe elites such as Ibn-el-Bilad has so far been rejected by the mainstream community. The underlying logic of the current thrust of the minority is that working within the framework of the democratic system would enlarge the civic realm of the state at the expense of the patrimonial Jewish dimension. Conversely, using confrontational violence would undermine the credibility of Israeli Arab quest for civic equality as well as obliterate the gains which had already been achieved.

The debate about the proper modes of activity has also led to a better articulation of the political goals of the Israeli Arab community. Theoretically defined, they amount to a demand that the collectively provided goods should be distributed on the basis of equitable individual criteria. The two criteria which are normally applied in the case of plural societies are *jointness of supply and allocation* and *nonexcludability*. The former entails that consumption by some members of the society should not preclude the consumption by others and the latter dictates that individuals should not be excluded for any reason from consumption and allocation of goods. The criteria of jointness of supply and nonexcludability are normally interpreted only in *civic*, i.e., individual terms.[9] Yet a careful analysis of this formula reveals that in a society with a superordinate majority and an ethnonational minority, the only way to achieve equality involves the recognition of group, rather than individual, rights. Since such a conclusion flies against the commonly held argument that the Israeli Arabs can achieve individual equitability in a civicly reconstructred Israel, it bears further elaboration.

An important part of the collective existence of society is defined in symbolic terms and involves national elements such as language, culture and religious heritage. Any partaking of symbolic collective goods thus mandates an equitable participation in the symbolic realm of a state. Even if the Israeli sectoral democracy is redefined in such a way that the distribution of nonsymbolic collective goods is not contingent upon Jewish patrimony or national service, the Israeli Arabs would be deprived of equality in the symbolic realm. Moreover, symbolic elements such as language have an important impact on the structure of opportunity and thus the individual's chance of success in a plural society. Under these circumstances, the only way to assure a truly equitable existence for Israeli Arabs as individuals would require the elimination of the Jewish character of the state. What is a suitable civic substitute for Hebrew is of course a moot question in view of the fact that no state can exist without some kind of tribally derived symbolic realm. Since the Arabs and the Jews have shared almost no cultural commonalities, the real meaning of the civic state formula is actually a binational state, with equality for Hebrew and Arabic.

The logical requirements of jointness of supply/allocation and nonexcludability, though not immediately obvious, have already surfaced in some advocacy themes of the Israeli Arabs. They repudiate the Jewish and Zionist character of Israel and the underlying assumption that Israel is the historical continuation of Jewish statehood and the exclusive patrimony of the Jewish people. They object that virtually all the state symbols—language, culture, holidays and national heroes—are Jewish. They argue against the monopoly of the Hebrew language in the daily affairs of the state. They strongly criticize the mechanisms for implementing the Zionist mission of Israel such as the Law of Return and the disproportional allocation of resources to stimulate Jewish immigration and development.

These themes generate a clear operational imperative for the creation of a binational state. The rationale for the proposed binationalism is that Israel is not only the historic continuity of the Jewish state in antiquity but also of the Arab community in Palestine. As a result, the state of Israel is seen as a cojoint patrimony of the Jews and the Green Line Palestinians. The binational rationale also mandates a more equitable sharing in state symbols whereby the Arabic language and other cultural elements would undermine the Jewish hegemony. Equally important, the Law of Return and other Jewish mission tools of the state, like the Jewish Agency, would be either abolished or matched on a one to one basis with mechanisms to promote Arab well-being.

The blueprint for binational revision which stems from the ethnonational preferences of challenge group members is inevitably difficult to implement because of the uninational preferences of the majority. The conflict between the superordinate and the challenge groups is an important part of the evolving binational reality. The exact nature and dimensions of the binational struggle are not easy to predict as there are many scripts available, reflecting the historical and cultural peculiarities of different societies.

One possible scenerio is based on the experience of Quebec. The French speaking Canadians waged a successful campaign to transform their country into a binational state. French was granted an equal status with English and Quebec aquired control over its political and economic affairs. However, in most ethnonationally divided societies active struggle seems to be the rule.

One of the best theoretical models of ethnic conflict was developed by Rabushka and Shepsle. The model suggests that the conflict would proceed through a number of stages. An initial period of ethnic cooperation would be followed by increased ethnic salience, electoral brokerage, gerrymandering and machination and ultimately violence.[10]

An examination of the Israeli case reveals a high level of ethnonational loyalty in both majority and minority mobilized by the Arab challenge to the Jewish character of the state. Even though Jewishness and Zionism enjoy a vast consensus among the superordinate majority, there is a slowly growing realization that these assumptions cannot be taken for granted in the future. The extremely popular theme of the "demographic threat," i.e. the growth of the Palestinian and Israeli Arab populations, reflects a vague and amorphous uneasiness among Jews that they may be required to defend the uninational status of the state. At the same time, there is also a growing awareness that Israeli Arabs, a traditionally passive and quiescent minority, are bound to press for binationalism once they reach critical mass, de-mographically speaking.

The issue of how to deal with the conflicting demands of the binational reality has fragmented the Jewish group. At the risk of some simplification, the response can be classified as *universalist, pragmatist* and *particularist.* The universalists, who politically overlap with the more leftist and liberal elements in the Israeli electorate, view the commitment to democracy as superceding the Jewish imperative of the state. Although most identify with Zionism, the advocates of universalism recognize that the Jewish hegemony of the state would have to be limited in order to enhance the civic realm. More specifically, the universalists argue for the dismantling of sectoral democracy and a distribution of public goods on the basis of civic criteria. Its adherents are more vague with regard to the symbolic hegemony of Hebrew language or Jewish culture; with few exceptions, there is no evidence that the universalists have embraced true binationalism.

The pragmatists who roughly correspond to the center and moderate right, are deeply aware of the inherent tension between the Jewish and democratic nature of Israel. The pragmatic advocacy hopes to avoid the hard choices between the Jewish and universal imperatives by restructuring sectoral democracy. A perusal of the pragmatic theme reveals a mixture of proposals. One proposal hopes to strengthen coalition making and brokerage institutions in order to reward Arabs willing to define their interests in individual rather than group terms. Another proposal involves the intro-duction of a national service for Israeli Arabs, so that allocation of goods based on service rights can be extended to the minority. Still another proposal calls for an additional transfer of state power to nonstate Jewish bodies such as the Jewish Agency and the World Zionist Organization. Since these organizations were created to enhance the Jewish mission of the state they cannot be legally challenged by the Arab minority. There is also some hope for a Jewish immigration to offset the Arab demographics, although the trend in recent years has not been encouraging. Working often at cross purposes, this mixture of proposals would presumably expand the civic realm of the state without undermining its Jewish character.

The particularists, who include right wing and national religious elites, are equally aware of the tension between the Jewish nature of Israel and democracy in a demographically binational state. Yet they argue that the choice should be dictated by the religious view on the redemptive destiny of Israel. Elaborated upon by Rabbi Zvi Yehuda Kook, the theory holds that Israel's political system should be inspired by the Torah and the writings of the great twelfth century Jewish philosopher Maimonides. The Abrahamic Covenant makes Eretz Israel Jewish and Palestinian Arabs, whether within the Green Line or the West Bank, are not entitled to *collective* rights in Palestine. The Torah defines them as *ger toshav*, i.e. aliens who can receive resident rights upon recognizing the full sovereignty and hegemony of the Jewish nation.

The principles of *ger toshav* delineate the limits of democracy in Israel. Since democracy is rooted in the fundamentally secular experience of the West, bolstered by the equally Western notion of sovereignty, it is not well equipped to cope with fundamentalist religious world views. Although the New Zionist advocacy does not demand an outright transition to theocracy, particularists justify amending of the rules of democracy to incorporate the Biblical concept of legal aliens. However, New Zionist elite has not evolved a consensus with regard to the specific ways in which the Palestinian and Green Line Arabs ought to be treated.

Gush Emunim's position is that under certain demographic contingencies, the Palestinian Arabs should be officially declared as resident aliens without voting rights. They would qualify for some civil rights as individuals, but would not be able to participate in the political decision making process. The scope of these rights has never been spelled out, but Gush spokesmen have repeatedly emphasized that Arab rights to stay in the entire territory of Eretz Israel would be respected.

On the other hand, Rabbi Meir Kahane has claimed that the status of *ger toshav* does not give Palestinian Arabs, whether within the Green Line or outside it, any automatic right to stay. In this interpretation, Arab residents of the state should not be regarded as citizens; they can be either encouraged to leave on a voluntary basis or subjected to an involuntary transfer, e.g. expulsion.

The broad spectrum of Israeli responses towards the increasing Arab population within the Green Line makes predictions about the future of the binational struggle difficult. It should be recalled that the theoretical model of Rabushka and Shepsle postulates that the initial increase in Jewish and Arab salience will lead to electoral competition and alliance making across the ethnic board. But as ethnic parity will increase by the middle of the twenty first century, Israeli Jews may be forced to act upon the more extreme advocacies. Which scenario for binational political reality will prevail in the next century depends on Jewish and Arab actions and responses.

At its face value, a policy based on the universalist advocacy seem to be the best way to avert a bitter struggle between the Jews and Arabs over binationalism. Yet such a policy can only work if two critical conditions are met. One is that universalism, at the moment confined to a marginal group in Israeli politics, would become a broadly based electoral movement. This condition is not easily met given the traditional weakness of left wing causes in Israel. The second condition pertains to the Arab willingness to accept the marginal civic rights reforms offered by the universalists. The observation that demographically prominent ethnic national minorities are likely to articulate demands for binationalism, makes the probability of acceptance of a modest reform rather low. Projection data based on a study of Israeli Arabs conducted between 1976–80 can be used to buttress the conclusion. The survey found that the Arab population is divided into accomodationists who accept Israel, strongly hesitant who question the state's legitimacy and radicals who reject the present ideology and political structure of the Jewish state. Although the proportion of radicals went down from 21 to 11 percent, and the percentage of those who have reservations declined to 30 percent, those numbers still indicates a fairly large core of Arabs who are unhappy about the Jewish state.[11] If the pattern of other conflicts holds true, this hard core of radicals will normally try to defeat the moderate reforms proposed by the Jewish universalists either through internal agitation or external circumstances.

The same type of dynamic usually applies to the efforts of pragmatists to control the situation through a mixture of carefully selected individual rights and efforts to fragment the Arab community through selective incentives. At this point, the theory and practice of ethnic conflicts predicts that Arab politicians would engage in outbidding each other in order to gain a broader base of community support. When the radical rejectionists join the outbidding process, the entire political spectrum in the Arab community would move in a radical direction forcing the demise of the Jewish-Arab brokerage institutions. In order to contain the demands for a binational state, the ruling pragmatists in the Israeli government would be tempted to engage in electoral machination and gerrymandering in order to curtail the electoral power of the Arab community.

In the final stage of the process we can expect the breakdown of the democratic system, often accompanied by violence. Democracy becomes a casualty of communal politics. The militant minority is willing to adopt nondemocratic and violent means to press for a binational system. In response the superordinate majority is tempted to strengthen its power through nondemocratic means and rely on these means, including violence, in order to maintain it. Moreover, the militancy of the challenge group and especially its willingness to use violence, undermine the credibility of the universalists and pragmatists in the superordinated majority, since their legitimacy is predicated upon the moderation of the challenge group. When legitimacy is lacking, the hard-line views of the particularists are strengthened and lead to hardline electoral success.

The final stage, that of substantial Israeli Arab demographic mass, will not occur for at least another century. Nevertheless, a reference to Northern Ireland where Catholics have reached 35 percent of the population, is instructive. The Protestant majority has become increasingly insecure while the Catholic group has been prompted to articulate binational demands which impinged on the traditional Protestant hegemony in Ulster. The Protestant response of electoral machination—majoritarianism, franchise qualification and gerrymandering—has only radicalized the Catholics. In turn, the extremely brutal terrorist campaign of the IRA has radicalized the Ulster Protestants to the point where the Unionists have come to identify with the extreme advocacy of Ian Paisley and his Ulster Volunteer Force, created to become a counterpart to the IRA.

The Ulster model seems especially fitting to describe the still distant scenario of binationism within the Green Line. A different but more immediate contingency involves the Palestinians in the West Bank and Gaza Strip. Psychologically, the Six Day War was a major catalyst in the crystallization of a full-fledged Palestinian identity. As a result, the group began to seek a state in the territory of Palestine legitimized as a patrimonial heritage. Yet, the Palestinians were also forced to acknowledge that their ideal national-state faced the reality of Jewish existence in the disputed land and the historic linkage with Jordan. The issue of what should be the membership and territorial structure of Palestine has generated bitter cleavages in the body politic of the Palestinians.

One early Palestinian response was linked to the traditional hamullah-oriented politicians who sympathized with the "old order" of King Hussein. Another response was the challenge of the modernized, free floating urban elements who soon became identified with the PLO. The former, though nominally committed to the idea of the indivisibility of Palestine, have shared in the traditional political culture where the individual and the community were assigned essentially passive roles in the universal order and the situational determinant was all important. As a result, the traditional elite had long accepted the territorial compromise imposed by the 1948 war as well as the ensuing linkage with the Hashemite Kingdom. Not surprisingly, the "old order" politicians argued for a continuous territorial compromise; the occupied territories would be returned to the Palestinians, who would be free to decide on either a uninational state or a binational confederation with Jordan.

The urban elite, reflecting important generational changes in the political culture of the West Bank, were more receptive to the PLO's revolutionary sociology of radical change. Derived from a combination of Marxist and Third-World liberation ideology, the new vision was essentially concerned with society's emancipation from structures which limit the potential of individual and national growth. The PLO advocacy has included a renewed emphasis on the indivisibility of Palestinian rights, including the right to the entire territory of mandatory Palestine. In essence this is a demand for Greater Palestine. The description of the proposed state as secular and democratic has civic implications but, as was already argued before, in cases of high ethnonational heterogeneity, civic aspirations cannot solve the problem of national hegemony. To confuse the issue more, the long standing PLO argument is that the Jews are not a national group. Even if they remained in Palestine, the Israelis would only enjoy rights as individuals. The most reasonable interpretation under these circumstances is that Greater Palestine would be a uninational state enjoying a Palestinian hegemony at the symbolic level of language and culture, with the Jews apparently relegated to a second class citizenship. From this inference it follows that Jews are expected to give up any claims to group legitimacy as well as territory and assume a civic existence as individuals in the proposed Palestinian state.

Though radical by accepted standards of the international system, this advocacy has been in line with the PLO's longstanding argument that Israel is a colonial society and thus nationally transient. An early variant of colonial imagery likened Israel to the medieval crusader state in the Holy Land, an equally powerful symbol of transient sovereignty. In order to carry out the liberation mission, the PLO has decided to adopt military struggle as the main form of its political activity. Given the radical nature of the PLO's goal and the reality of occupation, the choice of a military option is not entirely surprising. In fact, military resistance has been widely used throughout history in both colonial and occupation situations.

What is more difficult to explain is the choice of terrorist strategy as a technique of armed struggle. Because of its normative connotations terrorism here is defined specifically: the use of selective but intense violence by small organizations towards the civilian population of the target country in order to force its government to adopt certain policies. While there are certain advantages in the terrorist strategy, such as the relatively small number of operators needed and the relative ease of hurting unarmed civilians, the political costs of this strategy are normally high. The moral outrage which terrorist attacks create detract from the legitimacy of the liberation struggle of the group and even casts doubt on the entire national legitimacy claim which the group strives to represent. The psychological threat which terrorism generates normally prompts citizens to petition their government for strong countermeasures. Conversely, conventional military resistance and especially peaceful resistance have proved much more effective in promoting liberation struggles.

Whatever the reasons, the PLO's choice of terrorist strategy aimed at divesting Israel of statehood has by and large shaped the terms of the political context between the two national communities. On the Israeli side, the twin threat of terrorism and politicide has hardened mass political attitudes and delegitimized a Socialist Zionist ideology whose credibility was always dependent on the existence of Palestinian moderates. For its part, the New Zionist elite have utilized the PLO extreme advocacy in order to lend credence to its longstanding argument that a territorial compromise with the Palestinians is impossible because of the zero-sum nature of the conflict.

Ironically, the initial radical advocacy of the PLO has not only failed to produce a national consensus for giving up the territories but has driven some Labor supporters into the New Zionist camp, and thus contributed to the electoral consolidation of the cleavage between the two belief systems. Once this line of conflict was drawn and hardened, subsequent Israeli perception of the PLO has generally favored the New Zionist camp. First, the PLO has never amended its National Covenant to remove clauses about the liquidation of Israel. Second, the Palestinian organization has not curtailed the use of terrorism as a major form of liberation struggle. Although some of the more "spectacular atrocity" attacks of PLO have been eliminated, Israelis have attributed it to external circumstances such as the loss of Palestinians bases in Lebanon and improved Israeli security rather than a change in intent. Though there has been persistent speculation that the PLO leadership has adopted a more compromising attitude, uncertainty remains high among Israelis.

The ambiguity surrounding the PLO's real intent, and contradictory public utterances and private assurances has generated a debate in Israel with some taking the liberal position that threats should not be taken literally as they do not necessarily lead to bellicose behavior. However, the methodologically difficult question of whether the enemy really means what he says is normally interpreted by first-hand experience. In the case of the Holocaust, the aim of Jewish genocide was clearly spelled out by Hitler and later carried out by Nazi Germany. Hence an empirical precedent exists among Israelis for expecting that verbal threats derived from ideological dreams can become operational realities. The often ferocious nature of internal struggle between the PLO factions and the civil strife in neighboring Arab countries have done little to undermine the New Zionist and indeed national Israeli perception that military defeat will result in physical extermination.

The alternative argument, that the PLO and its formal proclamations such as the National Covenant are somewhat not representative of real

Palestinian beliefs, has also run into the methodological problem of sorting out the legitimacy base of the organization. If, as the PLO and its supporters claim, the organization is the legitimate representative of the Palestinian people, then its official ideology, its written documents and the official statements of its spokesmen should be construed as reflective of the underlying belief system of the society. Indeed, recent empirical research, confirming that the PLO and its key policies such as terrorism enjoy a broad support among Palestinians in the occupied territories[12] has validated the New Zionist claim that as long as Palestinians identify with the Covenant, they should not be trusted with an independent state.

Though the debate about the interpretation of reality in the West Bank has been long and often non-obvious, its cumulative effects lead to a major paradigmatic shift, whereby the New Zionist advocacy of nonreturn of the territories has become more accepted. The electoral support for the Likud government has enabled it to carry out a massive settlement drive and resist any external efforts to negotiate with the Palestinians. At the same time the paradigmatic shift has not been strong enough to produce a wide acceptance of the New Zionist vision of Greater Israel. In its bare essence, the operational plan of Greater Israel calls for a binational state with Jewish hegemony at the symbolic and political level. Unlike the Green Line Arabs, the West Bank and Gaza Palestinians are recognized as a national group. However, the exact legal status of the Palestinians in the evolving binational state has become a subject of extremely heated debate. In order to understand the complex nature of this debate a more systematic discussion of the legal nature of binationalism is required.

Binationalism as a Legal Entity

Law is most usefully conceived of as a conjunction of patterns of legitimacy and patterns of control. Legitimacy refers to the expectation that an action is consistent with community practices and controls ensure that the community can put its legitimized actions into effect or can sanction deviations. Conceived in territorial terms, the conjunction of patterns underpins the legal concept of sovereignty.

Historically, the concept of communal sovereignty evolved out of the struggle between state and society. Once resolved in favor of the principle that the people of a given territory have the sole right to declare themselves a state, sovereignty became translated into the principle of self-determination. The principle of self determination stipulates that the "broad population" of the self-determining community would act as a sovereign in the decisionmaking involved in the process. Thus, while the nation-state is the official subject of international law, the "broad population" is implicitly recognized as the self determining agent.[13]

The principle of sovereignty does not present any major problems in homogenous societies as long as there is a consensus on the national character of the state. However, in fragmented societies the definition of "broad population" and indirectly the national character of the state is often contested. It is the outcome of this political contest that ultimately dictates the national definition of the state. That is, whether a state determines itself as uninational, binational or multinational is dependent not so much on the national composition of the "broad community" but rather on *the relative balance of power between the various segments.* For instance, Sri Lanka, the home of the Sinhalese and Tamil groups, is described as a unitary state in the constitution. The original design in Cyprus acknowledged that the island has two national communities, the Greek and the Turk, but failed to define the state as binational.

In keeping with the sovereign rights of statehood, there are few if any binding legal conventions to denote the national status of a state. In some cases the national character of a country, whether unitary, binational or multinational is defined in a constitutional-statutory manner, that is, described in the constitution. Perhaps the most clearly stated case of such statutory binationalism is Czechoslovakia. The 1952 Czechoslovak constitution recognizes the inalienable rights of the Czech and Slovak people to self-determination and declares the union to be a voluntary bond contracted by two independent and equal nations. Other states either do not have a constitution or fail to indicate whether the state is unitary or not. For example, the South African constitution mentions "all national groups" which are granted rights to use their language and develop their culture. In the Malaysian constitution, there are numerous references to groups, but no one group is designated as the bearer of the national character.

To make matters more complex, statutory recognition of consequences of constitution of multinationality is not automatically translated into an operational reality. The highly centralized Communist system would de facto suppress any expressions of statutory binationalism in the Czech constitution, or the multinational autonomy recommended in the Russian or Yugoslav constitution. Conversely, in more liberal regimes, an ethnominority may be compensated for a lack of constitutional-statutory recognition by an elaborate network of laws and privileges on the nonstatutary level. Some of these paradoxes are actually enshrined in contemporary international practice. Soviet claim to statutory multinationalism was partially accepted by the United Nations when the Ukraine and Byelorussia were given separate representation. Yet neither they, nor any of the other Soviet republics can exercise their statutory rights.

The lack of clarity surrounding the legal conventions of uninational or multinational states has been especially evident in debates about the legal status of the Jewish and Arab communities residing in mandatory Palestine.

The great historical discontinuities in patterns of settlement and ownership in the Middle East have created what is known in international law as "limitrophe communities/countries," i.e., units where no precise boundaries coinciding with legal ownership by a national group could be established. The question of identifying the legal sovereign in charge of self determination has never been answered satisfactorily. As one legal source shows, the answer to this question potentially included the mandatory authority, acting with the consent of the League of Nations, the principal allied powers, and the inhabitants of the mandate areas.

The subsequent international recognition of the Zionist Organization as a public body closely connected with the Palestine Administration cleared up part of the legal ambiguity. The next to receive recognition was the Arab Executive Committee, but the question of who would represent the Palestine people was not fully resolved because the rival Arab High Committee laid claim to self-determination. The High Committee, reacting to the UN Partition Proposal of 1947, even declared itself the Government of All Palestine with its capital in Gaza and was recognized by six governments. The Arab High Committee adhered to the principle that all of Palestine, i.e., the territory under the Mandate, belonged to the Palestinian people and that the Palestinians were the only sovereign community in the entire territory for the purpose of exercising national self-determination.

Given these ambiguities it was no accident that in 1947 the United Nations, acting in its capacity as aco-sovereign recommended a partition. Legally speaking, the Partition Proposal amounted to a plan to eliminate the "limitrophe" of Palestine in terms of boundaries and establish two communities which would serve as agents of self determination. Once legally recognized, these two agents, the Jews and the Palestinians were free to accept or reject the Partition Proposal. The two sovereign communities used their self-determining power in very different ways. The Jews accepted the idea of a small but uninational state. The Palestinians, not recognizing Jewish sovereignty, argued for the right of self-determination over the entire historical "limitrophe" of Palestine with limited concessions to individual Jews. Only the marginal Jewish Brit Shalom group proposed what amounted to a statutory binational state where the Jews and the Palestinians would share coequally, but the proposal had virtually no public appeal.

The outcome of the 1948 war had settled part of the "limitrophe." The Jews were recognized as a sovereign community for the purpose of self-determination, and Israel was recognized as an independent state. Since the new state was left with a small Arab minority, the Jewish character of Israel was largely uncontested.

In the absence of a written constitution, the only direct statutory definition of Israel as a Jewish state was included in the 1950 Law of Return which gave Jews the right to unlimited immigration and citizenship status.

A somewhat more oblique statutory reference was made in the World Zionist Organization—Jewish Agency Status Law which was promulgated by the Knesset in 1952. The law charged the WZO and its operational bodies such as the Jewish Agency and the Jewish National Fund with the function of overseeing the absorption of new immigrants. In effect, it gave Israeli Jews priority over Israeli Arabs in developing economic resources. The Jewish character of the state was further enhanced by numerous nonstatutory political provisions. Hebrew was made into the official language and Jewish holidays and religious laws provided the basis for public observance. Jewish culture and history were incorporated into the social-ization and educational processes. Morever, the new state has also reaffirmed its Jewish-Zionist mission, that is, to cultivate the Jewish culture heritage which would facilitate the ingathering of the exiles.

The status of the Arab minority in Israel was defined by the demographic and power imperatives of 1948. The first census taken after the 1948 war indicated only some 69,000 Arabs but in 1949 there was an apparent increase to 160,000, or some 12.5 percent of the Jewish population. The minority lost its economic power and family links. Yet the Arabs won some legal concessions at both the individual and group levels. The Declaration of Independence, a legally nonbinding but influential document of intent, gave Arab citizens the same democratic rights as enjoyed by the Jews. The Arabs were also recognized as an official minority and Arabic was recognized as the second official language of the country. Administratively, their status was recognized first through the short-lived Ministry of Minorities (1948–1949) and later through the creation of special Arab departments in the relevant ministries.

In contrast, the issue of who should represent the "broad community" of the Palestinians remained unresolved. The Kingdom of Transjordan (later renamed the Hashemite Kingdom of Jordan) represented part of this community. Although a Jordanian nation did not exist in a historic or ethnocultural sense, the Hashemite Kingdom, which during the Mandate had sought to lead a large Arab state, began viewing itself as embodying the Palestinian right to self-determination. Whether the Palestinians, if left to make a free decision about sovereignty, would have chosen to join the Hashemite Kingdom, is difficult to know. The fact that the traditional Palestinian elites supported King Hussein indicates that the kingdom enjoyed a certain measure of legitimacy among Palestinians.

This legitimacy was subsequently challenged by the PLO, a self-proclaimed entity which emerged from the first Palestine National Council held in Jerusalem on May 20, 1964. The PLO claimed to be the legal heir to the defunct Government of All Palestine. Jordan objected to this claim on the grounds that the majority of the Palestinians are Jordanian citizens. These contradictory claims have never been settled by the Palestinian people acting as a self determining community, but Jordan was subsequently forced to accept the PLO legitimacy claim.

Another major legal dimension left open by the 1948 war pertained to boundary demarcations between Israel and the Arab states. In the process of fighting Israel expanded its territory beyond the Partition Proposal. Judea and Samaria were occupied by Jordan and annexed in 1950; the Gaza Strip was occupied by Egypt, but was never claimed or declared part of Egyptian territory. The Armistice Agreement of 1949 had legalized the cease-fire boundaries of 1948, although there was an understanding that the borders would be finalized in a peace treaty.

The 1967 war reopened the legal questions of both Palestinian self determination and the legal status of the territories. Disappointed with the record of Arab states in achieving a homeland, Palestinians under the PLO leadership reasserted their right to constitute the "broad community" for the purpose of self-determination. Moreover, acting in its own right and as a heir of the Government of All Palestine, the PLO claimed that this right to self-determination involved the entire territory of mandatory Palestine, including Israel.

Yet these territorial demands raised the question of whether an organization calling for the dismantling of a state recognized by the international system should have a juridical status in public international law. Contemporary international practice does recognize revolutionary or liberation movements, but in most cases the realization of such sovereignty claims does not involve the annihilation of another state. The legal status of the PLO has been disputed by Israel and its allies on the grounds that the PLO is not entitled to represent the "broad community" of Palestinians because the fulfillment of its legal claim would amount to the politicide of a member state of the international system. Conversely, the Government of Israel has expressed its willingness to negotiate with either the Hashemite Kingdom or with Palestinian representatives who do not subscribe to the legal claims of the PLO.

The legal stalemate over the interpretation of the juridicial status of the PLO and indirectly the question of who is legally entitled to represent the "broad community" for the purpose of self determination has informed the legal realities in the occupied territories.

With the exception of East Jerusalem, which was annexed by Israel in 1967 and the Golan Heights which were annexed in 1981, the bulk of the territories have been under an *occupation regime*. The legal framework of the occupation regime is well known. According to international law, the territories are administered by a military government which is defined as the form of government established by a country which has occupied enemy territory. The victorious belligerent does not acquire sovereignty over the territory by the mere fact of military occupation, but the occupation authority has the right to suspend the exercise of customary rights of the previous government. The absolute right of the belligerent's authority is tempered by both international and municipal law. Within this framework, the Israeli Military Government has followed but not officially acknowledged the major international law on occupation, the Fourth Geneva Convention. It also used selectively Israeli and Jordanian law.

In many ways though, the legal reality in the West Bank and Gaza constitutes a rare case in the legal history of occupation regimes. Because of the lack of clarity surrounding the question of who represents the Palestinian "broad community" and the conflicting claims to Greater Israel and Greater Palestine, the Israeli occupation has been extremely long by twentieth century standards. It has also differed from other occupation situations in its mixed application of municipal and international law. On the one hand, the Israeli occupation regime is fairly benevolent in its observance of customary norms of international law, whether codified or not. In some cases, Israel has actually gone beyond the letter of international law to liberalize punitive local measures, most notably the abolition of Jordanian capital punishment. The Military Advocate General has repeatedly called upon the Israeli legal authorities in the territories to go beyond the minimum standard laid down by the rules of war. Moreover, the Palestinians have enjoyed the unprecedented right of any occupied population to entertain an action against the occupying authorities in the Israeli Supreme Court sitting as a High Court of Justice.

On the other hand, Israel went beyond the right of a belligerent in allowing nonsecurity related Jewish settlement and expropriation of public land once owned by the Jordanian state. Although the Palestinians have the right to appeal such acts, the Israeli Supreme Court did not deem settlements illegal. This contention is based on the view that the extant international conventions, including the Fourth Geneva Convention, do not apply to the West Bank and Gaza, because of their former "limitrophe" status.

The pecularities of the occupation regime raise the issue of its legal link to the broader question of binational Israel. The most important consideration is whether a territory which is held under prolonged occupation can actually form a part of a binational state. A strict interpretation of international law would mandate against such a situation. In this sense, for Israel to become a binational state, it would have to annex the West Bank and Gaza. Presumably, if such an annexation was based on a voluntary agreement between the Israelis and the Palestinians, this binationalism would be acknowledged at the constitutional-statutory level. In the case of forced annexation of the territories, statutory binationalism would be only one among the possible options.

However, the stalemated political reality has produced the legal gray area of *extrastatutory binationalism*. The major feature of this arrangement is that the authority system over the occupied territories is not generated through the constitutional-parliamentary process. Control of the West Bank and Gaza is handled primarily through ordinances of the Israeli Military Government augmented by municipal law, regulations and bureaucratic regulations derived from Ottoman, British, Jordanian and Israeli sources. The legal linkages between the core authority of the state of Israel and the territorial annex of the West Bank and Gaza are handled in a similar, extrastatutory way. For instance, the extension of Israeli tax laws into the territories was implemented through an executive order rather than through parliamentary legislation. Another legal device in extrastatutory linkage pertains to the right of individual Palestinians to participate in Israeli organizations such labor unions. Union membership protects certain legal rights of the Palestinians without the need to apply the Israeli labor law to the occupied territories. Likewise, Israeli citizens in Judea and Samaria have been under the authority of Israeli law without any statutory adjustments in the legal framework.

The legal reality of extrastatutory binationalism may be peculiar by Western standards of stringently applied sovereignty where legal authority coincides with state boundaries. But recourse to a mixed legal authority structure has been traditionally practiced in the Middle East. In fact, the three legal actors involved—Israelis, Palestinians and Jordanians—have all had a long historical experience with particularly ambiguous legal cultures. Such cross-cutting legal interdependence, buttressed by variable degrees of "functional autonomy" and physical separation, has been highly effective in guaranteeing a working legal arrangement without the need for statutory commitment to binationalism.

Perhaps the most interesting feature of extrastatutory binationalism is its flexibility in terms of legal infrastructure and time span. Extrastatutory binationalism can exist with very little legal infrastructure because the authority system is not centrally legitimized and controls are not uniformly applied. Israel is an obvious beneficiary of the system since it does not depend on a Palestinian legitimization of its authority or require an extensive legal buildup. Conversely, a sketchy legal infrastructure makes the transformation or dismantling of binationalism quite easy. One possible change would be in the direction of autonomy. Should autonomy be voluntarily negotiated with the Palestinians, the legal basis of this autonomy, either personal or territorial, can be expressed by expanding the statutory basis of binationalism. If, on the other hand, Israel will give up or lose the occupied territory in a war, only minimal change would be required in the extant legal framework.

The extrastatutory binational model is also temporally flexible in the sense that it can be terminated on short notice or continue for a century. While these dynamics of occupation entailed the creation of some solid facts like Jewish settlements, there is nothing deterministic or "irreversible" in these statistics, as some observers allege.

Lustick captured part of the intrinsic unpredictability of the "permanent occupation," when he argued that the legitimizing debate in Israel may continue for another forty or fifty years.[14] During this time, the momentum may favor absorption rather than extrication from the territories. Whether the pendulum of the ideological debate can be expected to swing in the other direction would depend on the extremely complex interplay of factors which form the psychological and political realities of binationalism. The next section is devoted to an analysis of the possible outcomes of the legitimizing debate on binationalism.

Conclusion: Fateful Encounters of the Binational Kind

The most crucial issue in the pending binational debate is the legal status of the Palestinians. The specific nature of their rights has not been systematically elucidated but it has been widely assumed that they will be embodied in the framework of autonomy. The Camp David Agreement which sets out the parameters of transitional autonomy holds some clues to the permanent autonomy arrangement proposed for the binational state.

The latter is derived from the legal convention which makes a distinction between independence, that is complete self-determinance of people, and self-rule or self-government. When, for political or economic reasons, a particular area remains within the jurisdiction of another political entity, the people of this area may be granted political freedoms to regulate some of their affairs in preference to complete integration. Accordingly, under proposed autonomy, the Palestinians would enjoy the right to regulate municipal affairs without interference of the Israeli authorities, but would not share in the running of central affairs such as foreign policy or security.

As a rule, the autonomy model assumes that the members of the autonomous group have the same national status as the population of the larger unit. In other words, members of the autonomous group have the same rights—national and civic—as the other citizens. However, the New Zionist proposal is not easy to implement because Palestinians (as opposed to Israeli Arabs) are not citizens of the state of Israel. The public debate within the New Zionist circle reveals the dilemmas inherent in the permanent retention of the territories. The entire spectrum of the New Zionist advocacy is aware that, given the Palestinian demographic configuration, granting the minority full national and civic rights would undermine Jewish hegemony in Israel. This position was best summed by the Gush Emunim circles who recently claimed that giving voting rights to the Palestinians would turn Israel into an Ishmael state.

The New Zionists have been sharply divided, though, with regard to the alternative options. Some Likud elites adopted the Begin position that citizenship should be granted to those Palestinians who would request it and pledge loyalty to the state of Israel. Influential Gush Emunim circles have advocated the *ger toshav*, i.e., resident alien formula, whereby the Palestinians would enjoy presonal autonomy in Israel but would vote for the Jordanian parliament. The original Kahane advocacy of population expulsion has been increasingly adopted by some mainstream secular New Zionist politicians. The scheme, which calls for the transfer of the Palestinians to Jordan, would in effect make autonomy irrelevant.

The strains that have developed in the ranks of the New Zionist camp are reminiscent of the dilemmas which will face Israel with regard to the Green Line Arabs in the twenty first century. Since a *democratic, Jewish, and territorially extended Israel is a mutually exclusive proposition, some trade-offs between the three elements seems unavoidable.* In this sense, each of the options constitutes an effort to devise an optimal trade-off solution. The Begin formula of "voluntary citizenship" tries to preserve the facade of democracy by making democratic rights contingent on a loyalty oath which would de facto limit the political choices of the Palestinians to a range prescribed by the Jewish majority. The transfer option, although a short term violation of international norms and the spirit of democracy, strives to assure that in the longer run an expanded Israel would be both democratic and uninational. Bearing in mind the population transfers in Europe, this advocacy assumes that a democracy can withstand short term shocks such as expulsion but would succumb to an interminable ethnonational war of attrition. In spite of surface differences, the Begin and transfer formulas share the same ideological perspective that Jewishness and democracy should be preserved, though at cost.

The Gush Emunim argument deviates strikingly from this line of reasoning, as it clearly spells out that democracy should be sacrificed in order to implement the vision of Greater Israel. This thinking, already mentioned with regard to the Green Line Arabs, derives from fundamentalist religious perspective of the Gush. More specifically, it is grounded in the writing of Shabtai Ben Dov and his disciple Yehuda Etzion, a leader of the Jewish underground. Both argue that as a governing principle, democracy, though not alien to Judaism, can be implemented only to the extent that it does not clash with the messianic principle of Redemption. The arrival of Redemption would usher in a halakha-based theocracy; until such time, the democratic state of Israel can be tolerated as long as it fulfills the duty of securing the territorial integrity of Eretz Israel. As one scholar of Gush Emunim points out, in view of the Gush members, "Israel was not established to have another democracy under the sun . . . two thousand years after destruction it was revived for only one purpose, to redeem the nation and eventually the world."[15]

The meta-theoretical assumptions which underwrite Gush Emunim's paradigm derive of course from the centuries long messianic tradition of the Jews. Early efforts of Return to the Land have been always associated with an expectation of an imminent messianic transformation. Although secular in nature, the modern Return was imbued with a certain messianic fervor. Messianic motivation has not been clearly articulated in theories of electoral behavior and, as a result, it has not been tested in empirical surveys in Israel and elsewhere. How much popular support the Gush Emunim paradigm enjoys is difficult to evaluate, but apparently the messianic vision, far from been considered a lunatic fringe, has enough political vitality to stay a part of the political agenda of the society. At the same time, neither Gush Emunim's 'messianic polity' nor the other New Zionist formulas for Greater Israel have generated enough of a national consensus to provide a basis for action. This is nowhere better illustrated than in the continuous and bitter cleavage between Socialist Zionists who would engage in a territorial compromise to safeguard the democratic system and New Zionists. Since the commitment to democracy and territorial patrimony are both highly salient and intensely held values, there is little room for trade off and bargaining across cleavage lines. Moreover, intensely held issues do not lend themselves to democratic, majority imposed solutions. Thus, even if the Socialist/Zionist compromises could demonstrate that there is a moderate Palestinian elite which is capable of negotiating in good faith, the New Zionists would check any compromise initiative. In a mirror-image fashion, the Socialist Zionist camp would block moves toward de jure annexation of the occupied territories, even if the New Zionists could muster a majority.

As in other societies with extremely salient and intensely held values, the Israeli cleavage structure has led to the preservation of the status quo in the West Bank and the Palestinian question. The only consensus which this cleavage can generate is negative, that is, non-implementation of policies which may radically affect either the democratic legacy of the state or its Greater Israel historical heritage. In the absence of any active policy design binationalism occurs largely by default.

Interesting enough, this creeping extrastatutory binationalism has had a major impact on the cleavage structure of the West Bank and Gaza. In the initial post 1967 phase, the issue of how to achieve Palestinian independence pitted the "old-order" pro-Jordanian elite against the PLO. The latter based their strategy on the Algerian model of resistance whereby the Israelis were analogous to European colonialists who had to be driven out of the region. According to the model no Palestinian participation in the binational political process should be tolerated, as it amounts to legitimizing Israel's existance in the region and the occupation.

In the early 1980s, a new Palestinian elite of unaligned intellectuals, businessmen and former PLO sympathizers challenged this philosophy. Known as the "third way," their view was based on an analogy with South Africa whereby the Israelis are perceived as a deeply rooted population who wield a monopoly which can be gradually taken over "from within."

Hanna Sinora, the editor of Al-Fajr, Sari Nuseibeh and Rashid Shahadeh, were three prominent members of this advocacy. They pointed out that the Palestinians should utilize the extant binational framework rather than ignore political reality. Instead of using violence to dislodge the Israelis, the Palestinians should try to integrate themselves into the system in order to influence it. The demographic size of the Palestinians and the already high degree of integration, especially economic, should be used as a tool for future political gains. Unlike the PLO's Greater Palestine, "third-way" advocacy wanted to use binational integration in order to coerce the Israelis into creating a compact Palestinian state in the West Bank and Gaza.

As in the case of Israeli society, the Palestinian cleavage structure generated by the "old-order" PLO and "third-way" advocacy has become stalemated because no camp could muster enough political power to force its preferred solution on others.

The stalemated cleavage structure in both societies meant that for twenty years the political reality of binationalism had progressed in a fairly haphazard manner. Theoretically speaking, in the absence of a political consensus, the economic marketplace can generate common interests which promote binational integration. A momentum toward binationalism is created when new economic configurations are superimposed upon the traditional cleavage structure in both groups. However, economic integration between Israel and the West Bank has reflected the traditional ethnonational division of labor. The Palestinians have provided unskilled labor for the Israeli economy and a market for consumer products manufactured across the Green Line. This congruence with ethnonational division did not promote economic binationalism beyond its low entry level of integration. The developed Israeli economy was not irrevocably dependent on the Palestinians as suppliers of unskilled labor or consumers of products and services. The underdeveloped Palestinian economy, still dominated by agriculture like other nonspecialized economies, was flexible enough to absorb the shock of separation from its more advanced center. As long as economic binationalism has not completely disrupted the traditional pattern of land tenure and cheap imports have not undermined the local endeavors, such a separation would remain quite feasible.

Nor has this low degree of economic integration produced an autonomous binational interest which went beyond the goals of the primordial communities. First and most important, low economic integration has not generated the type of cleavages which can cut across ethnonational lines and unite Palestinian and Israeli along class lines. Second, the division of labor tends to reinforce the parochial views of the two communities. As a result, when economic or social conflict erupts, it is invariably viewed in exclusively primordial terms. With neither side ready to invest in the future of binationalism and with some elements in Israel and the occupied territories strongly opposing it, the laissez-faire economic process could not produce by itself a momentum for a more powerful binational integration.

In the absence of any real interest or a genuine market for integration, binationalism had survived for the past twenty years because of what may be described as a positive "binational viability calculus." Schematically put, this calculus is based on a type of cost-benefit analysis whereby the superordinate majority tries to keep the cost of coercive binationalism at a tolerable level. Since the idea of binationalism has been less than consensual in Israel, any rise in the cost of occupation tends to reopen the debate on the future of the binational order. High level of terrorist activity, frequent disturbances in the territories or massive civil disobedience are all considered by Israel as negative viability calculus. The Palestinian uprising, the *Intifadeh*, which started in December 1987 is a case in point. The protest, often nonviolent, has proved difficult to put down regardless of the means used by the Israeli authorities. The *Intifadeh* questions the continuous ability of Israel to contain Palestinian protest against enforced binationalism. Excessive use of force in quelling the uprising or Jewish acts of vigillantism are considered especially harmful to the binational calculus, because they compromise democratic values, provoking criticism at home and abroad.

Perhaps the most important consideration in the occupation policy is the political and strategic well-being of the Israel Defense Force. Since the IDF is in charge of both the security and administration of the territories, high levels of binational upheaval may cause the military a crisis of self identity. To complicate matters, the IDF is a citizen's army and thus extremely sensitive to political criticism and factionalism. Even if internal splits between units and individuals opposing/supporting the occupation are avoided, the tasks of policing a riotous population can impede the IDF's ability to fight a conventional war.

The "binational viability calculus" is of key importance in trying to predict the future binational reality. It was already emphasized that extrastatutory binationalism can theoretically exist ad infinitum. In a legal sense, extrastatutory binationalism is an open system, taking a variety of forms. Current extrastatutory binationalism can be expected to continue as long as the cleavage structure in both national societies is stalemated and any pro or antibinational activity is neutralized by the counter camp.

However, a major change in the "calculus" can destabilize the cleavage structure and force the system into a purposive action which would either terminate binationalism or provide a statutory basis for the de facto annexation.

An analysis of comparable historical cases suggests that the cost of coerced binationalism may prove too high when resistance, violent or peaceful, to the scheme becomes pervasive. In other words, if the Palestinians successfully mount a violent campaign which takes a heavy toll in terms of human and material losses, giving up the West Bank may be considered. Israelis may then perceive these losses as outweighing any gains from the strategic and normative value of the territories. Even then, this so-called "Algerian scenario" may take many years to implement. Alternatively, the Palestinians could successfully continue the current civil uprising. Peaceful resistance may be actually more effective, because democracies are sensitive to violence against an unarmed, Ghandian style opposition. As in the British encounter in India, such a use of power may produce a profound moral crisis in Israel and strengthen the anti-annexation camp.

A radically different route of terminating binational reality may involve a transfer script. The possible options of transfer involve voluntary migration of Palestinians, peacetime coercive exodus or wartime population expulsion. The probability of each transfer script occurring is difficult to estimate and depends on a large number of "unknowns." In terms of Israeli moral and political tolerance of transfer, the most favorable option would be a voluntary exodus of Palestinians. This scenario is least likely even if economic or political inducement is offered. There would be apparently little public support for expulsion of Palestinians during peacetime, but an exodus amidst large scale hostilities may encounter little opposition. Once such hostilities set in, regardless of who the primary instigator is, democratic norms are subject to matters of national. survival. Moreover, with few exceptions, the Middle East wars have served to crystallize the political consensus around the "national camp" in Israel.

The above scripts involve only purposive actions by the two core binational actors, without considering the regional and global players. As a rule, whenever two or more national units compete for one territorial space, the international system tends to favor partition. In spite of the shortages of partition, such a solution is deemed less disruptive to the stability of the international system than a continous binational struggle. The 1947 UN Partition Proposal reflected the philosophy that even minute uninational states are more viable than larger binational entities.

This philosophy has not changed much since 1947, especially as the Palestinians have evolved effective methods of gaining support from the international system. They exacerbate conflicts among Arab States, between Arab states and Israel, and enhance the danger of a regional or even international conflagration. To reduce the probability of these intrusions and to satisfy the legitimate rights of Palestinians, current international sentiments support the establishment of a Palestinian state alongside Israel. In sum, the international system is reluctant to sanction either the Greater Israel or the Greater Palestine vision.

Whether the system can impose a compromise solution on the core actors would depend on the degree of consensus among various international players. As other case studies of nonstate actors in international politics have demonstrated, such a consensus is hard to achieve. The situation in the Middle East is even more complicated by the large number of regional and international actors, deeply divided in their political sympathies. More-over, each side, particularly the Arab Rejectionist Front, has proved extremely effective in disrupting any consensual initiative. They have remained durable, audible and capable of conflict-widening strategies whenever an international solution is about to emerge.

In the absence of an imposed solution the encounter over nonstatutory binationalism may continue well into the twenty-first century. In fact, if the solution to West Bank nationalism is delayed long enough, this struggle will merge with the more endemic battle over Green Line binationalism. As already stated earlier, the Green Line scenariois expected to follow the Northern Irish rather than the Canadian model. If the Irish model is predictive, then binational tension is likely to undermine some important elements of Israeli democracy in the twenty-first century. The extent of the damage will depend on domestic as well as international factors. Domestically, the most important consideration is the pattern of Arab political action and the Jewish response. Extreme violence and Israeli countermeasures will delegitimize both Arab moderates and Jewish prag-matists whose position depends on the political moderation of the binational struggle. The resultant flight of pragmatists into the particularist camp will bolster radical right wing politicians, currently represented by Rabbi Kahane.

The temptation to manipulate or even abrogate the democratic process will also hinge upon market processes which are not easy to control politically. The model of a split labor market, based on experience in ethnically fragmented societies, predicts that the superordinate majority may block the subordinate minority through a caste or exclusion strategy. The caste method is used to limit the minority to low-status, poorly paid, marginal jobs. However, in economically depressed periods, the minority may be excluded from the job market altogether to guarantee employment to the lower status majority members. During economic hardship, the latter are also most likely to support highly particularist politicians. A harbinger of this pattern was already found in some studies on Israeli electoral behavior whereby lower class, unemployed Sephardi Jews from the economically stagnant development towns, tend to vote in disproportionally high numbers for Kahane's Kach party.

The most common methods of democratic manipulation derived from the Northern Irish model are changes in voting rules and representation. One way to preserve Jewish dominance entails switching from proportional representation to majoritarianism. The latter, based on territorial representation, lends itself to gerrymandering of electoral boundaries, allowing the dominant political group to continue its hegemony while retaining a semblance of democratic framework. Indeed, a number of leading Labor politicians such as Amnon Linn have already made electoral change a part of their advocacy. The effectiveness of gerrymandering Israel could also be ensured by adopting the Ulster method of controlling the geographic mobility of the Arab minority.

An additional method involves changes in the rules of universal franchise. Following the Ulster experience, Israel could institute voting qualifications such as property requirements. A slightly different approach was used in Malaysia in order to secure the ethnic hegemony of the Malay group. It involved granting equal representation to urban and rural constituencies, regardless of the actual number of inhabitants. In the Israeli case, urban districts, which are heavily Jewish, could be allocated more representatives than rural districts where most of the Arabs reside.

The Ulster model envisions the use of complementary methods to dampen the political competition from the minority. Some of them—refusal to register minority parties or deregistration of existing ones, jailing or house arrest of opposition leaders—have been already used under the Military Administration in the 1950s. Others, such as forced emigration, administrative arrests or violent intimidation may be used in order to respond to an expected violent reaction of the Arabs. Ultimately, Israel could adopt the Lebanese methods of freezing the census. While these measures erode the spirit and practice of democracy, they fall short of the radical step of disfranchising the minority or the ultimate solution of population expulsion. Given the fact that radical particularists like Rabbi Kahane have already demanded that the Israeli Arabs should be encouraged to leave, the pressures for either disfranchisement or transfer will increase in the twenty-first century. Yet even if there were enough domestic support for such a policy, it is unlikely that it would be tolerated by the international system.

As has been already pointed out, the Jewish claim to an independent state was legitimized by the international system in a highly conditional way. Although the international system has not delegitimize any of the Arab states for failing to create a democracy, it may react severely if Israeli democracy were compromised through disfranchisement or transfer. Population transfers are also difficult in an age of rigidly defined sovereign states which replaced the traditional permeable state units. Whatever limited transnational migration does exist depends on the agreement of the host country. As a result, a population transfer would have to be either negotiated with reluctant neighbors or imposed unilaterally by Israel at the risk of further undermining the legitimacy of the Jewish state.

Another and less familiar phenomenon may involve violence in settling the legitimization debates in both the Palestinian and Israeli communities. The history of similar conflicts indicates that intercommunal violence or even civil war are not uncommon when extremely highly salient national issues are settled. Actually the potential for intercommunal violence among the Palestinians is quite high. In the absence of a democratic tradition and deprived by the occupation of an opportunity to create one, the internal Palestinian dialogue may become increasingly violent.

Theoretically speaking, the Israeli democracy should be able to guarantee a peaceful resolution of the internal debate. Students of democracy have made many compelling arguments about the resilience of democracy to withstand tremendous challenges stemming from conflicting views of the moral and distributive justice order of the society. Other observers have demonstrated just as compellingly that democracy may be too fragile to handle peacefully certain types of legitimizing debates and most notably issues of ethnonationality. The current violence in situations as disparate as Lebanon, Cyprus, Northern Ireland, Sri Lanka or Fiji is cited as cases in point. Those who profess confidence in Israeli democracy cite the two thousand year Judaic tradition of peaceful conflict resolution. Those who are less sanguine point out that the Jews already resorted once to a civil war when they failed to resolve central issues stemming from the messianic revival after the first exile. This struggle led to the destruction of the Second Temple and an exile which only ended with the restoration of modern Israel.

On balance, any change in the extrastatutory binationalism model, either through statutory annexation or expulsion of the Palestinians, i.e. creating a uninational state, may involve violence. Ruling without consensus amid continous ethnonational strife may become the hallmark of Israeli democracy in the twenty-first century as the Jewish state follows in the well worn path of Northern Ireland.

Expectations about the binational state in the twenty-first century are purely speculative. They are derived from theoretical expectations, the experience of other countries, and the already evolving binational reality in Israel. Whether these predictions come to pass will ultimately depend on difficult-to-forsee exogenous events such as a major military upheaval in the region or the world, grave economic crisis or violent outbursts of anti-Semitism which might increase Jewish immigration to Israel. These random disasters, created by man or nature, are like tidal waves of history—

rising in the past and affecting the future in ways difficult to predict by scientific inquiry.

The following chapters reflect the inherent strength and weaknesses of the inquiry into binationalism. They ponder the binational past, they analyze the current binational realities and try to predict the binational future.

Notes

1. Ofira Seliktar, *New Zionism and the Foreign Policy System of Israel*, (London: Croom Helm, 1986).

2. Ferdinand Toennis, *Community and Association*, (London: Routledge and Kegan Paul).

3. Rupert Emerson, *From Empire to Nation*, (Cambridge Mass.: Harvard University Press, 1967), p. 92.

4. Arnon Sofer, "Geography and Demography in Eretz Israel in the Year 2000" in Alouf Harevan, ed., *Israel Towards the Year 2000*. Jerusalem, Van Leer Foundation, forthcoming.

5. Ibid., pp. 9–13.

6. Quoted in Ian Lustick, *The Arabs in the Jewish State*, (Austin, Texas: University of Texas Press, 1980), p. 65.

7. Sammy Smooha, *The Orientation and Politicization of the Arab Minority in Israel*, (Haifa: Jewish-Arab Center, 1982).

8. Ian Lustick, *The Arabs*, p. 77.

9. Alvin Rabushka and Kenneth A. Shepsle, *Politics in Plural Societies: A Theory of Democratic Instability*, (Columbus, Ohio: Charles E. Merrill Publishing Company, 1972), pp. 84–85.

10. Ibid., pp. 74–88.

11. Sammy Smooha, "Minority Responses in a Plural Society: A Typology of the Arabs in Israel," *Sociology and Social Research*, Vol. 64, July 1983, pp. 436–456.

12. Mohammed Shadid and Rick Seltzer, "Political Attitudes of Palestinians in the West Bank and Gaza Strip," *Middle East Journal*, Vol. Winter 1988, pp.16–32.

13. Francis H. Hinsley, *Sovereignty*, (Cambridge: Cambridge University Press, 1986), p. 107; p. 145; p.212.

14. Ian Lustick, "The West Bank: How Late is Too Late," in *Is Annexation Irreversible?*, (Tel Aviv: International Center for Peace in the Middle East, 1985), p. 23.

15. Ehud Sprinzak, *Fundamentalism, Terrorism, and Democracy: The Case of Gush Emunim Underground*, (Washington, D.C.: The Wilson Center, 1986), p. 49.

2

Binationalism Reconsidered: Ideological Continuity and Change in the Begin Era

Lilly Weissbrod

Introduction

The first Zionists following Herzl's call to establish a Jewish state naturally looked to the ancient cradle of Jewish statehood in Judea-Palestine. In staking out a claim to Palestine, the Zionists were also influenced by the European concept of sovereignty, that is the notion that people should have the right to define their national identity. Yet the realities of the Middle East were less than hospitable to the idea of a Jewish state.

Whatever perceptions or misconceptions the Zionists had about the Arabs, must have been dispelled by the early 1920s. In 1921, a major wave of riots swept Palestine, with the Arabs demanding an end to Jewish immigration, sale of land, and the creation of a Palestinian state. Strained and pressured by these events, the Zionist movement quickly became fragmented. On the one hand, there were the Socialist Zionists who felt that the historical boundaries of ancient Judea and Samaria should not be binding on the new state. Instead, they advocated a territorial compromise and a small and unmistakably uninational Jewish state.

On the other hand, the Revisionists came out very strongly in favor of the territorial patrimony principle. The Revisionists based their claim on a number of givens, namely that the Jews are a nation entitled to the territory of their historic homeland and that they have a right to sovereign determination in this territory. An analysis of the Revisionists' advocacy shows that they viewed the territorial patrimony as taking precedence over membership in the proposed state. In other words, the Revisionists were willing to have a considerable Arab minority in exchange for the proper historical boundaries of Eretz Israel.

Even so, the proposed state was not expected to be symmetrically binational with both the Jews and the Arabs enjoying equal rights. According to Jabotinsky, a prominent Revisionist leader, the Jews would form a political and demographic majority, preventing the Arabs from undermining the Jewish character of the state. Legally speaking, the Revisionist model was a type of "organic" binationalism derived from the minority experience in Europe and the millet system of the Ottoman Empire.

Since the option of a binational state was one among several considered in mandatory Palestine, it will be most useful to examine how the term was understood by the Revisionists and other Zionist leaders at the time. When the Balfour Declaration was issued, the Zionist movement at large envisaged the Jewish national home as a state with a large Jewish majority. To achieve this, the Revisionists and others in the movement hoped for a large Jewish immigration. However, by 1930 it became clear that an immigration large enough to ensure a Jewish majority was not forthcoming. Still, at the 17th Zionist Congress in 1931 Jabotinsky tabled a motion to declare that the aim of Zionism was to create a Jewish state. For this purpose, the Jews in Palestine were declared as an ethnic majority, so that Jewish control over the proposed state could be ensured.[1] Because of the Socialist Zionists' opposition, the proposal was never put to vote and the issue was avoided. Subsequently the Revisionists left the Zionist Organization and formed the New Zionist Organization.

The Revisionists used their new base of power to fight against the binational proposals of Dr. Haim Weitzmann and David Ben-Gurion, the leader of Labor. Following the 1936 Arab revolt, Weitzmann testified before the British Peel Commission, sent to investigate the situation, that the Jews would agree to a binational state in Palestine. He clarified that such a binational state would be based on a parity between the Jews and the Arabs irrespective of the actual numerical ratio between the two nations. One possible method to make the arrangement democratic was to get an equal number of Jewish and Arab cantons.[2] Even though the parity proposal was a practical solution given the demographic disparities between the Jews and the Arabs, the Revisionists considered it a betrayal of Herzl's vision of a Jewish state. In particular, they adhered to his dictum that Palestine should serve as a haven for all Jews whose "personal welfare is, or may become undetachable from actual membership in a Jewish state."[3] Since such a policy entailed, among others, that Jews alone should have a right to immigration, a viable democratic Jewish majority rather than parity was required.[4]

Ironically the issue of binational state which sparked off the long-lasting animosity between Labor and the Revisionists was settled by external circumstances. By 1947 the Mandatory power and the United Nations decided that binationalism, in whatever form, would not work due to the

Arabs' complete refusal to participate. The 1947 UN Partition Proposal which called for establishing two separate states followed. Labor, by then the uncontested leader of the Zionist movement, approved the Partition Plan as a "lesser evil." The ensuing war between Israel and the neighboring states ended with a small but uninational Jewish state holding only a small Arab minority.

The Six Day War and the
Delegitimization of Social Zionism

The process of consolidating a uninational Jewish state with a "managable" Arab minority was abruptly interrupted by the Six Day War. The extant evidence indicates that Israel was caught by surprise both strategically and in terms of the size of Arab territory captured. Israeli decision-making prior and immediately after the war reveals that territories were not considered in terms of national irredentism.

For instance, in a decision taken a few days after the end of the war, the Israeli cabinet proposed to exchange most of the territories for a comprehensive peace with Arab states. The message of the proposal was clear. With the exception of Jerusalem and the strategically located Golan Heights, Israel would prefer peace over the prospect of holding on to the historical boundaries of Eretz Israel.

The resounding Arab rejection of the Israeli proposal embodied in the three Noes of the Khartoum Conference (No Negotiations, No Recognition, No Peace) hardened Israeli attitudes. The Cabinet withdrew the peace proposal and official spokesmen became less clear on the subject of the territories. For instance, the Israeli Foreign Minister Abba Eban in a speech to the United Nations on October 8, 1968, did not mention the subject of return. The Prime Minister, Golda Meir, speaking to the Knesset (Israeli Parliament) on May 5, 1969, likewise ignored the issue.[5] On later occasions, e.g. a Knesset address on March 16, 1971, she mentioned the possibility of border adjustment in return for a peace treaty, but neither she nor other Israeli spokesmen were explicit with regard to the specifics.[6]

Even though Labor became less clear with regard to the issue of peace, its territorial policy did not indicate irredentist designs along the lines of Greater Israel. The Labor Government, including its two leading spokesmen on the territories, Yigal Allon and Moshe Dayan, conceived of most of the occupied land in strategic terms.[7] The pattern of Israeli settlements in the Rapha Salient and the Jewish settlements in the Jordan Rift Valley were strategically oriented. The Allon Plan clearly indicates that the Labor Party was faithful to its traditional policy of shying away from densely populated Arab areas in Judea and Samaria. Neither the original Allon Plan nor its successor, the Galilee Plan, would compromise the Jewish character of the state in order to secure the historical territorial patrimony.

The reason for Labor's territorial reluctance was rooted in the demography of the West Bank and Gaza. When Israel occupied the territories in the June 1967 war there were 670,000 Arabs in Judea and Samaria, the Golan Heights had a Druze population of 10,000, and the population of Gaza Strip and Sinai was 380,000. At the end of 1969, the population of Israel amounted to 2,776,300, roughly 16 percent of them Arabs. The annual growth rate of Jews was 1.6 percent and that of Arabs was 3.7 percent. Assuming that the natural growth rate of the population is a direct function of its stage of modernization, it followed that the growth rate of the population in the territories would be at least as high as that of the Israeli Arabs or higher. The Arab population of Greater Israel—Israel and the occupied territories—at the end of 1967 was 1,452,700 (including 392,700 Israeli Arabs) and the Jewish population reached 2,383,600. With a growth rate over twice as high as that of Jews, the Arab population could be expected to reach parity with the Jews at the end of the century.[8]

Labor's rule over a substantial and fast growing Palestinian population provoked a moral crisis in the Socialist Zionist camp. As the euphoria over the extent of the victory dissipated, doubts regarding the ethical right of retaining the territories started surfacing. The doubts centered mostly on the discrepency between Labor's claim to represent "the great apocalyptical vision of Israel's prophets, the vision of Jewish redemption within the framework of the salvation of humanity,"[9] and the reality of occupying an unwilling population. If Labor could present a credible claim that Judea and Samaria were part of the Holy Land given to the People of Israel by God, some of these ethical doubts could be alleviated. However, since Labor was a secular party and its ideology was largely disassociated from traditional Judaism, claims to represent the patrimonial heritage were less than convincing.[10] The security argument was even less helpful to Labor's position, especially as Israel had existed without the territories for almost twenty years and repelled successfully an attack of three Arab countries from strategically inferior borders.

Initially, the contradiction between Labor's ideology and its praxis bothered only a few. They were primarily Kibbutz members, sons of the Socialist Zionist vanguard. In two widely read books published after the Six Day War, these dissenters criticized the bankruptcy of the Israeli ideology and searched for a new solution.[11] The delegitimization of Social Zionism reached a peak after the 1973 October War. In its wake, large scale protests broke out aimed first at the conduct of the war and later at the entire Labor leadership. The protest movement brought to fore a number of pressure groups whose ideological reasoning had a great impact on the growing debate over the territories.[12]

Known as the Peace Movement, the advocacy comprised a number of loosely knit groups associated in a pattern of changing coalitions. The groups shared one theme: They called for peace in exchange for a withdrawal from the territories. The Movement had a harder time in agreeing on the extent of the territories to be returned, or on the question as to whom they should be returned. But a consensus prevailed that the return of the territories would be both moral and demographically prudent. The peace activists believed that unless there was a constant annual immigration of thousands of Jews to Israel, annexation of the territories would lead to a binational state within the next 20-30 years. Israel would then either lose its Jewish character or its democratic character and, either way, cease to conform to Zionist ideals.[13] In fact, the need to secure the Jewish nature of the state remained one of the few concerns shared by all Israelis.

A large group in the protest movement criticized Labor's conduct of the war but implicitly condoned government policy in the occupied territories. They offered no alternative course of action and seemed to be content to support the official "wait and see" policy. Yet in the absence of ideological reasons in support of territorial occupation, the Peace Now movement was determined to monopolize the territorial debate.

Yet the Peace Now was progressively challenged by another group which emerged from the protest movement. A loose coalition of Revisionists, neo-Revisionists, Laborites turned nationalists and national religious circles, the New Zionists strove to provide a convincing answer to the moral doubts regarding the occupation of land. The New Zionist ideology, largely shaped by Gush Emunim and the Greater Israel Movement, also tried to address the problems of Israel as a Jewish state.

The New Zionist basic premise was that there is a strong and irreversible link between Jewish religion and Jewish nationalism. The occupied territories, and most notably Judea and Samaria, are part of the Holy Land. Holding onto the territories is a sacred duty and not an act of high immorality as alleged by Leftist critics. The land is Israel's patrimony through the Abrahamic Covenant. "All this land is ours, absolutely, belonging to all of us; it is nontransferable to others even in part because it was promised to us by God, Creator of the World."[14] Because of it, the occupied territories should be settled by Jews. For instance, in an appeal to the High Court, a Gush Emunim settler claimed that security considerations notwithstanding, the settlement of the West Bank is required "by token of the mission (of the Jewish people) and the return of Israel to its land."[15] Settling the liberated parts of the territories will hasten the redemption, i.e., the coming of the Messiah.[16]

The New Zionists also addressed themselves to the whispered fears that Palestinian demography would undermine the Jewish character of Greater

Israel. Initially, they claimed that the 1973 demographics were similar to the situation in 1948, when 45 percent of the Israeli population were Arabs.

Mass Jewish immigration tipped the scales in favor of Jews and then revised the ratio. Gush spokesmen expressed confidence that Palestinian emigration to seek work in Arab states and Jewish immigration to Israel would produce a tolerable balance in the future. Gush members even advoated that the Arabs in the occupied territories should be granted Israeli citizenship on their way of becoming loyal citizens.[17] However, when by 1982 mass Jewish immigration did not materialize, Gush Emunim altered its stand. Hanan Porat, a founding member and leader of the Gush, suggested that the Palestinians had to accept Israeli sovereignty in the Holy Land. They could either forego all claims to independence and become loyal Israeli nationalists including military service, remain resident aliens, or emigrate.[18]

Capitalizing on the widespread political trauma of the Yom Kippur War, the Gush challenged the weakened Labor Government of Yitzhak Rabin to implement some of the New Zionist ideology. The most successful Gush campaign focused on forcing the Government to establish Jewish settlements in the heavily populated Arab Samaria, the heart of the biblical Eretz Israel. Yet New Zionism had to wait for a change in political power in order to establish it as an operational policy for Israel.

Attempted Routinization of New Zionism

The political turnaround came in the 1977 election where Labor lost its relative majority to the Likud party headed by Menachem Begin. Likud was a merger party whose core constituent was the Herut party, the successor of the pre-state Revisionist movement. During its long years in opposition, Herut was the bearer of Revisionist ideology. However, the Revisionist ideology had failed to elicit mass electoral support. Indeed, the Revisionists and later Herut-Likud were considered illegitimate competitors for power by the dominant Socialist Zionists.[19]

To bolster its appeal, Likud enthusiastically adopted Gush Emunim ideology, as it was both compatible with Revisionist and neo-Revisionist tenets and proved powerful in electoral mobilization. The elements of New Zionism most compatible with Likud's interest were the issue of settlements in the West Bank and Gaza Strip and the Gush position that Israel's right to the occupied territories stems from Jewish sovereignty to the entire mandatory Palestine. As is common in cases of co-opted ideology, Likud presented Gush Emunim as formulators and implementers of the entire New Zionist ideology, including its religious-mystical aspects. Begin paid symbolic respect to the spiritual leaders of the Gush, but in practice confined

Likud to implementing the political aspects of New Zionism and, most notably, settlement policies.[20]

Theoretically speaking, this process of co-option can be explained in terms of the phenomenon known as routinization of revolutionary ideology. Revolutionary precepts are an important resource for mobilization, electoral appeal, and support. As was suggested elsewhere, once a party becomes entrenched in power, the revolutionary ideology undergoes a process of routinization. In a step-by-step elimination and selection, some components are pushed to the background, whereas others are emphasized.[21]

Indeed, already in its platform paper for the 1977 election, a short version of which was mailed to almost every household in Israel, Likud tried to routinize New Zionism.

> The right of the Jewish people to Eretz Israel (the entire Holy Land as distinguished from Israel in its present borders) is an eternal right linked to its right to peace and security. Therefore, Judea and Samaria will not be handed over to any foreign rule; between the Sea (Mediterranean) and the Jordan (river) there will be Israeli sovereignty only.

Furthermore,

> The Likud government will call upon the young generation . . . to redeem its inheritence in all parts of Eretz Israel and will help every group and individual in the task of settling the country.

Clearly, Likud tried to balance the secular principles of settlement and security with the more spiritual elements of patrimonial possession of the Land. As could be expected from the routinization imperative, Likud did not incorporate any of Gush Emunim advocacy of messianic redemption. Moreover, Begin took a fairly civil stand on the thorny issue of the Palestinian demographics. The platform paper offered citizenship to all those Arabs of Eretz Israel who wished to opt for it and undertook to be loyal to Israel. Those who preferred their former [Jordanian] citizenship could retain it. "The Likud government will guarantee to members of the Arab nation of Eretz Israel cultural autonomy . . . (and) economic integration."

The party program was in line with the traditional Revisionist vision of binationalism in Palestine. The plan would guarantee a Jewish majority even if all the Palestinians were to opt for Israeli citizenship after the annexation of the territories. In any case, Likud probably considered such an event unlikely, since the Arabs were offered the alternative of living as resident aliens. The platform was also loyal to the Revisionist view of cultural nationalism. The Arabs of Eretz Israel were not considered to be a distinct nation of the binational state. Rather they were offered a cultural autonomy which the Israeli Arabs have enjoyed all along.

For all its efforts at routinization, the New Zionist ideology reflected in the policy platform was a product of a party with little practical experience. With the short exception of the 1967 National Unity Government, Herut or Likud never wielded power and bore executive responsibility. The party leadership apparently did not anticipate the 1977 electoral victory and had even less faith that its annexationist advocacy would be implemented in the near future. As a result the party's leadership probably did not feel any urgency to provide a truly workable formula for solving the demographics of the proposed binational state. However, the political events surrounding the Sadat initiative triggered off steps towards further routinization of New Zionism. The historical development thus accelerated a process which might have occurred at a much slower pace.

First Ideological Shift

President Sadat of Egypt paid his historic visit to Jerusalem in November 1977, just six months after Likud assumed office. This extraordinary event set in motion the first ideological shift in New Zionism. In December 1977, the Likud cabinet of Menachem Begin formulated the Autonomy Plan for the West Bank and Gaza Strip.[22] The Plan was presented to President Sadat in February 1978.

Unlike the 1977 policy platform which offered cultural autonomy to Arabs opting for Israeli citizenship, the Autonomy Plan proposed to create an autonomous administration for all the residents of the West Bank and Gaza Strip. The Military Administration was to be replaced by an autonomy administration by and for the Palestinian residents, irrespective of their nationality. Israel would retain responsibility for security and public order, but the autonomous administration would have a police force of its own. Most important, the Autonomy Plan reflected a changing perspective in the issue of sovereignty of Eretz Israel. Although the Plan reiterated Israel's claim to sovereignty over the West Bank and Gaza, it also recognized similar claims by unspecified others. Any final decision about sovereignty claims was deferred for at least five years.

Quite clearly, the Autonomy Plan constituted a break with the call for an immediate and total annexation included in the 1977 platform. The proposed Palestinian self administration would have resulted in creating a separate national and civic identity even for those inhabitants of the territories who opted for an Israeli citizenship. The effort to defer the final decision on the territories was an obvious attempt to hedge an ideological shift forced on Likud by the Sadat initiative.

On the one hand, the Egyptian move occurred so early into Likud's tenure that the party had no time to legitimize the New Zionist quest of

TABLE 2.1
Percentage of Respondents in Public Opinion Polls Opposing Territorial
Concessions in Return for Peace

Date	% Opposing Concessions
September 1975	40.3
November 1977	51.3
October 1978	32.1
July 1979	46.3
May 1980	60.0
April 1981	62.5
September 1982	58.3
June 1983	49.9

Sources: Pori Public Opinion Polls, Haaretz 11/7/77, 11/17/78, 7/3/79,
4/1/81; Mabat Lekalkala Vehevra 5/20/80; Jerusalem Post 9/3/82, 6/10/83.

annexation. On the other hand, the visit produced strong pressures from
the U. S. to settle the Middle East conflict and a corresponding sentiment
in Israeli public opinion. Likud, on its way to consolidate its newly acquired
legitimacy, could hardly ignore both. As the public opinion polls summed
up in Table 2.1 show, the percentage of respondents who objected to
territorial concessions for peace decreased from 51.3 in October, 1977 to
32.1 in October 1978. Although the decline, related to the Sadat initiative
and the signing of the Camp David Accord, was short lived, the public
sentiments did not support a creation of a binational Israel through
annexation. Moreover, the dynamics of Camp David prompted Likud to
routinize New Zionism in ways which shifted the ideology away from its
religious-national origins.

Second Ideological Shift

The second ideological shift coincided with the signing of the Camp
David Accord on September 17, 1978. The Accord provides for the
abolishment of the Israeli military and civilian administration. More important, part of the military force would be withdrawn and the remainder
assigned to specific security locations. Finally, the claim to sovereignty in
the territories would be settled in negotiations between Israel, Egypt, Jordan,
and elected representatives of the inhabitants of the West Bank and Gaza
Strip.

TABLE 2.2
Trends in Likud Support - % Support in Public Opinion Polls and in Elections

Date	% Support
Elections 1977	33.4
December 1977	58.3
January 1978	50.0
December 1978	33.3
December 1979	18.7
November 1980	21.1
Elections 1981	37.1
December 1982	40.6
July 1983	35.4

Sources: Mabat Lekalkala Vehevra 3/24/78; Pori Public Opinion Polls, Haaretz
2/2/78, 12/22/78, 12/21/79, 11/9/80, 12/24/82, 8/1/83.

The last provision represented the most far-reaching shift from the
original Revisionist ideology and, even more significantly, from New Zionism.
If the final status of the West Bank and Gaza is to be determined by
negotiations, this implies Israel's willingness to relinquish part of its claim
to some unspecified parts of Eretz Israel. The deviation from the original
New Zionist binational vision was even more striking when it is considered
that the Camp David Agreement did not include any provisions for acquiring
Israeli citizenship for willing Palestinians. Indeed, the entire issue was
omitted from the Accord, so that it would not raise the specter of Israeli
sovereignty. The comparison between the Autonomy Plan and the Camp
David Agreement puts the Likud's dilemma in routinizing New Zionism
into sharp focus. In omitting the claim to Israel's sovereignty over Eretz
Israel, Likud could forfeit its claim to represent New Zionism. Indeed, both
before and after the signing of the Accord, Gush Emunim protested
emphatically. The scope and bitterness of this protest embarassed Likud
and forced Begin to appease the Gush by invoking religious symbols of
solidarity.[23] On the other hand, adopting the Gush position could have
led to the creation of a binational state for which the Israelis were not
prepared. The opinion polls summarized in Table 2.2 reveal that most of
the Israelis supported Likud on the issue of autonomy. For instance, 44.3
percent of the respondents in a January 1978 poll were happy with the
autonomy agreement, and 69 percent respondents in a June 1978 poll were

satisfied with the government's security policy. Overall, the percentage of those who were satisfied with Likud went up from 33.4 at the 1977 election to 50 in January 1978.

Likud would have been largely contended with the broad legitimacy it acquired after the two ideological shifts in New Zionism. However, the party leadership in general and Menachem Begin in particular faced an increasing challenge from the Gush. When some hawkish secular members of Likud, notably Geula Cohen and Yuval Neeman, left the Likud to form the radical right wing *Tehiya*,[24] Begin was forced to readjust New Zionism.

Reaffirmation of Unadulterated New Zionism

Protest action against the Camp David Accord was prompt. On September 18, 1978, one day after the signing of the Accord, 700 Gush Emunim members established an unauthorized settlement in Samaria, to provide "an answer by the Land of Israel Faithful to the Camp David Accord."[25] On the same day Herut and Gush Emunim leaders launched a campaign against their leader, Begin, and called for a new election. On October 4, 1978, the Gush organized a mass rally against the Accord in the West Bank.[26] The Accord was confirmed by the Israeli Cabinet on September 24, 1978, with two ministers voting against it and one abstaining. In the following Knesset debate Begin came under heavy criticism from the right wing and more surprisingly from the dovish Labor opposition and even the liberal Israeli press. Yet after a two day debate, 84 out of the 120 Knesset members ratified the Accord.

It is interesting that the parliament ratified an Accord which differed somewhat from its written official version. During the debate preceding the vote, the Likud leader provided a slightly different interpretation of some of the key provisions of the Accord. He claimed that

> We have left no doubts and stated that after the interim period of five years (of autonomy), when the issue of sovereignty is raised for a final decision, we shall claim our right to sovereignty in Judea, Samaria and Gaza. If an agreement is reached on the basis of contrary claims, fine; if no agreement is reached, the result will be the autonomy and Israeli security arrangements will continue.[27]

Quite clearly, the Prime Minister was retracting for fear of losing the support of his ideological vanguard, Gush Emunim, and those within his party who were committed to the principle of Greater Israel. Although the percentage of the public who were unwilling to make territorial concessions rose to 32.1, this was still a substantial number to bolster Begin's critics.

To shore up his position with the ideological hard core of New Zionism, Begin went further in qualifying the Camp David Accord. By spring 1979 he claimed that autonomy is personal rather than territorial, meaning that Arabs would be in charge only of their civil affairs. This interpretation became generally accepted by the public: in a May 1979 poll, 58.4 percent of the respondents supported this arrangement.[28]

The new interpretation was used in writing the Likud platform for the 1981 elections. The document reaffirmed Israel's right to sovereignty in the West Bank and Gaza and promised that Israel will claim this right at the end of the five year interim autonomy period. "The Likud will act to resume negotiations on implementation of full autonomy to the Arab residents of Judea, Samaria and the Gaza Strip." However, "the autonomy which was agreed at Camp David is not a state, is not a sovereignty and is not self-determination."

In line with the reasserted claims to binationalism, the 1981 platform offered Israeli citizenship to any "resident of Eretz Israel who applies for it and undertakes to be loyal to the State of Israel." This position completely voided the second ideological shift contained in the Camp David Accord and retained only part of the shift in the Autonomy Plan. The 1981 document specifically precluded any possibility of self-determination for the residents of the West Bank and Gaza. By omitting any mention of cultural autonomy it also made Israeli citizenship less attractive to any Palestinians. This time around, references to "any residents of Eretz Israel" were made even more vague, apparently in order to obfuscate the demographic cost of the proposed binational state.

Begin backed up the renewed adherence to the original version of New Zionism by a policy of settlements. The 1981 platform revealed that between 1977–1981, 55 settlements were set up in Judea and Samaria and 6 in the Gaza Strip. In spite of the intense pressures from the United States and Egypt to freeze the settlement drive which threatened the Camp David Accord, the Likud policy platform promised more settlements. In giving in to hard core New Zionist demand, Likud had also to contend with public opinion. Though in May 1979 40.4 percent of the respondents agreed that these settlements are an obstacle to peace, in December of the same year 64 percent supported the Gush Emunim quest for more settlements. As Table 2.3 shows, the percentage supporting settlement policy, despite its cost to peace, remained considerable.

Moreover, Likud was facing an added challenge from the newly established Tehiya party which was making a competing claim to represent true New Zionism. Tehiya's policy program proposed the immediate annexation of the occupied territories. To solve the demographics of the binational state Tehiya suggested an intensive Jewish settlement in Judea and Samaria and an accelerated immigration of one million Jews over the next ten years.

TABLE 2.3
% of Respondents in Public Opinion Polls Supporting Continued Settlements on
the West Bank and Gaza Strip

Date	% Support
December 1979	64.0
July 1980	47.0
August 1981	48.8
October 1982	48.5
October 1983	36.9

Sources: Mabat Lekalkala Vehevra 12/11/79; Pori Public Opinion Polls, Haaretz
7/4/80, 8/13/81, 10/8/82, 10/5/83.

Under any circumstance, a splinter party claiming to represent and
implement the original ideology would be highly threatening to the mother
party. In this specific case, the threat was amplified because Likud was new
to government and not entirely sure about its own legitimacy. Public opinion
polls were less than reassuring. Table 2.2 indicates that after an initial jump
in popularity after the 1977 election, Likud's support took a downward
turn, reaching a lowpoint of 35.4 percent in July 1983.

This decline in popularity was not necessarily linked to ideological
routinization per se. In June 1978, 69 percent of respondents in an opinion
poll were satisfied with the security performance of the government, 35
percent were happy with its foreign policy, and 37 percent agreed with its
economic performance. By February 1979 these percentages declined slightly
with regard to security and foreign policy (66 and 32 percent respectively)
but dropped to a dramatic 14 percent with regard to economic performance.[29]
Whatever the reason for the drop in popularity, Likud's doubts about its
popular legitimacy apparently contributed to a renewed populist commitment
to New Zionism. Coupled with new economic measures, Likud's policy
resulted in a new upsurge in popularity. In the 1981 elections, the party
received 37.1 percent of the popular vote, some 4 percent more than 1977.

After the lessons learned in 1978–1979, Mr. Begin never again attempted
to shift the ideological emphasis away from the purist New Zionist version.
Until his resignation in October 1983, Begin continuously reiterated that
Israel's sovereignty in Judea and Samaria is undisputed and that the
settlements are totally justified. Since Egypt did not abrogate the peace
treaty with Israel on this account and Jordan did not challenge Begin's

true intention by entering the autonomy negotiations, there were no powerful external factors to test the renewed adherence to hard core ideology. Domestically, Likud's principled stand on the binational state issue generated considerable support at a time where its other policies fell into disrepute. Whether intentional or not, Begin's many shifts were construed as brilliant diplomacy aimed at negotiating the historical peace treaty with Egypt without betraying Likud's commitment to binationalism. But as the following discussion will show, the policy of "having the cake and eating it too" can only continue as long as no major peace initiatives, internal or external, are undertaken.

Discussion: Romancing the Binational State

In order to discuss the continuity and change in the Begin era, we have to make a distinction at two conceptually different levels. At one level, we shall look at the ideological change in New Zionism which occurred at the time when Likud came to power and the subsequent changes taking place in the Begin era. On another level, a distinction should be made between changes at the fundamental level of an ideology and changes in the operational level related to actual policy formulation.

When Likud assumed power in 1977, it did not initiate a new settlement policy. It merely pursued energetically what Labor had done reluctantly. Where Labor largely responded to the Gush engineered settlement *fait accompli*, Likud initiated and sponsored new settlement activities. Yet at the fundamental level, New Zionist ideology constituted a dramatic break with Socialist Zionism promulgated by Labor. New Zionism justified the ongoing occupation of territories occupied by war as an act of reclaiming the national heritage bestowed on the People of Israel by God.

The change from a secular to a religious world view was the most significant contribution of New Zionism. This change had a profound impact on the issue of territorial occupation. A secular world view requires human action to be ethical in the sense that it conforms to principles of inter-human relations determined by men. The responsibilty for the outcome of these actions, including the need to adopt them to changing circumstances, rests with man.

A religious world view regards human action ethical if it conforms to the commandments of God. Men are not expected to question these commandments and their possible outcomes, nor to adapt them to changing circumstances. This principle was applied by Gush Emunim to the political sphere. Annexation of Judea and Samaria is a Divine Imperative, and none of the practical considerations such as international censure or Palestinian demographics should be relevant. In other words, God would be ultimately responsible for solving whatever international problems Israel may incur as a result of annexation or balancing the demographics of the binational state of Greater Israel.

The religious world view imbedded in the fundamental level of New Zionism proved difficult for Likud's operational policy of advocating a binational state. Disregarding future hopes of mass Jewish immigration and/or mass Arab exodus, the reality of higher growth rates of the Palestinians presented an immediate problem of demography for the binational entity. Possibly realizing the implications of such a development, but certainly compelled by the historic peace offer from Egypt, Likud went through the two ideological shifts. If either the Autonomy Plan or the Camp David Accord were implemented, the demographic problem would have been resolved or at least deferred. As already indicated, the operational tenets represented in the Autonomy Plan and Camp David Plans did not conform to the fundamental religious component of New Zionism. Pressed by religious and secular ideologies and lacking a sufficient base of popular legitimacy, Begin felt compelled to retreat to the ideological purity of early New Zionism.

However, compared with the early pre-1977 policy of ignoring the specifics of the binational state, Likud's stand since 1979 tried to ward off the demographic problem. To this effect, the party adopted the vague formula of autonomy in conjunction with annexation. The Palestinian population is not given Israeli citizenship and is referred to by the cryptic name of 'Arabs of Eretz Israel'. This may mean that the Palestinians should not be compared to Israeli Arabs who have voting rights within the Green Line. Since the population of the territories does not have political rights, the binational state de facto becomes uninational. Such a political structure is somewhat similar to Athenian style democracy where a large part of the public is excluded by law from political participation. The ingenuity of the 1979 Likud formula is especially striking in view of the fact that binationalism raises doubts about the Jewish nature of Greater Israel. While the opponents of New Zionism define the Jewish state as one in which the *population* is principally Jewish, New Zionism in the Begin era defined it as a state in which the *citizens* are largely Jewish.

The success of Begin's formula depended on a number of factors. Perhaps the most crucial one was the problem of finding enough moderate Palestinian leadership willing to accept the autonomy. Since by 1979, most of the elected political leaders in the West Bank and Gaza were among PLO supporters, they rejected the autonomy proposal. The Israeli response amounted to an exercise in political engineering. The Military Administration in the territories was restructured as a Civil Administration. In autumn 1981, Menachem Milson, the newly appointed Adminstrator, set out to foster a more moderate Palestinian leadership. When the experiment failed, the Israeli authorities attributed it to the PLO influence on the West Bank and Gaza Strip.[30] The Lebanon war, begun in June 1982, can be viewed as part of an attempt to eliminate the PLO as a political force in the territories. Yet in spite of the apparent success of the war in dismantling the PLO infrastructure in Lebanon, the quest for a moderate Palestinian leadership thus remained.

The resignation of Prime Minister Begin in 1983 left the autonomy question open. The change of political leadership in Israel and Egypt further detracted from Begin's binational design. As the Middle East peace process came to a standstill, the new generation of New Zionist leaders were less pressed to forge a link between fundamental ideology and the binational reality.

Notes

1. *Stenographic Protocol of the 17th Zionist Congress*, (German), London, Central Office of the Zionist Organization, 1931, pp. 164–178, p. 397.

2. Walter Laqueur, *A History of Zionism* (Hebrew), (Jerusalem: Shocken, 1974), pp. 405–406.

3. *Blue-White Papers*, (London: the World Union of Zionist Revisionists, 1935), p. 6.

4. It was by no means the only cause. For a detailed discussion, see Lilly Weissbrod, "Economic Factors and Political Stategies: the Defeat of the Revisionists in Mandatroy Palestine," *Middle Eastern Studies*, 19(3), July 1983, pp. 326–344; "The Rise and Fall of the Revisionist Party, 1928–1935," *The Jerusalem Quarterly*, 30, Winter 1984, pp. 80–93.

5. Joseph Nedava, (ed.), *The Israel-Arab Conflict* (Hebrew), (Ramat-Gan: Revivim, 1983), pp. 48–51.

6. Ibid, pp. 86–88.

7. One of the few is Meir Pail, now a leading member of the Sheli party, a left-of-center party advocating peaceful coexistence with the Arab neighbors. He claims that Jewish settlements and military units on the West Bank are sitting ducks in case of a surprise attack and would have to be rescued by massive forces anyway, so that the Israeli presence on the West Bank is no safeguard against attack. See Meir Pail, "A Palestinian State Alongside Israel" in Alouf Hareven (ed.), *Is there a Solution to the Palestinian Problem? Israeli Positions*, (Hebrew), The Van Leer Jerusalem Foundation, 1982, pp. 123–150.

8. According to Aaron Yariv, a leading Israeli strategy expert, Arabs will constitute 50% of the population of Israel by the end of the century if the West Bank and Gaza Strip are retained by Israel (A. Yariv, "The Solution of the Problem and Its Price to Israel" (Hebrew), in *Is there a Solution to the Palestinian Problem*, op. cit., pp.11–24. Moshe Arens, former Israeli Minister of Defense in the Likud government, claims that emigration from the West Bank is a decisive factor which halves the population increase, bringing it near that of the Jewish population (Moshe Arens, "The Palestinian Problem as a Jewish Problem," (Hebrew), ibid, pp. 199–205.

9. David Ben Gurion, *Israel and Zionism As I See It*, (London: Poalei Zion, 1951), p. 10.

10. For a detailed discussion of ideological change in Israel, up to the Six Day War and after it, see Lilly Weissbrod, "From Labor Zionism to New Zionism; Ideological Change in Israel," *Theory and Society*, November 10, 1981, pp. 777–803.

11. *Talks of Warriors* (Hebrew), published by a group of young Kibbutz members, 1967; *Talks in the Kibbutz Among Young People* (Hebrew), (Tel-Aviv: Am Oved, 1969).

12. For a fuller discussion, see Lilly Weissbrod, "Core Values and Revolutionary Change" in D. Newman (ed.), *The Impact of Gush Emunim*, (London: Croom Helm, 1985), pp. 70–90.

13. Arie Eliav, *Glory in the Land of the Living* (Hebrew), (Tel-Aviv: Am Oved, 1971), pp. 159–160.

14. "Manifesto of Rabbi Zvi Yehunda Hacohen Kuk" (Hebrew), *Gush Emunim*, September 1, 1977.

15. *Haaretz*, August 31, 1979.

16. Mendelson, M. "Gush Emunim Plans Fourth Settlement," *Maariv*, June 24, 1975.

17. Eliezer Livne, "Nor Will I Hide My Face Any More From Then" (Hebrew), *Moznayim* 25 (2), July 1967, pp. 102–104; "Debate With Gush Emunim" (Hebrew), *Yediot Ahronot*, November 3, 1976.

18. David Richardson, "Special Responsibility," *Jerusalem Post*, December 31, 1982.

19. Lilly Weissbrod, "Economic Factors and Political Strategies: The Defeat of the Revisionists in Mandatory Palestine," *Middle Eastern Studies*, Vol. 19 (no. 3) July 1983, pp. 326–344.

20. For a discussion of these points, see Lilly Weissbrod, "Delegitimation and Legitimation as a Continuous Process," *op. cit.*

21. Lilly Weissbrod, "From Labor Zionism."

22. Reproduced in Itamar Rabinovich & Jehuda Reinharz (eds.), *Israel in the Middle East*, (New York: Oxford University Press, 1984), pp. 327–328.

23. Lilly Weissbrod, "Delegitimation and Legitimation as a Continuous Process," *The Middle East Journal*, 35 (4), Autumn 1981, pp. 527–543.

24. Yuval Neeman, "Samaria as the Basis of Israeli Security" (Hebrew) in his *The Policy of Distorted Vision*, (Ramat-Gan: Revivim, 1984), pp. 155–170.

25. *Jerusalem Post*, September 19, 1978.

26. *Jerusalem Post*, October 5, 1978.

27. Joseph Nedava, ed., *The Israeli-Arab Conflict*, (Hebrew), (Ramat-Gan: Revivim, 1983), p. 395.

28. Pori Public Opinion Poll, *Haaretz*, May 21, 1979.

29. *Yediot Ahronot*, July 20, 1979.

30. For a discussion of the Israeli economy during the Begin era, see Doron Weissbrod and Lilly Weissbrod, "Inflation in Israel: The Economic Cost of Political Legitimation," *The Journal of Social, Political and Economic Studies*, 11 (2), Summer 1986, pp. 201–226.

3

The Binational Idea in Mandatory Times and Today: A Personal Evaluation

Susan Hattis Rolef

In the years 1918–1948 and again since 1967, Jews and Arabs have lived in western Palestine, or Eretz Israel west of the River Jordan, under a single ruler but in a state of conflict. In the earlier period it was a foreign power, Great Britain, which ruled in Palestine in accordance with a Mandate granted it by the League of Nations. Since 1967 it has been Israel, which occupied the West Bank and Gaza Strip in the course of the Six Day War, which is the de facto ruler.

Both in the earlier period and today the status quo was/is not generally accepted as permanent, the future of the territory being undecided. The theoretical options then as now are almost identical. The territory could be divided between the two peoples; it could remain united under the rule of one of them, with the other enjoying at most minority rights; it could be shared by the two as a binational state.

The subject of this essay is binationalism. Was it ever an option? Is it still an option today?

Binationalism—A Definition and Theoretical Background

Binationalism in the political sense involves a system of government in which the two nations concerned are viewed as the primary components, or state-forming elements of the state, where the status of neither depends on the good will or generosity of the other, and the government and state institutions are shared by the two, not necessarily in proportion to their respective numerical strength but as a fundamental principle of the system. While the component nations share a common patriotism, each national group maintains its own separate national identity, the use of its language and its own cultural and religious heritage. In this system the language, culture and religion of neither enjoys a superior status.

It follows that the fact that two nations live in the same state does not automatically mean that the state is binational. In fact, most states in which two nations live are not binational. They are either ordinary democratic states in which the majority rules and the minority enjoys minority rights, or "apartheid" states in which one of the nations does not enjoy equal rights and suffers from discrimination and segregation.

The number of functioning bi- or multinational states is not large, but they all share several features worth mentioning:

- All of them are free associations. None developed from a situation in which one of the component nations dominated the other or others. Such a situation is not conducive to the development of bi- or multinationalism since a ruling nation is never willing to give up its dominance in favor of a condominium, while subject nations invariably seek independence. Furthermore, a binational or multinational state cannot be kept together by force.
- In all existing bi- or multinational states there is one nation which is substantially larger than the other or others, a fact which appears to contribute to the system's stability since there is never a struggle for predominance.
- All these states have suffered from problems of unrest resulting from uneven levels and rates of development and prosperity. However, what has kept them together has been the absence of a better alternative and the application of policies designed to gradually reduce economic and social inequalities.[1]

Though theories of bi- or multinationalism have not been developed as such, as concepts or ideals they were advocated in the 19th century and the beginning of the 20th by those who viewed the prospect of the European multinational empires breaking up into so many nation states as regressive and sought to reform these empires into multinational states.[2]

In more recent academic jargon such systems have been included in the concept of the "consociational democracy"—a model for democracy in pluralistic societies which avoids the dictatorship of the majority.[3]

The prerequisite for any successful consociational democracy is said to be "cooperation attitudes and behavior of the leaders of the different segments of the population" in order to counteract the centrifugal tendencies inherent in a plural society."[4] This applies to different national groups as much as to other categories of groups in a pluralistic society.

Chauvinism and national liberation movements are, by definition, the greatest opponents of the ideal of bi- or multinationalism.

Jews and Arabs in Mandatory Times

In the years 1918–1948 Great Britain was the ruling power in Palestine, having succeeded the Ottoman Empire. After conquering the country in 1917–1918 it administered it by power of a League of Nations Mandate which formally came into force in July 1922. The text of the Mandate did not foresee any particular type of state evolving in Palestine, though as in the case of all mandates the Mandate for Palestine was not designed to continue to exist in perpetuity, and the mandatory power was supposed to prepare the country for independence.

However, the Jewish national home provisions of the Mandate[5] ensured that a major change in the country's demographic make-up and consequently in the options open for the country's future would inevitably occur. It was this change which the Palestinian Arabs resisted throughout the mandatory period—to the extent of refusing to recognize the Mandate by force of which the change was allowed to take place—and which the Zionists struggled to realize, against the persistent hostility of the Arabs and the growing coolness of the mandatory power.

Throughout the mandatory period the country was administered by British officials on the basis of directives from the Colonial office, and then the Foreign Office, in London. Attempts were made to establish a legislative council in which representatives of both communities would participate.

The debate over the establishment of a legislative council was, inter alia, the background for one of the first binational proposals for Palestine, but the legislative council never materialized due to the impossibility of finding a mutually acceptable formula for distributing seats between the Arab and Jewish communities.[6] As a result, the mandatory government continued to administer the country without the participation or formal representation of the two communities until the bitter end in 1948.

While this ensured that the country was administered relatively efficiently, despite the fundamental conflict between the two national communities inhabiting it, this form of administration also facilitated the political separation between them. "It relieved the need for Arab and Jewish political elites to cultivate direct relationships . . . This technical possibility of avoiding direct political contacts was exploited by both sides in ways which reflected their respective national aspirations."[7]

Why the two communities should have sought segregation is not difficult to understand. For the Arabs direct contact and cooperation with the Jews would have implied recognition of the Jews as a national entity with a legitimate claim to Palestine. While the Jews did not object to direct contacts and cooperation on principle, they did not accept the Palestinian Arabs as a separate national entity distinct from the Arab nation as a whole. In fact, they were almost exclusively concerned with their own national

development and crystallization and the establishment of autonomous institutions representing and serving the Jewish community only.

The establishment of these institutions further contributed to the process
of political separation, and though one does not know what would have
happened had the Arabs chosen to be cooperative, one may assume that
the separatist tendencies would still have been strong.

The two communities were in the process of crystallizing their national
identities, and the rivalry which developed between them was a major
component of this process. The two were also developing in very different
directions. While the Jewish community, made up predominantly of immigrants from Europe, developed as a democratic society with elected
institutions, the Arab society was still traditional and autocratic.

However, the separation and differences did not only have political
causes.

> Differences between the two communities were apparent in all areas of life.
> The Jewish sector was mainly urban while the vast majority of the Arab
> sector was rural . . . In the economic sphere, two levels of wages existed for
> the same occupations and even two levels of prices for the same agricultural
> produce . . . Estimates of national per capita income clearly show different
> levels of development for the Jewish and Arab economies . . . No less significant
> were the differences between the two communities in the sphere of education
> and culture.[8]

Under the circumstances there were only two possible forms of social
structure. "The two populations (could) be aligned in the same hierarchy,
with the more 'developed' population . . . located in the upper stratum
and the less developed in the lower stratum. Or, each population (could)
maintain a hierarchy of its own, which implies that the populations are,
to a considerable extent, segregated from each other."[9]

The first pattern might possibly have developed if the British administration had not been present and had the Jews been able to mobilize
sufficient force to impose their rule over the Arabs at this early stage. But
the circumstances encouraged the development of the second pattern. The
development of binationalism under the circumstances never really stood
a chance.

A Brief History of the
Binational Idea in Mandatory Times[10]

The fact that binationalism was not a realistic option did not prevent
the emergence of a diverse group of binationalists within the Jewish
community in Palestine.

The binationalists stood apart from the rest of the Jewish community in their viewing the Arab-Jewish conflict as a conflict between two nations, both having national rights and aspirations in Palestine. They sought a solution to the problem within an undivided Palestine—a solution which would avoid one nation dominating the other, and which would avoid an armed conflict. They sought to avoid an armed conflict either because they had pacifist inclinations or because they did not believe in the Jews' ability to survive such a conflict.

The group included *humanistic liberals*, mostly academics who were disturbed by the fact that Zionism did not seem to be interested in the political rights of the Arab population and tended to regard the Arabs as a nuisance rather than prospective partners with whom the country would have to be shared.

There were *idealistic socialists* for whom the binational solution, possibly within Palestine on both banks of the River Jordan, was the only way out of the inherent contradiction between Zionism as a national movement and socialism based on international working class solidarity.

There were the *pragmatic old-timers* who were individuals strongly rooted in the Jewish community but at the same time spoke fluent Arabic and felt comfortable in the Arab milieu. These individuals wished their personal experience on a national scale.

Fourthly, there were the *pessimists* who were skeptical about the prospects of the Jews ever having the power to establish their own national state and viewed binationalism as the only feasible tolerable option.

Finally there were what one may term *"tactical binationalists"*—those who did not believe in binationalism as an ideal or as a last resort but merely used the idea as a tactical lever to achieve other aims.

The 1920s

The history of binationalism in mandatory times opened and closed with constitutional plans. In the early 1920s these plans proposed parity (equal numerical representation) in the legislative council which the British administration seemed bent on setting up. In the early 1940s much more elaborate binational plans were proposed by two Jewish committees appointed to examine various constitutional arrangements for resolving the conflict. The first proposal which advocated parity in the institutions of government (as well as in the army) was made by Ze'ev Jabotinsky at the end of 1922. Jabotinsky, who had earlier advocated the conquest of the whole of Palestine by the Jews and to his dying day in 1940 continued to advocate the establishment of a Jewish state on both banks of the River Jordan, was no binationalist, and the purpose of his proposal was purely tactical. In 1922 the Jews constituted only 11 percent of the population and Jabotinsky raised the proposal in order for it to be rejected and for the whole legislative council idea to be dropped.[11]

Parity in the senate, in a two-chamber legislature, was again mentioned in 1924 at the conference of the *Ahdut Ha'avodah workers party* by Shlomo Kaplansky, who remained a proponent of binationalism until the end of the Mandate. However, his was a minority position within the pragmatic Zionist labor movement. The first serious study of the binational idea as a solution to the Arab-Jewish problem in Palestine began in 1925 with the foundation of the Jewish *Brit Shalom* (Covenant of Peace) society. The group was made up primarily of intellectuals, most of them of central European origin, and a number of "practical" Zionists who had settled in Palestine before the First World War.

The society was founded by Arthur Ruppin, head of the Zionist Palestine Land Development Company, following an impressive lecture by the German-Jewish orientalist Professor Joseph Horowitz. Ruppin wanted it to be a study group on Jewish-Arab relations, which might contribute to a more active Zionist policy aiming at cooperation with the Arabs. He did not want it to produce constitutional blueprints or enter into active politics. However, the 1929 disturbances, which involved murderous attacks by Arabs on Jews, brought about a change of leadership in the society, and the so-called "university group," led by Professors Hugo Bergmann and Gershom Scholem, became predominant. *Brit Shalom* started to prepare memoranda containing plans for a solution of the Palestine problem based on binational lines and considered entering active politics within the framework of the Jewish community in Palestine.

Despite its strong impact on the Jewish community, which stemmed from the quality of its members and the public controversy which its views generated, *Brit Shalom's* membership never rose above 200.

Nevertheless, in the early years it had the sympathy of certain official Zionist circles, including the President of the World Zionist Organization, Haim Weizmann, who, after realizing that his hope that the Balfour Declaration and the British Mandate would lead to the rapid establishment of a Jewish state would not materialize, was intellectually inclined to consider binationalism as an alterntive. However, as a realist Weizmann soon realized that the idea was impractical since binationalism appealed to neither the Jews nor the Arabs and the British were in no mood to impose a policy which was unpopular in both camps. After a while the society also began to clash with the Zionist and local Jewish establishments which it accused of shortsightedness concerning the Arabs. While the ideological principles of *Brit Shalom* were not radically different from those on which the official Zionist policy was based (the need for accommodation and the principle of non-domination over the Arabs), both the officials and many private persons became increasingly irritated by the self-righteousness of many of the society's members and their apparent lack of faith in the absolute Jewish right over the historical homeland, in the ability of the Jews ever to become a majority in the country or to survive in Palestine without British protection. However, it was *Brit Shalom's* implication that the Jews might have avoided the outbreak of the 1929 disturbances through greater foresight which finally brought a flood of abuse on it in the Jewish press, and its members found themselves labelled as traitors and defeatists.

Perhaps if *Brit Shalom* had managed to find adherents among local Arab circles it might have gathered a greater following in the Jewish community as well. But it never made any serious efforts to establish Arab contacts or to propagate the binational idea among Arab circles, and even if it had it is doubtful whether Arab support for binationalism could have been elicited at this stage.

Lack of funds was the immediate cause for the termination of *Brit Shalom's* institutionalized existence in 1933.

Though all the various Jewish workers' parties accepted the principle that neither of the two peoples in Palestine should dominate the other, it was only the peripheral Marxist *Hashomer Hatza'ir* which called, in 1929, for the establishment of a binational socialist state in Palestine on both sides of the River Jordan in which the Jews would constitute a majority. In other words, unlike the binationalism of *Brit Shalom* which was minimalist in territorial and immigration terms, that of *Hashomer Hatza'ir* was maximalist.

Another basic difference between the two brands of binationalism was that while the ideology of *Brit Shalom* was based on liberal principles and a perception of the Arab-Jewish conflict as a national one, that of *Hashomer Hatza'ir* was based on a social approach which saw the clash as stemming from social and international causes.

The socialist binationalists were convinced that the Arab masses were not concerned with politics and nationalism and could be drawn away from their bourgeois *effendi* leaders on the basis of working class solidarity and by means of programs of social and economic betterment. In addition, the left-wing binationalist approach argued that the national alienation (between Arabs and Jews) had been created, at least in part, by the imperialists' policy of "divide and rule."[12] In other words, the clash between Arabs and Jews was artificial—created by the traditional Arab leadership and the British.

The 1930s

While several individual members in the pragmatic Mapai workers' party, founded in 1930, were active binationalists, Mapai as such never adopted binationalism as an ideology. Nevertheless, for a number of years in the early 1930s it formally supported the idea of parity in a legislative council, should the British have decided to establish such a council in Palestine.

In addition, several prominent members of Mapai, including David Ben-Gurion, gave the Swiss cantonal model—one of the few functioning multinational systems—some serious thought. However, like Victor Jacobson, the representative of the Zionist Organization in Geneva, who in 1929 proposed a cantonization plan for Palestine, so they too soon abandoned the idea in favor of the concept of partition, i.e. the partition of Palestine into two separate independent states.

The Mapai proposals regarding parity in a legislative council and cantonization differed from similar proposals made by the binationalists in that they did not seek to bring the two peoples—the Jews and Arabs—closer together in the process but rather to maximalize Jewish gains under the given circumstances.[13]

The 1930 Passfield White (policy) Paper once again raised the prospect of a legislative council being formed within the framework of constitutional developments in the country. In fact, the legislative council idea remained on the British agenda until the outbreak of the 1936 disturbances, and some of the senior civil servants in the Colonial Office in London, as well as one Colonial Secretary, Malcolm MacDonald, considered the introduction of a system of parity in such a council favorably before giving the whole idea up.

The cantonization idea was less popular in the Colonial Office, but there were several influential British personalities who favored and advocated it towards the mid-30s. In the years 1933–1936 most of the Zionists were preoccupied with the massive Jewish immigration into Palestine which resulted from the rise of National Socialism in Germany and anti-Semitic forces in Eastern Europe, and with the economic prosperity which accompanied it. For the first time the chances of a Jewish majority and state in Palestine in the foreseeable future seemed feasible. Under those circumstances, who needed binationalism? Thus, it was the British dabbling in ideas conducive to binationalism which encouraged the Jewish binationalists in these years.

In the years 1937–1938 it was a sudden apparent Arab interest in plans based on binationalist principles which kept the binationalists going. This was in the period between the publication of the Peel Commission Report of 1937, which recommended partition, and the publication of the Woodhead Commission Report the following year, which temporarily buried the idea. As long as the threat of partition was in the air, some Arabs seemed willing to consider a modified form of binationalism as the lesser evil.

This resulted in a long series of exploratory probings, of which the best known and most intricate evolved around the so called Hyamson-Newcome plan. Albert Montefiore Hyamson was a non-Zionist English Jew who had served with the Mandatory administration in Palestine, and Colonel Stewart Francis Newcome was a pro-Arab Englishman working for the Palestine Office in London. Three different plans emerged from this effort. None of the three—the first prepared by Hyamson and Newcombe themselves, the second by Haj Amin al-Husseini, the exiled Mufti of Jerusalem, and the third by Nuri Said of Iraq—would have permitted free Jewish immigration into Palestine, or the Jews ever reaching numerical equality with the Arabs in the country. The plans were all rejected out of hand by the Jewish Agency, though Judah L. Magnes, Chancellor of the Hebrew University in Jerusalem, stubbornly continued in efforts to start some form of negotiations between the two sides on the basis of these plans.

This was not the first time that Magnes had been involved in contacts with Arabs in an effort to bring about an agreed settlement of the Palestine problem based on binationalism. Magnes never belonged to *Brit Shalom*[14] though he had supported its activities. Following the 1929 disturbances he had carried on discussions with St. John Philby, an Englishman closely associated with King Ibn Saud of Saudi Arabia, in an attempt to find a basis for an agreement between Jews and Arabs. At the same time Magnes, a rabbi and pacifist, also published several articles in which he advocated the binational idea. He was severely criticized by the official Zionist leaders for holding negotiations with Philby on a topic which only the official Jewish institutions were authorized to deal with. In 1938 he once again came under fire for the same reason.

In between these two episodes he introduced Ben-Gurion to several of his Arab acquaintances, and in 1936, following the outbreak of the disturbances of that year, joined with four other highly respected Palestinian Jews[15] in an attempt to find some sort of breakthrough in the apparently insoluble Arab-Jewish conflict. The activities of the five were based on the premise that an agreement was possible between the Zionist leadership and the existing leadership of the Palestinian Arabs.[16] Had they been right then the main condition for working out a "consociational democracy" in Palestine would have been possible.[17] But an ex post facto study of the period and the actors involved on both sides suggests that this was an illusion.

Another Palestinian Jew who was active in trying to foster better relations between Jews and Arabs on a binational basis during these years was Haim Margalit Kalvarisky. Kalvarisky, an agronomist who had lived in Palestine since 1895, started to initiate political talks with Arab personalities as early as 1914. Unlike Magnes, he joined *Brit Shalom*, and following the 1936 disturbances became one of the founders of an association called *Kedma Mizraha* (Eastwards to the Orient) which sought to bring the Jews closer to the peoples of the Orient. Not all the members of *Kedma Mizraha* were binationalists, and the association soon ceased to function on a regular basis, though Kalvarisky continued to carry on talks with various Arab personalities in its name until 1939.

Both Magnes and Kalvarisky were constantly turning to the Jewish Agency Executive with what they believed to be real opportunities for furthering understanding between Jews and Arabs. Of the two Magnes was more highly respected, but both were given a hearing. Their influence however, was, minimal.

In these years the *Shomer Hatza'ir* continued to advocate binationalism, though most of its members did not go beyond general declarations. One of the exceptions was Mordechai Bentov who in 1936 started to struggle within his movement against its disinclination to adopt an explicit binational program.[18] It was not until 1942, after the Biltmore Program was adopted by the Zionist Organization, calling for the establishment of a Jewish "commonwealth" in Palestine, that Bentov managed to convince the *Shomer Hatza'ir* to advocate binationalism openly as an immediate policy goal, even if this meant reaching an agreement with the existing reactionary Arab leadership.[19]

The pre-Second World War era ended for Palestine with the London "Round Table Conference" at which the British met separately with Jewish and Arab delegations (the Arabs refused to sit formally with the Jews at the same table). At the Conference several different plans for Palestine were discussed, some of them bearing distinct binational features. But the meetings ended in deadlock, and within several weeks the British published a new White Paper which foresaw the termination of Jewish immigration to Palestine after five years and the establishment of an independent Palestinian state in which the Arabs would remain the dominant majority.

The 1940s

The outbreak of the War found most of the Palestinian Arab leaders in exile and the Mufti of Jerusalem supporting the Axis powers. This raised hopes amongst the Jewish binationalists that in the absence of the extremist Arab leadership the two peoples in Palestine might find ways to cooperate and that at the end of the War the Allies might seriously consider a binational solution for the Palestine problem.

Several weeks after the breakdown of the London Conference the various groups and individuals in Palestine who had traditionally advocated bi-nationalism managed to get together in a single organization—the League for Jewish-Arab Rapprochement and Cooperation.

One of the groups, which assumed the name *Ihud* (Union), was led by Magnes and the philosopher Martin Buber, who had arrived in Palestine from Germany on the eve of the War, and was made up primarily of *Brit Shalom* and *Kedma Mizraha* veterans. A second group included members of the two socialist parties *Hashomer Hatza'ir* and *Poalei Zion Smol*, both of which joined the new organization en-bloc in 1942. A third group was made up of some of the leading figures among the new immigrants from Germany who founded their own political party *Aliya Hadasha* (New Immigration) in the Autumn of 1942.

The League declared its goal to be the advocacy of a binational solution to the Palestine problem and attempted to get the Zionist Organization to adopt it officially.

Soon after the outbreak of War, two committees were established within the Jewish community in Palestine to study the subject of Jewish-Arab relations in Palestine and possible solutions to the conflict. Both committees had a strong binational bias, which created the false impression that the binational idea might be progressing towards victory.

The first committee was established by the Jewish Agency in January 1940 under the chairmanship of Shlomo Kaplansky to gather information and hear evidence from experts. It was made up of seven members of whom four (including Magnes and Kalvarisky) were known proponents of the binational idea. Why the Jewish Agency should have set up a committee with such a bias might have one of two explanations: firstly, following the breakdown of the Round Table Conference, Ben-Gurion had seriously considered the possibility of a federal solution to the Palestine problem, involving free Jewish immigration into an autonomous Jewish region and a federal government based on parity,[20] and he may well have wanted the idea to be examined more thoroughly. Secondly, the Jewish Agency leaders might have seen the committee as a way of keeping the binationalists busy—a sort of occupational therapy which would keep them out of mischief in those troubled times.

The second committee, the "Constitutional Committee," was set up at the same time by the League for Jewish-Arab Rapprochement and Cooperation under the chairmanship of Mordechai Bentov, not to do research but to design a binational constitution.

Due to their composition, the two committees started their work from the same basic premises, namely that neither the Jews nor the Arabs could have all they wanted, that partition was undesirable, and that the domination of one people over the other was unacceptable.[21]

Both committees ended up by examining two forms of federalism: personal-communal federalism based on the sharing of power between the two national groups irrespective of their territorial base, and territorial federalism based on the division of the country between the two nations but with a central government based on parity. Both published reports which favored the latter solution, though the Kaplansky committee did so more unequivocally than the Bentov committee.[22]

The two committees completed their work before the full dimensions of the Holocaust were known. If in 1941 there was still a chance that binationalism might be seriously considered by the Jewish leaders, in 1942 none was left.

When the Zionist Organization came out officially with the Biltmore Program in 1942, the members of the League became its most active opponents. But those demanding the establishment of a Jewish state, whether in the whole or part of Palestine, were the majority, and their determination was now greater than ever before.

The binationalists had always been the subject of criticism and attacks, but now, under the influence of the Holocaust, the criticism turned into unrestrained abuse and demands that the binationalists be removed from all official positions and stopped from holding unauthorized negotiations.[23]

Nevertheless, the League members did not give up their struggle and continued to advocate their ideas to the very end—namely, May 1948. In 1943 it established contacts with one of the Arab parties in Palestine the *Istiglal* (Independence), but the interest of this party's leaders in negotiating an agreement was short lived. In 1946 the League succeeded in finding an Arab group in Jerusalem which was willing to advocate binationalism, but its leader, Fawzi Darwish al-Husseini, was murdered shortly afterwards by Arab extremists.

As the hopes of getting Jewish and Arab endorsements for binationalism vanished, the League's last hope were the two international committees which were sent to Palestine after the Second World War to investigate the situation and recommend a solution.

The first was the Anglo-American Committee of 1946, and the second the UN Special Committee on Palestine (UNSCOP). Magnes appeared before the first committee and left a strong impression on its members, while a long memorandum prepared by the *Shomer Hatza'ir* was given serious consideration. Both the League and *Ihud* appeared before UNSCOP, but had no influence either on the majority report which proposed partition or the minority report which proposed leaving Palestine as a unitary state with the Arabs in de facto control.

The departure of Britain on May 15, 1948, and the proclamation of the State of Israel in part of Palestine the previous night sounded the death knell to the binational idea in Palestine—at least until June 1967. The deaths of Kalvarisky in 1947, of Magnes in 1948, and of Kaplansky in 1950 were, in a way, symbolic of the whole movement.

Most of the persons who had been involved in the struggle for binationalism and were still active after the establishment of the state shifted their efforts to the struggle for the abolition of the military administration applied to the Arab population of Israel and to secure equal rights for Israel's minorities.

Despite the total failure of the binationalists, the study of the binational idea in mandatory times is important both from a purely intellectual point of view and as a way to understand the nature of the Arab-Jewish conflict in Palestine until 1948 and the Arab-Israeli conflict since.

In theoretical terms, the Jewish binationalists in mandatory times made a major contribution to political thinking regarding the inadequancies of the nation state in certain circumstances, proposing various constitutional solutions to certain problems stemming from the requirements of pluralistic societies.

In concrete terms, through their obstinate insistence on pursuing every apparent opening for finding a solution to the conflict which would not lead to either the domination of one people over the other or to partition and would avoid war, the binationalists provided ample proof (though they themselves would never admit it) that there was really no alternative to either partition or the domination of one people over the other and that war was unavoidable.

In other words, the reasonable, humane, and just solution to the Arab-Israeli conflict was not realistic because it did not take into account the historical forces which motivated the two camps. It was a detached intellectual idea which went against the mainstream developments in both camps.

Zionism was a "national Liberation movement" which sought national sovereignty for the Jewish people, and the Zionists were people who came to Palestine to realize this goal.

Though the Zionists had to address themselves to the problem of Jewish-Arab relations in Palestine, they could hardly be expected to do so at the expense of their primary goal, especially since most Zionists believed their rights in Palestine to be superior to those of the Arabs and expected the Jews to become an overwhelming majority in the country in the foreseeable future through mass immigration.

For most Jews in Palestine the "second best solution" to a Jewish state was living in the diaspora—not sharing sovereignty in a state with the hostile Arabs.

As to the Palestinian Arabs, none of them doubted that if only the foreign power, Great Britain, got out and left them to take care of the situation without intervention, they could reverse the "Zionist invasion" and reclaim the whole of what they believed to be rightfully theirs. Rejection of any compromise was the cornerstone of their position then and the position of the Palestinian rejectionist camp to the present day. It made no difference if the compromise took the form of partition or condominium—it was rejected out of hand.

We have no way of knowing what the Palestinian leaders in mandatory times would have done had they foreseen the consequences of their "all or nothing" policy. Perhaps they might have accepted partition. It is difficult to imagine that they would have opted for binationalism.

The Situation Since 1967

From 1948 to 1967 binationalism became a purely academic issue. In the territory of mandatory Palestine there was now one predominantly Jewish state with an Arab minority seeking equality. Transjordan and what now came to be known as the "West Bank" became the "Hashemite Kingdom of Jordan" (some might say a Jordanian-Palestian binational state, but one in which the Jordanians were predominant), while the Gaza Strip was occupied by Egypt, which left it in the status of an occupied territory. If anyone thought in terms of reuniting Palestine—or Eretz Israel—it was certainly not for the purpose of resolving the Arab-Israeli conflict through binationalism.

But in 1967 the situation changed again. The Six Day War resulted in an outcome which had not been planned. Israel embarked on what it regarded as another war of defense and ended up in occupation of the whole of Mandatory Palestine west of the River Jordan and more. Once again western Palestine, or Eretz Israel west of the River Jordan, was ruled by a single power, only this time it was not a foreign power but one of the two nations which claimed rights of ownership over the whole country— Israel.

However, while East Jerusalem was annexed soon after the termination of the War, and the Golan Heights (not part of Palestine) was annexed in 1981, the bulk of the West Bank and the whole of the Gaza Strip have been kept under occupation and the future of western Palestine remains open, at least in theory. Again, theoretically speaking, binationalism has reverted to being an option for the future, though unlike the mandatory period this time there is no organized, systematic, and coherent force advocating it.

Are the objective conditions more suitable today than they were in mandatory times for the development of a binational state? The factors working against binationalism seem insurmountable. On the Israeli side one may enumerate the following factors which are working against binationalism:

• It is Israel which is in occupation of the whole territory. It has full sovereignty of close to 80% of the territory and is in military occupation of the rest. As was pointed out in the beginning of this essay, there is no example in history of a ruling people voluntarily entering an arrangement of condominium with a people it has occupied. At the same time binationalism is the solution least likely to be imposed from the outside, supposing a solution is eventually imposed, since it is wanted by neither side.

- The Jewish Israeli public is becoming progressively more nationalist and less tolerant, both characteristics which make the concept of binationalism less likely to be accepted by it than ever before.
- Within the camp which is more inclined to compromise and keep an open mind with regards to the national ambitions of the Palestinians, the largest bloc—the Alignment—openly rejects binationalism.

  It justifies its advocacy of a territorial compromise and rejection of annexation by arguing that unless Israel gives up the densely populated territories in the West Bank and Gaza strip it will either cease to be democratic or cease to be a predominantly Jewish state, i.e., it will turn into a binational state.

- In the last 40 years the political, social, cultural, and economic gaps between Jews and Arabs have not closed to any substantial degree, while distrust, animosity, and mutual dehumanization have grown as a result of the constant torrent of terrorist acts, or the "armed struggle" carried out by Palestinian forces against Israeli and Jewish targets, and unrelenting retaliatory attacks by Israeli forces. The wave of violent demonstrations which broke out in the occupied territories at the end of 1987 and the harsh measures taken by Israel to quash them has added an additional layer of hatred and suspicion which makes cooperation on equal terms seem totally unlikely.

From a superficial standpoint one would have assumed that the main proponents of binationalism would now come from the Palestinian side as the weaker of the two and the one with less to lose after having lost almost everything in the last 40 years. But the reality once again, is different.

- 40 years of deprivation have increased the Palestinian national consciousness, have make the Palestinians more eager than ever before to become masters of their own destiny and to acquire a state of their own. If the Palestinians have become more willing to compromise (and it is at best debatable if their "sole legitimate representative," the PLO, really is willing to compromise), it is in the direction of willingness to accept a state in only part of western Palestine—not in the direction of sharing power with the "Zionist entity" with which they still still find it difficult to come to terms.
- The Palestinians perceive the Israelis as domineering occupiers who do not recognize the Arabs as their equals and whose overwhelming military force the Palestinians are not likely to match for many years to come. Arab Knesset member Mohammad Wattad from Mapam describes this perception in the following terms: one could observe a

wolf and a sheep sitting every morning together in a meadow and conclude that this is co-habitation on equal terms. But is it the same sheep which one sees every morning?[24] In other words, Jewish-Arab coexistence on equal terms within the framework of a binational state is perceived as unlikely as a wolf and sheep grazing together in the meadow. At most it might be a utopia.

And yet, there are those who continue to advocate binationalism. On the Jewish side since 1968 various individuals have come up with proposals for federal or confederal solutions to the conflict which bear distinct binational features. Some involve Jordan as well and are thus trinational.[25] However, most of the individuals involved are eccentrics working on their own, with no influence whatsoever in the Israeli mainstream.

Israeli public opinion is, in fact, divided into two main groups: those who call for Israeli withdrawal from all or most of the territories occupied in June 1967, in other words who call for a repartition of western Palestine, and those who call for annexation of the territories.

Meron Benvenisti, director of the West Bank Data Center, has developed what he terms the "irreversibility prognosis." The "crawling annexation," says Benvenisti, has gone so far that it is highly unlikely that Israel will ever withdraw from the West Bank and Gaza Strip. Since annexation is inevitable, Benvenisti argues that Israel has three options: to maintain the Jewish character of the state by ceasing to be democratic; by granting the Palestinian minority national autonomy; by finding some arrangement based on the association of the Arab population of the West Bank and Gaza Strip in the regime, side by side with the Jews and Israeli Arabs—i.e., a binationalist solution.[26]

Benvenisti does not say which of the three options he believes to be the most realistic. Though he has his own preferences, he views himself primarily as an observer and documenter.

On the Arab side three concepts are worth taking a look at. It is frequently suggested that the "democratic-secular state" which some members of the PLO advocate, or claim to be the true long term goal of the organization, is binationalism. It is not.

In a binational state there remain two distinct nationalities, with their own languages, cultures, and in this case religions. Only the governmental institutions are shared, as is a common patriotism. The "democratic-secular state" seeks to blur the national differences, to mold a new consciousness free of the old nationalisms.

Another idea which PLO leaders have said they are willing to consider and which may be mistaken for an acceptance of the principle of binationalism is the idea of an Israeli-Palestinian confederation. PLO chairman Yasser Arafat actually stated that he would be willing to discuss the idea with

Israelis.[27] However, on other occasions he and other PLO personalities have made it clear that the Palestinians must first have full independence in their own sovereign state before entering any confederal arrangements with any other state.

Dr. Sari Nuseibeh, a lecturer of Islamic philosophy at Bir Zeit University in Ramallah, is one of the few Palestinians to advocate binationalism. But even for Nuseibeh binationalism is only a transition stage, not an end goal.

Since he shares Benvenisti's skepticism regarding the likelihood of an Israeli withdrawal from the West Bank and Gaza Strip Nuseibeh advocates that the Palestinians should ask Israel to annex these territories. Such an annexation will formalize the de facto state of apartheid which exists, in his opinion, vis-à-vis the Arabs in the territories. The Palestinians should then start to struggle for equal rights and Israeli citizenship. By the year 2020 there are good prospects that the Arabs living in Palestine West of the River Jordan will be the majority, and when they are finally given full rights they will control the Knesset and other institutions of government and be able to pass a Palestinian "Law of Return" which will enable all the Palestinian refugees to return to Palestine, if they chose to do so. At this stage Israel/Palestine will turn into a binational state in the full sense of the word. However, Nuseibeh's ideal is the democratic-secular state, and nationalism is but a tool to reach the higher ideal of secular internationalism.[28]

It is a clever scenario, but one which merely strengthens those forces in Israel which call for Israeli withdrawal before it gets caught in the web.[29]

Nuseibeh's scenario assumes that at a certain point Israel will have no alternative after annexing the territories but to grant the Arabs equal rights. In fact, annexation is much more likely to lead, after a stage of apartheid, to a forced transfer of the Arab population than to binationalism.

In the *Al Fajr* opinion poll of September 1986 no question was asked about a binational solution, but one may infer from the answers given to the questions asked that binationalism would not have gained any support. It is also a safe guess that an Israeli public opinion poll which would present the binational state as an option would reveal that the Israelis do not consider it acceptable either. Nobody wants or believes in binationalism. Thus binationalism as a system of government and state organization, as opposed to a demographic reality, is, unfortunately, no more than a pipe dream.

Notes

1. See for example, Susan Hattis Rolef, "The Multinational State," *Res Publica*, Vol XVI, No 1, 1974, pp. 89–116.

2. Ibid. pp. 90–96.

3. Arend Lijphart, *Democracy in Plural Societies,* (New Haven: Yale University Press, 1977).

4. Ibid. p. 1.

5. The Mandate for Palestine included the Balfour Declaration in its preamble which spoke of "the establishment in Palestine of a national home for the Jewish people."

6. Dan Horowitz and Moshe Lissak, *Origins of the Israeli Polity,* (Chicago: University of Chicago Press, 1977), p. 19.

7. Ibid. p. 33.

8. Ibid. pp. 20–21.

9. Ibid. p. 26.

10. This chapter is largely based on Susan Hattis Rolef, "The Binational State and the Challenge of History," *New Middle East* No. 35, August 1971, pp. 24–27.

11. Susan Hattis Rolef, "Jabotinsky's Parity Plan for Palestine," *Middle East Studies,* Vol 13, No 1, January 1977.

12. Shmuel Dotan, *Hama'avak al Eretz Israel* (The Struggle for Palestine), (Tel-Aviv: Defense Ministry Publishing House, 1981), pp. 67–68.

13. Ibid. p. 95.

14. It is curious how Magnes' name continues to be associated with *Brit Shalom* to the present day and how many people still believe that he was its leader. He was never even a member.

15. The four were Pinchas Rutenberg, Moshe Novomeysky, Gad Frumkin, and Moshe Smilansky.

16. Dotan, op. cit. p. 115.

17. See above p. 3 and footnote 3.

18. Dotan, op. cit. p. 125.

19. Ibid. p. 235.

20. Ibid. p. 185.

21. Ibid. p. 194.

22. For further details see Susan Lee Hattis, *The Binational Idea in Palestine during Mandatory Times,* (Haifa: Shikmona), pp. 231–249, and Dotan, op. cit. pp. 185–201.

23. There is a similarity with the way the Israeli public today reacts to those who advocate recognition of the contacts with the PLO.

24. Discussion between author and MK Mohammad Wattad, January 6, 1987.

25. Arie Hess, a member of the Labor Party Central Committee, has been advocating the idea of an Israeli-Palestinian-Jordanian confederation for several years. So far he has not gained any formal support for his ideas in Israel, though Yasser Arafat offered to discuss the idea with him (see p. 31).

26. See Meron Benvenisti "Benvenisti Prognosis" in Susan Hattis Rolef ed. *A Political Dictionary of Israel,* (New York: Macmillan, 1987).

27. See interview with Yasser Arafat in *Le Nouvel Observateur,* January 1, 1988.

28. See interview given by Dr. Sari Nuseibeh to the author in *Spectrum* (the English language monthly of the Israel Labor Movement), May, 1987.

29. Israeli Minister of Economics and Communications Gad Yaacobi first reacted to Sari Nuseibeh's ideas, as published in an interview in *Newsweek* on January 23, 1986, in an article "Talks or Autonomy," *Jerusalem Post,* January 28, 1986.

PART 2

The Politics of
the Second Republic

4

Fragmentation and Polarization in Greater Israel: Political Behavior in Perpetual Crisis

Shlomo Aronson

Introduction

The binational reality, an interim reality that came into being after the Six Day War, is a result of a long-standing political stalemate in both the Israeli and Arab societies. The Arabs and Jews are immobilized politically and deadlocked with regard to most of the issues related to the Middle East conflict. As a result, they tend to adopt a status quo posture hoping to serve their contradictory interests. Recently, the Arab population of the West Bank and Gaza deviated from this pattern by resorting to riots and political protests. Beforehand, each side believed that a solution would be found in the remote future. The previous deadlock contributed to the emergence of a binational Israel by default rather than by design. Yet the riots, which had started in December 1987, did not produce a practical solution to the conflict, acceptable to all parties concerned.

The deadlocked political reality in the Middle East suggests that it is not enough to identify steps conducive to conflict resolution in general or devise diplomatic schemes designed to break the stalemate. Rather, the focus should be on the analysis of the cleavage structure of the conflict actors.

The major purpose of this chapter is to illustrate how the political system in Israel contributed to the deadlock. Accordingly, the current Government of National Unity which has ruled Israel since 1984 is a symbol of this deadlock. It has been brought to power by often imperceptible historical changes in the Israeli parliamentary and parity system in reaction to the political realities at home and in the Arab world. The historic dynamics of the cleavage structure are important in their own right and as a basis for assessing the prospects for a renewed diplomatic effort in the Middle East.

This chapter analyzes principally the history of cleavage structure in the Israeli society. The politics of the Arab society is discussed only in a marginal way. Such an asymmetrical presentation may create the impression that the major blame for creating binationalism by default falls on the Israeli society. Yet as the following discussion indicates, the struggle and the ensuing paralysis in the Arab camp were fully functional in creating the present situation. On many occasions the stalemate within Israel was generated and exacerbated by the divisions within the Arab camp.

Historical Background: The Emergence of the Cleavage Structure in the Israeli Society

The political system which evolved after the establishment of Israel in 1948 is in a large measure the legacy of the Jewish Yishuv in Palestine. The present party system grew out of a history of political struggles which were partly Western and partly peculiar to the Jewish society in Palestine and to "Jewish politics"—or political habits—in the diaspora.

It is commonplace to use 1882 as the starting point of modern Israeli politics. It was in this year that the first wave of Jewish immigrants (the First Aliyah) established farming communities in Palestine. They joined the Jews of the old Yishuv (those who lived in Palestine for centuries) in forming a fairly traditional society. Politically, this partially secular and partially religious orthodox community drew from the experience of the *kehillah*, the Jewish community councils of the diaspora.

This traditional structure was radically transformed during the next and most important Second Aliyah (1904-1914). The young, mostly Eastern-European immigrants were influenced by the revolutionary movements in Europe. They first adopted the Socialist creed in their struggle against the traditional Jewish middle class, and Jewish life conditions abroad. In Zion, they tried to build a socialist-agrarian society which emphasized collectivism, a fair division of labor, and egalitarianism, cultural revival and normalization of Jewish life in terms of proletarization and return to nature. These early Socialist Zionists were strengthened by the Third Aliyah (1919-1923), eventually becoming the dominant Mapai party.

The Revisionists offered the only serious political challenge to the dominant Socialist Zionist ideology. Originating in Eastern and Central Europe, the Revisionists arriving in the later immigration waves, i.e. the Fourth and Fifth Aliyah (1924-1944), challenged the Socialist value system of Mapai. Bitter clashes occurred over issues such as social change first versus political independence and a Jewish military posture first. Mapai and the left were a protest movement against Jewish diaspora habits in the socio-moral sense. The Revisionists were a protest movement against the political and moral harassment of the Jews by the European right and the left.

At the founding of the state the existing cleavage structure was already well entrenched. On the one side of the divide were the Socialist Zionists. On the other side were the disparate forces of the orthodox, liberal, and former Revisionists embodied in the right wing Herut party. Although the clashes between the various political groups involved concrete political issues, the underlying tension pertained to the ultimate character of the new state.

The socialist camp was deeply divided between elitists, whose interest was centered around the small collective unit, the Kibbutz, and who adopted, at first, a Soviet orientation, and those who stressed the needs and the problems of the masses. Led by David Ben-Gurion, the moderate, popular oriented left became, at first, the pivotal power between far left, center, and right. Ben-Gurion dreamt about a secular state based on the selective Jewish humanistic tradition of social democracy. The Israeli elite under Ben-Gurion legitimized its claims to Eretz Israel through the use of biblical and historical symbolism combined with a quest for social justice. The Land of the Bible was conceived of as a modern refuge and a moral inspiration to both Jews and humanity at large.[1]

An important component in Ben-Gurion's thinking was based on a selective adaptation of some universal values derived from the prophetic ethos of the Bible and from modern social democracy. They included an exemplary and even ascetic way of life and personal sacrifice for the collective good. This behavioral pattern was exemplified in the Kibbutz, the Labor movement's use of capital and profits for the common good and other pioneering institutions of that movement such as health services, cooperative agriculture, and settlements in empty territory (i.e. not inhabited by Arabs). The moral and social ethos of the Socialist Zionists was designed to create a sense of mission and a vehicle for mobilizing and integrating the large masses of Jewish immigrants who came to Israel out of necessity or cultural-political reasons. The former, like the Sephardi Jews, were motivated by the age-old messianic spirit, and the hatred of Arabs in their neighboring countries, whereas the latter were driven out of Europe by the Holocaust or the yearning for a safe haven.

The final goal of Socialist Zionists was the return to nationhood of an historical nation to be accompanied by a process of national and social reeducation of the Jews. In Ben-Gurion's opinion this process of reeducation involved the development of a virtuous national ethos while pursuing the national interests of a nation state in a hostile world. It should be noted that Ben-Gurion's "messianism" did not fully correspond to a religious belief system or the "secular religion" of the type practiced by the radical political left. Rather, it derived from the rational pantheism of Spinoza, though without Spinoza's distinction between the Godly "general substance" and man. Quite clearly, Ben-Gurion strived to fill the moral vacuum typical of a secularized society by adopting a higher set of moral values.[2]

Ben-Gurion's "messianism" had many important foreign policy ramifications. Perhaps the most crucial one pertained to the territorial integrity of Eretz Israel. Although Socialist Zionists recognized the Biblical Jewish patrimony over the Land, they felt that ruling over a large Arab population would not only compromise the Jewish character of the state but also undermine its moral mission.[3] Thus, a territorial partition was both a practical demographic necessity and a moral imperative stemming from Ben-Gurion's unique brand of secular "messianism."

The national ethos dictated other foreign policy stands. Ben-Gurion tried to balance a proud and sovereign Israeli stand with the requirements of realpolitik at the international and regional level. At the operational level, Israel under Ben-Gurion adopted the cautious policy of limited retaliation in response to Arab raids across the borders. Another highly successful operational policy was the breaking of Israel's international isolation by acquiring access to vital foreign aid such as the delivery of French conventional weapons and Israeli-French nuclear cooperation.[4] A hallmark of Ben-Gurion's policy was the limited Sinai campaign of 1956 which served both to provide an answer to the guerrilla border raids, deter Israel's enemies, and break the Arab blockade over the Gulf of Eilat.

Yet for all its visionary reach Ben-Gurion's formula lacked a coherent theory of government. Ruling Israel amounted to maneuvering among heterogenous elites of the Left (Mapam), the Nationalist-Left (Achdut-Ha'avoda), the Center-Left (Mapai), the Right (Herut), the Right-Center (Liberals) and the religious parties. Ben-Gurion's personal efforts to reform the party system inherited from the Yishuv period failed. His subsequent moves to adopt the British procedures of a majority ballot, two party system, and a strong cabinet were challenged by the Israeli left, the smaller parties of the Center and the moderate Right which adhered to the radical, continental-European tradition.

Ben-Gurion's decline paved the way for the growing delegitimization of the dominant Mapai. To be sure, there were additional forces at work during the long and complex process of undermining his formulae. There was an increase in bureaucratization and the formalization of the Socialist dreams. The emergence of young, politically aggressive, Israeli born aspirants for power and the influx of immigrants whose political beliefs were at odds with the secular and pioneering vision of Ben-Gurion challenged his leadership from several directions. Yet the final blow was administered by the elitist left and the intellectuals, who resented his strong rule and his method of finding a common language with the Sephardi masses by invoking a "messianic" terminology. Having disposed of Ben-Gurion, a Center-left coalition took over in 1963. Yet the initially amorphous and passive, emergent groups of religious and Sephardi Jews joined hands with the Israeli right to challenge this coalition in a lengthy process that culminated in 1977 and was very much influenced by foreign political developments.

The first structural result of the changing cleavage structure was a new form of party alliance known as the bloc system. The new system emerged before the 1965 election when Mapai's pivotal role was challenged by an alliance between Herut and the Liberals who formed the Gahal bloc. Gahal countered Mapai by creating its own alignment with the liberals. The Left-Left Center coalition led to the creation of Labor and subsequently to the Labor Alignment bloc. After the Six Day War the Likud bloc, put together by Ariel Sharon from Gahal and several smaller parties, under Herut's leader Menachem Begin, was able to decisively delegitimize the Socialist Zionist belief system.

The Legacy of the 1967 War and the Ascendence of Begin

Even before the Six Day War, the Labor bloc was changing rapidly. Following Ben-Gurion's departure the party assumed new characteristics.[5] Ben-Gurion's successors recognized the new mass character of the Israeli society,[6] including consumerism and materialism. To meet the new demands, the party became responsive rather than mobilizing. Economically, it moved from the legacy of equalitarian socialism to a "capitalist welfare state" without dismantling the old, now bureaucratized, socialist ventures and trade-union dominated spheres of public life. At the same time the spirit of "state capitalism" created new, largely European-born or Israeli-born, business and bureaucratic elites.

Begin's Herut-based movement, on the other hand, was far more populist. It capitalized on the built-in resentment of the Socialist Zionist elite and its bureaucracy, the hatred toward the elitist, kibbutz-oriented left, and its pragmatic, secular ethos, among Sephardi immigrants. While having no coherent economic policy of its own, Herut was able to tap into the wells of social protest and combine a nationalist zeal with a positive though basically secular approach to Jewish traditional religious values.[7] This mixture of politics was particularly successful in mobilizing the Sephardi Jews and forging the initial ties with the orthodox camp.

However, there were some more general factors working for the right wing bloc. First, Begin's emerging nationalistic vision was able to fill the spiritual-cultural vacuum created by the demise of Ben-Gurion's legacy. This trend was particularly noticeable because of the continuous inability of the successor generation of Labor to provide a new ideological vision.

Second, Herut could capitalize on the growing right wing sympathies of the native born generation of Ashkenazi Israelis. Unlike their European-born parents, the native born sons had little understanding and appreciation of the Socialist egalitarianism and social morality. Their political beliefs were forged against the background of a harsh and continuous struggle for national survival.

Perhaps the most decisive factor in shaping the new Israeli belief system was the belated impact of the Holocaust and the cumulative Arab threat.[8] Initially, Israel was too preoccupied with survival to dwell on the real meaning of the Holocaust. The Eichmann trial in 1960-1962 proved a turning point in coming to terms with the tragedy. But the evaluation strengthened the perception that international relations are a Hobbesian arena where justice and morality rarely exist. Coupled with the perceptions of the Arab danger, the Holocaust theme reinforced the Revisionist appeal to the national ethos of fight and survival.

The developments preceding the Six Day War deepened these perceptions. Israel's international isolation in the face of a united Arab threat conjured up classic images of Jewish helplessness throughout ages of anti-semitism culminating with a new Holocaust. Even though the Six Day War ended with an unprecedented victory, the crisis left an indelible imprint on the collective psychology of the Israelis. Moreover, the war reopened two traditional Herut foreign policy themes which were particularly near and dear to several leftist groups.

The first theme was included in the debate on the concept of "secure and defensible boundaries" and the meaning of peace. The latter included demands that any future agreement with Arabs should be based on a binding peace treaty rather then the pre-1967 armistice arrangements. Needless to say, a peace treaty entailed an Arab recognition of Israel's legitimacy. The second theme embraced the long-standing Revisionist contention that Israel has a historical right to the entire territory of Eretz Israel.

The concept of territorial integrity of the Land of Israel, never formally abandoned by Herut, seemed particularly irrelevant in the 1948-1967 period. Any territorial claims were confounded by the political reality of the 1949 borders and the Ben-Gurion national ethos, which negated Israeli rule over many Arabs, i.e., the occupation of the West Bank. Rather, the empty Negev desert was to be populated and eventually the Sinai (1956). However, after the 1967 war, Begin's claims seemed more justified. The occupied territories provided the missing "strategic depth" deemed to be necessary for Israel's defense. More significantly, the territories became increasingly imbued with a symbolic and moral value transcending security considerations. Begin's newly acquired legitimacy was duly recognized when Labor invited the Right-Center bloc to participate in the 1967 National Unity Government.[9]

The political bloc led by Begin gained further impetus because of the events surrounding the 1973 Yom Kippur War. Domestically, the Israeli-born middle class became resentful of Labor's bureaucratic policies and the numerous corruption scandals associated with the party's "state capitalism." Internationally, Arab refusal to negotiate with Israel, Soviet involvement in the Middle East, and U.S. pressure in the form of the Rogers Plan of 1969 inflamed nationalist sentiments among Israelis.[10] Thus a division between "hawks" and "doves," those who viewed the Arabs and "the world" with mistrust and those who were more inclined to concessions due to moral considerations and the fear of the Arabs and the "world's" wrath emerged in the general public and were honored by the politicians.

Labor elite came under particularly severe criticism in the wake of the Yom Kippur War. Demands for more party democracy such as respect for grass root sentiments and open candidate lists mingled with the criticism of the management of the war. One prevalent criticism was that a more open and democratic debate within the government could have prevented the intelligence and military debacles during the first stage of the war. This criticism sharply contrasted with the perception that Israel was saved from almost certain destruction in the War by the "Likud general," Ariel Sharon. Sharon's leadership, disputed by other IDF generals, was credited with turning the debacle into a victory.

Labor suffered further because two of its legendary leaders, Moshe Dayan and Golda Meir, fairly hawkish but pragmatic leaders, paved the way to a collective, highly competitive leadership under Rabin and Peres and a growing dovish element. The dovish ascendancy in Labor, coinciding with a surge of hawkish public opinion, delivered many traditional Labor voters and new political cohorts into the Begin camp. The tenure of Meir's successor, Yitzhak Rabin, did nothing to reverse the Labor decline. The perception of Rabin as an inept politician heading an administration plagued by corruption and scandal alienated even the most faithful of Labor partisans.

The massive shifts in voting behavior were actively helped by Likud's interpretation of international events. Both Begin and Sharon emphasized that the Yom Kippur War was far from being a limited Arab offensive. They were also extremely critical of the role played by the American Secretary of State, Henry Kissinger, in the post-1973 negotiations with Arab states. Kissinger was accused of playing into the hands of the rich Arab countries and of selling Israel out for the sake of American oil interests. Above all, the Yom Kippur War confirmed to many the long standing Likud argument that the "strategic depth" prevented the Arabs from overrunnning Israel.

The changing perception, long in the making, eventually legitimized Begin's belief system. In many ways, the Revisionist vision was an anathema of Ben-Gurion's formula. It called for a Greater Israel, a Jewish state dominating a large Arab minority.[11] The moral underpinnings of the state were derived from the traditional and religious elements of Jewish heritage. As Begin drew closer to the national religious circles, Ben-Gurion's "secular messianism" was gradually replaced by the myth of a Greater Israel and messianic redemption related to it. Yet Likud's victory in 1977 was possible due to the split among traditional Labor voters, who resented its long rule, bureaucracy, and uninspiring leadership.

The Cleavage of 1977 and Beyond: The Rise and Demise of Begin

Likud's political platform in the 1977 election specified the failures and mistakes of its Labor rivals while underlining Israel's "rights" in "Judea" and "Samaria," i.e. the West Bank. To manage the demographics of the binational state, Begin proposed the formula of voluntary citizenship for loyal "Arabs of Eretz Israel," and avoided outright annexation of that territory, due also to a certain liberal-legalistic element in his political behavior. It was expected that Likud would honor the Labor-initiated settlements in the Sinai Desert and the Gaza Strip.

Thus, many of Begin's old guard supporters and newly acquired voters were surprised when Likud responded to the peace overtures of President Sadat of Egypt. Indeed, most of the Israelis and the world were taken aback when the first Begin Cabinet (1977–1981) negotiated the peace treaty with Egypt conditioned upon Israel's return of the Sinai as a whole. Palestinian autonomy as negotiated in the Camp David Accord were bitterly criticized by Gush Emunim allies of Begin. Begin himself, however, might have hoped to secure Israel's presence in the West Bank and Gaza in exchange for Sinai, while driving a wedge between Egypt, the PLO, and the radical Arab states.

The second Begin Cabinet (1981–1983) reiterated Likud's commitment to the West Bank. A major force in the renewed drive for the practical annexation thereof was Ariel Sharon, who became Begin's Defense Minister. Together with the Chief of Staff, Raphael Eitan, another ardent ideologist of Greater Israel, Sharon devised an ambitious scheme to secure the territorial integrity of Eretz Israel while minimizing the political costs of binationalism. The keystone of Sharon's position was that Jordan is the legitimate Palestinian state and thus there is no need for a second Palestinian state between Jordan and the Mediterranean. Begin himself devised a formula calling for a narrow interpretation of Camp David autonomy as opposed to the broader territorial autonomy which could potentially lead to national sovereignty.

In order to implement his scheme, Sharon took two important policy steps. The first step was expressed in the new "security doctrine." Based on his lessons from the 1973 War (in which the Arabs took the initiative, chose the time and place, and attacked Israel simultaneously, eventually winning great-power support toward a political process at their favor), Sharon conceived of a new strategy of deterrence, Israeli military initiative, and a political change at her favor. As he saw it, Israel's main problem in the past was a lack of credible deterrence. To increase credibility, the Arabs must be led to believe that the cost of hostilities undertaken against Israel would exceed the benefits.[12] Israel's security should be aimed not only at insuring survival but also at preventing limited wars and wars of attrition such as the 1969–1970 Canal War. To this effect, Israel should draw "red lines," i.e., specify contingencies considered as casus belli, and "security fuses," while threatening that Israel will hit the very centers of the offensive capability of the enemy at the first phase of Arab-initiated hostility.

Thus Sharon's doctrine could be interpreted as if Israel might use its nuclear option. The Israeli drive for nuclear monopoly in the Middle East was already underscored by the 1981 raid on the Iraqi nuclear facility Osiraq. The Israeli Government did not deny reports that it would further pursue the nuclear option in order to save on the cost of conventional weapons. While never made official, the nuclear option was clearly emphasized to bolster Sharon's "security doctrine."

Sharon's second step was more directly involved with political reality in the West Bank. The limited personal autonomy could be successful only if there was enough Palestinian support for the scheme. The civilian administration, designed by Sharon and supervised by Chief of Staff Eitan, was designed to encourage moderate Palestinian leadership ready to cooperate with Israel. When the effort failed, partially because of the PLO campaign of intimidation, the situation in Lebanon seemed to offer a radical solution to Israel's problem in the East and in the North alike, while the South was secured due to the peace treaty with Egypt. This led to the 1982 War in Lebanon. The invasion of Lebanon had two major goals. First, the war aimed at reestablishing Israel's deterrence credibilty vis-à-vis Syria, the most active among the hardline Arab states. Syrian entrenchment in Lebanon coupled with the introduction of the SAM batteries in the Bakaa Valley were increasingly perceived as a threat to Israel. Sharon also hoped that Israel could establish a friendly Maronite-controlled government in Lebanon which would be ready to sign a peace treaty with the Jewish state.

Second, and more important, the war was planned to dislodge the PLO from Lebanese soil. Denying a territorial base to the PLO was a long standing tenet of Israeli security policy. This principle was made even more urgent because the PLO utilized its territorial infrastructure in Lebanon to stage terrorist raids across the border at will. Terrorist attacks and shelling of Northern Galilee put the Likud government under severe domestic pressure. Needless to say, eliminating the PLO structure was expected to diminish the international standing of the organization and its overwhelming influence in the West Bank.

There is considerable public and academic disagreement to what extent Sharon's vision and policy were shared by the cabinet of Begin. Whatever the initial degree of support for Sharon's "grand design," however, it quickly dissipated when the war developed into a complex foreign and domestic failure. The Israeli army was slow in acting against the Syrians and the U.N.-sponsored cease-fire left the Syrians well entrenched in the Bakaa Valley and Tripoli. The long siege of Beirut and the massacre in the Sabra and Shatila camps damaged Israel's image abroad. Even the forced departure of the PLO, the major success of the war, was temporarily overshadowed by the assassination of Bashir Gemayel. But it was mostly the growing casualty list prominently publicized by the media which drew home the cost ofthe war.

The first reaction came from within Likud, when both Herut and Liberal ministers criticized Sharon publicly. The Labor Alignment that first half-heartedly supported the war turned critical when the mood of the country changed. Actually the change in the public atmosphere suited the new image of Labor developed by Shimon Peres. Departing from the tough legacy of Meir and Dayan, Labor resumed its traditional Center-Left posture while also capitalizing on its stand as a "cautious and prudent" opposition party.

The increased criticism of the Begin cabinet culminated in the public demand to appoint a commission of inquiry into the Sabra and Shatila massacres. The blow to Begin's standing was compounded by the Reagan peace initiative which called for a stop to settlements and negotiation between Israel, Jordan and the Palestinians. Succumbing to political pressures and personal problems, Begin resigned in 1983.[13]

Begin's political demise raised the question of the continuation of the Likud belief system. As in the case of Ben-Gurion and Mapai, much of Likud's legacy was bound up with Begin's personal vision. Likud under Begin's leadership assumed the character of a populistic movement based on several principles. First, there was the principle of Israel's historical and legal rights to Eretz Israel. This element in Herut's ideology is based on the idea of working back from a desired future to the present by trying to create this future through both military settlement and diplomatic tools. As a secular, modern mass party, Herut's ideology was not solely based upon a total religious world view but rather on a historical-biblical interpretation of the Jewish fate in the Diaspora and the Return.

Second, there was always a liberal democratic element present in Herut's view of the Arabs in Eretz Israel. Rather than outright annexation, Begin felt that the Arabs should be given a choice between accepting Israeli sovereignty and complete civil rights or partial rights under occupation until the future of the West Bank was resolved. The resolution itself, in his view, required negotiations (with Egypt and representatives of the Palestinians in the West Bank) in which he did not intend to make any territorial concessions. In practical terms, this meant continued Israeli rule over that territory without annexing it.

Third, Herut's social and economical ideology was a mixture of populist welfare and conservative economy. Instead of the pioneering and voluntaristic ethos of Ben-Gurion, Begin offered classical liberalism such as individualism, competition, less bureaucracy, and less government, but combined them in fact with enormous welfare state benefits to the lower strata, "his" voters.

Whether Begin's vision could continue in his absence depended to a large degree on the political structure of Likud and to a lesser degree on the Israeli political system in the closing decades of the 20th century.[14] Formally, Begin presided over a very democratic party structure. Herut officers were chosen by a 1000-member committee but informally the wishes of the Herut leader were undisputed. After Begin removed himself from office, this "thousand Indians" could dictate the choice of the new leader in a highly independent way. Whether the new leader would continue the Begin vision or try to take Likud into new ideological territory would depend on the balance of power in the party. The election of Yitzhak Shamir was at first a caretaker arrangement in the forthcoming power struggle.

Ben-Gurion's inability to reform the political system resulted in an ever increasing proliferation of small and medium parties. Traditional party allegience likewise slackened, forcing both major parties to scramble in putting together coalitions of disparate groups. The political system was awash with floating voters who moved from one party to another at first, but many stayed with Likud, which gave them a sense of pride and emancipation vis-à-vis the old, bureaucratized, upper class, elitist left.

The voting fluidity in the 1980s indicated that neither the Socialist Zionist creed nor the binational vision of Likud were dominant among the Israeli public. The former was still suspect and disliked by many who suspected that Labor has not changed sufficiently from its elitist and corrupt ways. The latter was blamed for the failure in Lebanon and the human price of the war and its populist, inflationary economic policy. At the same time, the society was almost equally divided with regard to the most salient issue of territorial retention and the wisdom of binationalism.

The 1984 Election and the
Government of National Unity

The 1984 elections were fought in a political-ideological vacuum created first by the departure of Begin. Shimon Peres, who led the Labor Alignment,

in 1981 sought at first to recover the traditional Labor vote lost in 1977
and retain the votes of the left that might have otherwise wandered to
extreme left parties, or to a centrist party who might be ready to join
forces with Likud. This strategy drove him from a "hawkish" stance in
the 1970s to a center-left plank. In 1984 he produced a new formula for
the occupied territories, a vague notion of a "territorial compromise" to
be negotiated with Jordan and the Palestinians but not the PLO. The latter
was not only perceived as a terrorist organization, but as the spearhead of
the Palestinians who left in 1948 and who wished to return to the pre-
1967 Israel; thus, Israel had nothing to offer to them, unless they recognized
Israel, gave up their right of return to the pre-1967 Israel and renounced
terrorism. The formula was agreed upon in internal party deliberations
and satisfied the left and the center because of its pragmatic and less
nationalistic nature, while the more "hawkish" element in labor endorsed
it as well since it seemed to be theoretical and totally unacceptable to any
Arab partner. Should the Arabs be ready to concede territory to Israel in
the West-Bank and allow Hussein rule over the rest rather than the PLO,
then why not?

Peres also sought to erode the electoral support of Likud, especially by
appealing to the Sephardi Israelis and the native-born generation. In spite
of the economic situation, Labor failed to make significant inroads into the
right-wing camp. The fragmented, polarized, but stalemated cleavage of the
Israeli political system was faithfully reflected in the 1984 election result.

With both Labor and Likud reduced to a tie that could not be broken
through coalition machinations, the Government of National Unity between
Labor and Likud became inevitable.

When Peres became the first Prime Minister of the National Unity
Cabinet, he was well aware that the stalemated political cleavage would
leave him few options in most foreign policy areas. Typical of his political
style, Peres sought to divide the big issues into smaller, more manageable
parts. First he managed to split the Likud ministries on the issue of
withdrawl from Lebanon. When the IDF left Lebanon in May, 1985, the
move was well received by the public alarmed with the seemingly endless
list of battle casualties.

Peres was also successful in improving relations with Egypt which bogged
down because of the Taba issue. However, Labor's effort to cooperate with
Egypt on the stalled autonomy talks were less encouraging. The major
obstacle to any meaningful progress in finding a formula for negotiation
between Israel, Jordan, and the Palestinians was the issue of the PLO.

The PLO's failure to recognize Israel, either independently or under the
auspices of Jordan, enabled Likud to reiterate its commitment to Israeli
control over the West Bank. Peres counteracted by revoking the traditional
Labor hope that King Hussein of Jordan might be willing to accept a

"territorial compromise" in the West Bank, and step in instead of the PLO, thus paving the way for a moderate Palestinian-Israeli-Jordanian dialogue.

Apart from the domestic, "dovish" pressure on him to show flexibility in foreign affairs, Peres was motivated by the need to cut a different posture domestically in comparison to Likud without taking any risks. A genuine concern of his, however, seems to have been the nuclear and missile issue. Expressing a sense of urgency, Peres repeatedly reiterated, in public, the need to arrive at a territorial compromise before the enemy states could achieve nuclear potential of their own. In any case, the availability of nuclear weapons and missile technology would make holding territory for defense purposes obsolete. At times, Peres came close to advocating territorial compromise, based on a nuclear deterence stand, and some deal with the Russians, should Israel be willing not to deploy its Jericho 2 intermediate range ballistic missile, while Moscow would exert moderating influence over the Syrians. However, neither Peres nor any of the other Labor leaders could ignore the fact that about half of the population formed a normative attachment to Judea and Samaria. The significance of the West Bank as an ideological vacuum filler was especially appreciated by Peres who tried to unite the floating center-left groups into a coherent Labor lead force.

Thus, Peres arrived at a conclusion that his personal future and the future of the Labor movement were to be sought in less controversial subjects at first. The state of the Israeli economy, chronic inflation, and low productivity posed a formidable challenge. By providing considerable leadership and tackling some of the most structurally difficult elements in Israel's economic malaise, Peres and the National Unity Government were able to curb inflation and restore confidence in the economy.

The Labor leader tried to use this newly won political capital to push his political agenda. Peres embarked on a successful round of negotiations with moderate Arab leaders. He restored the relations with Egypt to their pre-Lebanon level. Then he utilized all of his diplomatic maneuvering in order to work out a blueprint for an international peace conference on the Middle East. The peace conference would have enabled Israel to show good will toward a territorial compromise to be negotiated with Jordan under international auspices. However, like any previous Labor initiatives potentially threatening Israeli control over the West Bank, it was soundly rebuffed by Likud and Yitzhak Shamir, who became the new Prime Minister of the National Unity Government in 1986.

Once again, the Peres-Shamir encounter was symptomatic of the underlying stalemate created by the political cleavage in Israel. In order to evaluate the possibility for any future dynamics, it is imperative to look again at the political right.

The Israeli Right and Its Future

It was already indicated that Begin's departure left an ideological and leadership vacuum among right wing voters. After Sharon failed to fill the slack, the radical right wing Tehiya Party and Rabbi Meir Kahane moved in. In addition, the mainstream Israeli Right is split between the populist Herut and the Liberals. Their historical alliance in Likud was strained over the war in Lebanon and economic programs.

Peres exploited these tensions in order to obtain the support of the cabinet for his policy in Lebanon and the economic program. Yet the Labor elite is well aware that in the minds of the Israeli masses Likud is still perceived as the party which gave the Sephardim better living standards and increased their social status. These are strong ties that can be enhanced by foreign challenges.

Still, the most divisive issue for the Right is the binational future of the territories. Theoretically the Begin liberal-national formula of settling all of Palestine with civil rights to Arabs may easily lead to an Arab majority within the next twenty years. The specter of a binational Israel with a legal Arab majority has already provoked a non-liberal fundamentalist backlash among the national and religious right. The Gush Emunim proposition of a resident alien status for the Palestinians or Kahane's advocacy of transfer are all harbingers of the bitter debate to come.

These tensions can become easily inflamed because of the explosive relations between Jewish settlers and Palestinians and the campaign of terrorism. Things grew even more complicated following the riots in the West Bank and Gaza since December 9, 1987. The ensuing peace initiative by Secretary Shultz was welcomed by Peres but practically rejected by Likud under Shamir.

The crisis and deadlock in the Israeli cleavage system makes any step-by-step or comprehensive solution to the Arab-Israeli conflict difficult. A number of "blockage scenarios," along the lines of the recently failed Peres initiative for an international conference, can be readily imagined in the future. Ironically, the deadlock in Israel always has been fed and sustained by the spiritual and political paralysis among the Arab states.

Historic and Contemporary Cleavages in the Arab Camp

The cleavages in the Arab world have been subject to an extensive scholarly debate. As suggested by Walid Khalidi, the Arab world is torn between three kinds of contemporary logic: the logic of Arab unification, the logic of the status quo, and the logic of social and political revolution. One may add to Khalidi's classification the logic of the Arab-Israeli conflict as reflecting all other "logics." The conflict became a major factor in Arab reality as it relates to problems of Arab and Palestinian identity, the relation between Arab states, and contacts with global powers. All four logics form the basis of serious cleavages in the Arab world.

Tensions exist between "revolutionary" Arab regimes who seek to alter traditional social and political structures and the conservative regimes who seek to maintain the status quo. A different type of revolutionary versus status quo cleavage pertains to religious divisions. The Suni-Shia scheme is the most obvious one. There are other regime divisions such as moderate/ modern traditionalism (Egypt under Sadat), modern fundamentalism (Qadafi's Libya), and modern/revolutionary secularism (Ba'ath in Syria and Iraq). Those ideological conflicts are all represented in the PLO, with the current mainstream Moslem leadership maintaining a tenuous compromise among the various factions.

The logic of unification stems from the Pan-Arab versus regional-particularist ideology. At the height of the Pan-Arab ethos of Gamal Abdel Nasser, partial unification was attempted but invariably failed. The Egyptian-Syrian union and the short lived Egyptian-Libyan encounter left the parties frustrated and suspicious.

To complicate the situation further, these tensions were all played out and exacerbated in the course of the Arab-Israeli conflict. Religiously and in terms of the Pan-Arab ethos, the Arabs believed that Palestine belonged to them, especially as the Middle East was conjured under Islam. In this sense, the return of the Jews not only undermined the Pan-Arab physical continuity but offended their sense of Islamic justice. Modern Arabs have apparently perceived the establishment of Israel as a cosmic catastrophe which threatened their historical and religious identity. Not surprisingly, they were totally unwilling to recognize the competing Jewish religious-historical legacy in Eretz Israel. Instead they preferred to define modern Israel as a "Western imperialist" or colonial exploitation of the native Middle East. This religious, cultural, and political apprehension of Israel required a theory that could explain the reality of the Jewish state and provide a praxis of power to defeat it.

The theoretical underpinnings for Arab and Palestinian nationalism were derived from the German rather than French or British political model. According to Bernard Lewis,[15] the Arabs found the Western individualism and liberal democracy irrelevant to their political experience. The National Socialism of the Third Reich, albeit without its racism and vulgar Darwinism, appealed better to the Arabs who were trying to unify into a nation in the face of past political divisions.

The Holocaust, in which the Palestinian leader, Haj Amin El Husseini, was involved as a Nazi supporter (he moved his headquarters to Berlin in 1941), was perceived by the Arabs as totally irrelevant to their ethnocentric view of the Middle East and the world. Not surprisingly, since the Arabs did not accept the Western moral political heritage, they felt no compulsion to share in the Western moral obligation for the Holocaust. Paradoxically, they felt threatened and victimized by its survivors. Repeating the classic European logic of anti-Semitism, the Arabs depicted Israel as a sinister conspiracy of "world Jewry" to invade and control the Arab nation.

The praxis of power derived from this theory was an all-out war of destruction against Israel, following the German resurrection after Jena and Napoleon's initial victories. Defeat should be turned into victory and division to unification. Thus, partition, negotiations, or any other diplomatically derived solutions which would have enshrined Israel's existence in the Middle East all fell short of the imperative of total elimination. However, the repeated Arab failure to destroy Israel militarily generated bitter tensions among the participants of the crusade against the Jewish state. The new cleavage structure which crystallized after the Six Day War featured the rejectionists as opposed to the moderates. The Rejectionist Front led by Libya, Iraq, and Syria argued for a continued commitment to the theory and praxis of destroying Israel. The moderates argued that given the power reality in the Middle East, compromise with the Jewish state is necessary. The PLO, both generating and symbolizing the conflict, was rent by the same cleavage, with Yasir Arafat presiding over a tenuous coalition of rejectionists and compromisers.

The paralysis in the Arab camp was only broken after Sadat replaced Nasser as the leader of Egypt. Sadat's various initiatives such as the Yom Kippur War and the peace mission to Jerusalem have been extensively discussed in academic and public literature. However, these politics should be analyzed with a view of isolating the specific considerations which enabled Egypt to break out of the deadlocked Arab cleavage structure. Three important inputs into Sadat's decision can be surmised. First, Egypt under Nasser failed in the German model of national management and Pan-Arab unification. The pro-Soviet orientation, the foreign policy currency of Nasser's model, proved equally unsatisfactory in helping Arab interests. Second, the economic and social cost of the rejectionists, posture proved prohibitive. Third, and perhaps most important, a total destruction of the Jewish state became unfeasible because of Israel's nuclear option. While never publicly stated, Sadat was aware that Israel would use nuclear weapons, when faced with annihiliation, regardless of the eventual introduction of an "Arab bomb."

Having achieved a psychological breakthrough, Egypt was able to devise the realistic strategy of the limited 1973 War. Thus, Sadat's road to Camp David was based on a somber analysis of the political impass in the Arab camp. He realized that the Arab-Israeli conflict was not only ideologically motivated but perpetuated for reasons of political expediency by rejectionist actors like Syria and Libya. Unlike Nassar, who actively sponsored the radical PLO, Sadat was reluctant to support Arafat's survival strategy of maneuvering among the deadlocked factions of the organization. Above all, Sadat hoped to show that Camp David could be a political alternative for breaking the stalemate in the Arab camp.

However, Sadat's departure from traditional Arab policies has not produced enough momentum to alter drastically the overall Arab picture. The dynamics of Arab rejection isolated Egypt and discredited other moderate regional actors. To make matters worse, the internal cleavage in Israel prevented the moderate Labor from giving credibility to the autonomy plan envisaged in Camp David. The renewed paralysis in inter-Arab relations feeds into the status quo spirit in Israel.

Conclusion: The Status Quo Syndrome and Binationalism by Default

As shown above, the blocked cleavage structure in Israeli society has been reflected in the National Unity Government. Begin's own peace strategy contributed to the dynamic of war and finally to his personal demise but not to the demise of Likud. Begin's successor, Yitzhak Shamir, and Moshe Arens refused to vote for the Camp David Agreement. Egypt's "cold peace" did not make the Camp David Accord popular among Israeli voters, especially Likud partisans. The saliency of the West Bank grew rather than diminished following Camp David. Right wing and possibly centrist voters were upset because of the traumatic withdrawal from Sinai, Arab ostracism of Egypt, and the continuous exposure to PLO ideology and its terrorist activities. These developments were overlayed by historical inertia which transformed occupation from an anomaly to a fact of life.

Because of these circumstances, Labor's official plank regarding negotiations with Jordan on a "territorial compromise" in the West Bank was played down by its own authors during the 1984 election campaign. During his two years as prime minister, Peres succeeded in improving relations with Egypt's Mubarak and met in public with King Hassan of Morocco. He capitalized on the PLO's failure to recognize Israel publicly or negotiate with King Hussein over the West Bank. As a result, Labor was able to resurrect its former policy of cooperation with the King. Yet the "London Agreement" between Peres and Hussein in 1987 was ignored and shelved by Shamir.

Both Peres and his rival and successor Shamir are committed to a strategy of no recognition and no negotiations with the PLO. Peres, however, is not committed to add settlements to the Arab-populated West Bank as Shamir is. Both were unable to prevail over each other and thus were forced to shelve the issue of the territories in the anomalous Government

of National Unity. Both are dependent on a public that is almost evenly
divided between "hawks" and "doves" and upon smaller parties, either far
Left or far Right, to form a coalition. The result was an uneasy status
quo which has led to a complete standstill in Israel's foreign policy.

For their part, the PLO, Syria, and other radical Arab states believe
that the prolonged occupation would transform Israel into a South Africa.
While waiting for his South African dream to materialize, Arafat tried to
establish a renewed autonomous base in Lebanon. Should Israel be transformed into a South Africa, he hopes to use the base in Lebanon for a
guerrilla warfare against Israel, supported by one or more nuclear-armed
Arab states. Thus the Arabs in the West Bank and Gaza were torn between
radical obligation and reality; frustrated with others who failed to solve
their problems, they turned to mass riots of their own since December 9,
1987. Yet they were unable to suggest to the Israelis, nor to Secretary
Shultz, a positive program of their own. They recognized the PLO's inner
division and lack of realism, but they won't defy their commitment to
Arafat.

Thus, both sides are divided and yet they hope that third parties (the
U.S., the U.S.S.R., and the Arab states) will sooner or later salvage them
from their own deadlock. Yet never were the parties more deadlocked,
tired, and devoid of a daring leader who like Sadat would prevail over
historical and psychological obstacles.

Notes

1. See Peter Y. Medding, *Mapai in Israel*, (Cambridge, London: Cambridge
University Press, 1972), regarding the early history of Ben-Gurion's political party,
and C. Natan Yanai, *Party Leadership in Israel: Maintenance and Change*, Vol. 13,
The Modern Middle East Series, Middle East Institute, Columbia University, (Ramat-
Gan: Turtledove, 1981).

2. These statements are based on the author's recent research in the Ben-Gurion
archives, S'de Boker; the final results of the research are scheduled to be published
in 1988 under the title, *History of Israel's Domestic and Foreign Policy*. See also,
Michael Keren, *Ben-Gurion and the Intellectuals: Power, Knowledge, and Charisma*,
(DeKalb, Illinois: Northern Illinois University, 1983).

3. See Shlomo Aronson, *Conflict and Bargaining in the Middle East*, (Baltimore:
John Hopkins University Press, 1978).

4. See Michael Bar-Zohar, *Ben-Gurion*, Vol. 3, (Tel Aviv: Am Oved, 1977);
regarding the nuclear issue and the Israeli-French cooperation see Matti Golan,
Peres, (Tel Aviv: Shocken, 1983), G. Pierre Pean, *Les Deux Bombes*, (Paris: Fayard,
1983).

5. See Natan Yanai and Shlomo Aronson, "The 1984 Elections—Testing the
Israeli Political System," in *State, Government and International Relations*, no. 25,
Spring 1986, pp. 78–85.

6. This dualism was common among Fabians in England, who exercised some influence on future Israeli Labor leaders such as Moshe Sharett. See William F. Stone and David C. Smith, "Human Nature in Politics: Graham Wallas and the Fabians," in *Political Psychology*, Vol. 4, no. 4, 2983, pp. 693–712.

7. See Shlomo Aronson and Natan Yanai, "The 1981 Elections: A Framework for Analysis," in Emanuel Gutmann, Abraham Diskin, Dan Caspi (eds.), *The Roots of Begin's Success*, (London: Croom-Helm, 1983).

8. See Sophie Kav-Venaki and Arie Nadler, "The Impact of Massive Traumatization on Holocaust Survivors and their Families," paper submitted to the Annual Conference of the International Society for Political Psychology, Manheim, Germany, 1981.

9. For details, See Aronson, *Conflict and Bargaining*, Ibid.

10. Named after the then Secretary of State, William P. Rogers; for details, See Aronson, Ibid.

11. For the impact of the 1973 War on Israeli domestic politics, see Aronson, Ibid.

12. Regarding Sharon's security doctrine see Shlomo Aronson, "The Theory of Nuclear Deterrence and Middle-Eastern Reality," in Avner Cohen, ed, *Humanity and the Atom*, (Tel Aviv: Hakibutz Hameochad, 1988).

13. See Shlomo Aronson, "Israel's Leaders, domestic Order and Foreign Policy: June 1981–1983," in *Jerusalem Journal of International Relations*, Vol. 8, no. 1, 1984. For Begin's political legacy see Ilan Peleg, *Begin's Foreign Policy, 1977–1983: Israel's Move to the Right*, (Westport: Greenwood, 1987).

14. See Samuel H. Beer (ed. and his first chapter on Britain), *Patterns of Government: The Major Political Systems of Europe*, (New York: Random House, 1978).

15. Bernard Lewis, *Semites and Anti-Semites: An Inquiry into Conflict and Prejudices, 1st edition*, (New York: Norton, 1986).

5

The Political Road to Binationalism: Arabs in Jewish Politics

Ian S. Lustick

From the establishment of "the Jewish state" in 1948 Israel has included within its jurisdiction very substantial numbers of non-Jews. From 1948 to 1967 the proportion of non-Jews (Arabs) living under Israeli jurisdiction averaged about 13 percent. Virtually all were Israeli citizens. After the 1967 war the proportion of Arabs living under the jurisdiction of "the Jewish state" has risen from 34 percent to 38 percent. Of the 2.3 million Arabs only the 650,000 living inside the Green Line have Israeli citizenship (15.0 percent of all Israeli citizens).[1] But if one considers that even the Arab minority within the 1949 armistice lines represents nearly twice as large a proportion of the population as do blacks in the United States, one can appreciate the extent to which the image and reality of Israel as a "Jewish state" are contingent upon political and ideological contrivance. From the standpoint of political science, in other words, the shape of the Israeli political order as mononational, not binational, can certainly not be taken as a permanent given of Israeli life.

From Mononational Control to Binational Democracy

Theoretically Israel could become a "binational state" as a result of explicit decisions by the duly constituted authorities to "redesign" it. Such formally implemented federalist or consociational schemes would represent a radical break from the substantive thrust of statist-Zionist ideology as it crystallized in the 1930s and 1940s, but it would be consistent with the

---

This chapter was submitted to the editors in its completed form in October 1987. A related article was published in the July 1988 issue of *New Outlook*, under the title "Creeping Binationalism inside the Green Line."

conceptual approach embedded within the tradition that the shape of the political order is an architected function of the plans and programs of dominant elites. To consider the possibility that Israel may be evolving toward binationalism, we must loosen both our conceptual harnesses—that which requires us to believe that the statist Zionism of the 1930s and 1940s is the only version which can ever make sense to the Yishuv, and that which leads to the view that state decisions alone will determine the shape of the political order, not the cumulative consequences of social, economic, and demographic trends and the political dynamics attendant upon them.

It is indeed most unlikely that a binational Israel will be the product of a transformation of the political order guided by an elite aware of the need to accommodate the needs and grievances of non-Jewish Israelis. Political orders change their shape according to complex processes which combine the cumulation of incremental stresses with ruptures in the legally established pattern of institutional life. Consider the United States as an example. The formal integration of black Americans into the white political order created by the founding fathers could not have occurred without the gradual diffusion of abolitionist sentiment, long tortuous campaigns for "free soil," and judicial struggles over the fugitive slave law. But changing cultural norms, and new political bargains mediated through stable forms of political competition, brought an end to slavery only in combination with a long and bloody civil war. Realization of the biracial society implicit in the thirteenth amendment to the Constitution has still not been achieved, but the great distance toward that goal since Reconstruction would not have been travelled without sustained campaigns of patient political pressure, civil disobedience, and, sometimes, violence. In a particularly instructive case, George Wallace's transformation from segregationist politician par excellence, to a Governor of Alabama elected by black votes on the basis of his repudiation of segregationism, reflects the specific kind of contribution which political participation by effectively enfranchised but previously excluded minorities can make to changes in the political order itself.

My purpose here is to address the question of the long-term response of the Israeli political order to the increasing size and sophistication of a formally enfranchised Arab electorate. I take as a starting point Israel's 40-year history as a deeply divided society in which a state constructed and maintained to serve the interests of the Jewish majority has been used to control the Arab minority—to prevent Arabs from using their legal status as Israeli citizens to bargain for bigger slices of the economic, cultural, and political pie. The general argument I wish to explore is that in certain kinds of deeply divided societies, and under specifiable conditions, democratic political competition can move a deeply divided system of control toward integration and effective binationalism. I shall begin by identifying those conditions and circumstances. I shall then make a case that within the last five years Israeli politics has come to approximate them, and that the political consequences of these developments are already apparent and likely to become increasingly salient.

The literatures on the origin of political cleavages and the implications of politicized communal identities strongly suggest that once a society emerges as "deeply divided" the ordering of political competition will be more or less frozen along those lines.[2] Reinforcing this tendency in bipolar democratic systems is a pattern which most analysts appear to expect, of out-bidding by parties within the dominant segment, i.e. competition among those parties which produces increasingly tough policies and appeals with respect to the status and claims of the minority. Stripped to its essentials, the argument runs as follows: If the most important dimension of political competition is ethnic or communal, if the basic character of the intercommunal relationship is antagonistic, and if it is presumed by parties within the larger of two segments that votes can only be drawn in substantial numbers from members of that segment, then each party within the larger segment will strive to appear at least as vigorous in its defense of the majority's prerogatives as its competitors.[3]

This overall perspective and the specific theories attached to it help explain the stability of the relationship between Jews and Arabs in Israel—a relationship of dominance in which most Jewish parties have sought consistently to avoid being labelled "soft on the Arabs." But accepting the assumptions of this approach, analysis suggests that under certain conditions the political dynamics of democratic competition may lead to coalitions which cross ethnic/communal lines. Such a dynamic could even transform the political order from one characterized by the unilateral dominance of a majority over a minority to one in which bargaining plays a key role in the authoritative allocation of political, cultural, and economic resources. Specifically, if the majority segment becomes divided within itself with sufficient intensity, and if the minority is large enough to be politically useful to one side of the majority segment but not so large as to threaten it with achieving dominance in a coalition with it, the stage would appear to be set for acentripetal political dynamic. The key element in this dynamic would be that previously peripheral elements of the system (minority, outgroup voters) could become significant resources in competition for control of the center.

The question posed in this study may now be restated in more refined form: To what extent does this theoretical possibility exist in Israel? That is to say, to what extent has increasingly polarized competition between dovish, secularist Labor-oriented Jews and hawkish, religious, Likud-oriented Jews, resulted in attempts to mobilize Arab political support in return for a more equitable distribution of resources and effective if not official movement toward the crystallization of a binational political order.[4]

Polarization and the Collapse
of the Gentlemen's Agreement

An important element in Israeli political life has been the absence of independent Arab political activity. For 18 years, a military government, established by Israel during the 1948 war, closely regulated many aspects of life in Arab areas of the country. Fledgling attempts to form political organizations, newspapers, and protest movements were thwarted relatively easily during this period by military governors who used their power, not only to prevent independent Arab political activity, but to deliver large majorities of the Arab vote to the dominant Labor Party and its "Affiliated Arab Lists."

The military government was abolished in 1966, but its functions continued to be performed by a network of ministerial Arab departments, the Arab department of the Histadrut (Israel's dominant trade union organization), and the Office of the Adviser to the Prime Minister on Arab Affairs. This later bureau worked closely with the internal security services and the police. The primary objective of the policies carried out by this bureaucratic array was to prevent independent Arab political organization. Through policies which kept the Arab minority internally fragmented, economically dependent, and bereft of credible leadership, this overall objective was reliably achieved at relatively low cost. This success was particularly striking in view of the intense discontent of the Arab population, its high rate of voter participation, and the overall conduciveness of Israel's proportional representation electoral system to the development and growth of small parties.[5]

The effective exclusion of Arab citizens from Israeli political life was made possible by a gentlemen's agreement within the Jewish sector to unite behind the policies which maintained it, to ostracize individuals or political groups (particularly the Communist Party) seeking to mobilize Arab discontent for electoral purposes, and to prevent the emergence of representative Arab political organizations. In 1980, for example, Arabs from all over Israel chose delegates to a congress to be held in Nazareth for the purpose of establishing an all-Israel Arab political party. Several days before it was to have taken place, the Likud government ordered the event banned. It also banned all meetings that might be called to protest the proscription of the congress itself. In accordance with the gentlemen's agreement, neither the Labor party nor its allies made any serious objection to this order, which destroyed the embryonic Arab organization.

Since the 1984 elections, however, evidence has begun to accumulate that this gentlemen's agreement is breaking down in the face of processes of political and religious polarization among Jewish Israelis. Before 1967 differences among leading political parties over important aspects of national security and foreign policy did exist. To be sure, Herut, formally at least, continued to support claims to Jewish sovereignty over both banks of the Jordan. In the early 1950s Mapam advocated closer ties with the Soviet bloc than any other Zionist party was willing to contemplate. Ahdut Haavoda and Rafi tended to advocate more militant stances toward regional issues, such as the appropriate scale and frequency of retaliation raids, then did Mapai or the religious parties. But the one issue that had helped bring the Yishuv to the brink of civil war, the question of borders of the state, was pushed from the center stage of national politics by the 1949 Armistice Agreements, and eliminated from the political agenda altogether by the withdrawal from Sinai and Gaza in 1957.[6] An impressive consensus among Israeli Jews existed, before 1967, which combined acceptance of the 1949 armistice lines with perceptions that Arab hostility was so intense and resilient that Israel's foreign policy had to be subordinated to a prudent, pessimistically based, national security policy. Such perceptions and judgments meant that the deep yearnings of Israeli Jews for peace, their equally deep concerns about protecting the state from threats of destruction, and the powerful, but latent, visions of a grander implementation of the Zionist ideal than had been achieved in 1948, hardly intruded upon electoral politics.

The Six Day War, of course, changed all that. As virtually every observer of contemporary Israel has noted, the Six Day War, including in particular the extension of Israeli rule over the West Bank and the Gaza Strip, with their large Arab populations, unleashed powerful forces within Israel, resulting in dramatic changes in the country's cultural, psychological, and political landscape.

Immediately following the Six Day War a wave of emotional enthusiasm for the Jewish people, its history, and its connection to the land of Israel swept the country. Religious symbols and traditions which had been discarded by a sabra culture imbued with cynical disdain toward them took on new meaning for many Israeli Jews. As Charles Liebman and Eliezer Don-Yehiya argue, the Six Day War contributed mightily to the creation of a new "civil religion" in which Jewish religious traditions have been much more widely honored, if not observed.[7]

Closely associated with these developments was emergence of the "generation of the knitted skullcap." It had grown up within the state-religious educational system, the National Religious Party's Bnei Akiva youth movement, and the network of field seminaries known as "Yeshivot hesder." In the wake of the Yom Kippur War this subcultural cohort group produced the most effective extraparliamentary movement to emerge in Israel since 1948—Gush Emunim, dedicated to territorial expansion as a means of hastening the Messianic Redemption process. Gush Emunim drew most of its leadership from circles close to the "Young Guard" of the National Religious Party. Their influence within the NRP led it to adopt an activist, even ultranationalist stance on foreign policy issues. Its militant inclinations toward the Arabs and toward the permanent incorporation of the West Bank and Gaza into Israel, combined with a substantial increase in the size of the Party's Knesset delegation, interfered with efforts by important elements within the Labor Party to slow settlement of the occupied territories and promote proposals for a negotiated territorial compromise with Jordan.

Quite apart from developments within the religious sector, but occurring approximately at the same time, the simmering discontent of Israel's Oriental Jews finally found its political voice. The resentment of the "Edot HaMizrah" (Eastern communities) against the Labor Party controlled Ashkenazic establishment, combined with their attraction to Menachem Begin's charismatic and oppositionist leadership style and his militantly patriotic, vigorously anti-Arab rhetoric, created the electoral basis for the first successful challenge to Labor's political hegemony.

The issues and trends which appeared in the decade between 1967 and 1977 set the stage for an historic realignment, in which both the National Religious Party and the ultra-orthodox Agudat Yisrael shifted their support to the right. This enabled the Likud, which received the majority of Oriental Jewish votes, to form the first non-Labor government in Israel. Associated with their increased political clout and the improved climate surrounding religious observance, the religious parties (including, since 1984, Shas) have subsequently enlisted Likud assistance in repeated attempts to move Israel beyond the "status quo" in sensitive areas such as abortion, amendments to the "who is a Jew" law, Sabbath observance, etc. Meanwhile many Oriental Jews, energized by the defeat their support of Likud had helped inflict upon the Labor Party, escalated their attacks upon the Labor leadership, the kibbutz movement, and upon the Ashkenazic establishment in general.

But what makes the political divisions among Israeli Jews so significant, and what has spurred so many observers to use terms such as "polarization," breakdown of "consensus," and "crisis of legitimacy," to characterize contemporary Israeli politics, is the extent to which sociological and cultural cleavages—between religious and non-religious Jews, Orientals and Ashkenazim, lower class and less well-educated Jews vs. middle class and better educated Jews—reinforce one another in their relationship to the dominant political-ideological issue before the country, i.e. the ultimate disposition of the occupied West Bank and Gaza Strip.[8] Thus polls consistently show that those refusing to consider any territorial concessions, and who vote for Likud, Tehiya, the National Religious Party, and Kach, tend to be religious, Sephardic, and less well educated than the secular, Ashkenazic, and relatively well-educated strata of Israeli Jewish society who tend to support at least the principle of territorial compromise, and whose votes tend disproportionately to go to Labor, Shinui, the Civil Rights Movement, and, in 1984, Yahad.[9] Since the late 1970s public opinion polls have also shown that the Jewish population of Israel has been virtually evenly divided over whether, in principle, and under any circumstances, territorial concessions in the West Bank and Gaza should be made.[10] The following data are representative.[11]

Responses to the question: "Do you favor a peace agreement with Jordan that would call upon Israel to give up territories in Judea and Samaria?"

	percent responding that they were "against any concession"	percent responding that they were willing to concede parts or all of the area
March 1986	44.9 percent	52.5 percent
October 1986	47.7 percent	49.3 percent
April 1987	46.4 percent	51.8 percent

Reinforcing this split in Israeli society even more forcefully is that differences on the future of the territories appear to be closely linked to attitudes on one other issue of fundamental importance to Israelis—the question of peace. Before the Six Day War, whether or not Israelis believed peace with the Arab world was likely to be achieved, virtually all believed that a genuine peace agreement with the Arabs was worth foregoing opportunities to extend Israeli rule over East Jerusalem, the West Bank, and the Gaza Strip. Now, despite a yearning for peace among many of those willing to make territorial concessions that is as strong as ever, the fact is that for most of those who favor complete absorption of the territories, the attractiveness of a genuine peace agreement with the Arabs seems to have declined, at least relative to the value placed upon consolidating Israeli sovereignty over the "whole Land of Israel." In a July 1984 poll 54 percent of the Jewish Israeli public chose "annexation" when asked whether, if forced to decide, they would choose peace or annexation of the territories held since 1967.[12]

Increasingly, the profoundly ideological character of the division among Israeli Jews has become clear. Gradually the debate has shifted, influenced in part by increasing signs of Arab moderation, to the deeply divergent images which Israeli Jews have of the nature and purpose of the country. This split within the Jewish sector divides both the elite and the mass. Indeed, despite its relative social and educational homogeneity, Israel's political elite is at least as deeply and evenly divided on the issue as is the Jewish public in general. This view is held, for example, by Amnon Sella, who argues that in the 12 years following the Six Day War a fundamental split developed within the Israeli elite over the most basic issues of foreign policy and national security. Whereas before 1967 the elite was essentially united on these issues, it subsequently split into "custodians" and "re-deemers." Sella uses these labels to refer to those who would use the occupied territories to negotiate for peace with the Arab world vs. those for whom the permanent incorporation of the West Bank and Gaza into Israel is a national mission of paramount importance. Sella characterizes the idelogical differences between these two groups as "irreconcilable" and "unbridgeable."[13]

What is particularly consequential for political relations between Arabs and Jews is the depth, intensity, and bitterness of the dispute between significant groups on each side of this controversy. Many of those who favor permanent incorporation of the territories tend to do so on the basis of beliefs that a negotiated peace with the Arab world is impossible and even undesirable. Heavily influenced by the Redemptionist ideology of Gush Emunim, the integral nationalist thinking of Revisionism, and the rabidly anti-Arab sentiments most explicitly expressed by Kahane, they condemn Israeli Jews willing to contemplate territorial concessions as overly sensitive "pretty souls." Other epithets for doves, that have become regular parts of right wing Israeli political discourse, include "nowists," "meists," and "traitors." "Leftists," has become, in their parlance, virtually a curse word. Peace Now activists, on the other hand, view many within the hawkish camp as mystical, primitive, and utterly irresponsible in their insistence on policies seen to jeopardize the democratic and Jewish character of the state by incorporating 1.6 million Arabs from the occupied territories into the body politic. A 1983 poll asked Israeli Jews whether they would favor outlawing certain political organizations, including Gush Emunim and Peace Now, the two movements most directly and importantly involved in the struggle over Israel's future relationship to the West Bank and Gaza. The results of the poll showed that 22 percent of those responding favored banning Gush Emunim and 27 percent favored banning Peace Now.[14]

In addition to such polls, the hatred that exists between these groups is readily apparent in arguments on the street and in the need for heavy police involvement to prevent violence between demonstrators and counter-demonstrators. The intensity of feeling and the extent of polarization are also apparent on the floor of the Israeli parliament. Early in 1984, for example, one of the founders of Gush Emunim, Member of Knesset Rabbi Haim Druckman, spoke at length of the disrespect toward religious and national values displayed by increasing numbers of theatre productions and in the electronic and print media. Supported by ultra-nationalist Knesset Members such as Miriam Glasser-Tussia, Druckman proposed establishment of a government censorship board empowered to ensure that the media would fulfill its proper function: "to serve the good of the state and of Judaism."

In the response of Amnon Rubinstein, head of the liberal-dovish Shinui Party, the categorical differences in fundamental values which account for trends toward polarization in Israeli are apparent.

When I hear Rabbi Druckman and Miriam Glasser-Tussia I conclude each time anew that we are speaking in two worlds, really two separate worlds, and on two planets far from one another that have no contact with one another, and I don't believe it is possible to bridge this gap between planet and planet. I just don't believe it.[15]

A subsequent interchange between two Knesset Members would seem to bear out Rubinstein's opinion that the ideological schism within the Jewish population is unbridgeable.

Eleazar Granot: There is a culture war in this land.
We have stopped deluding ourselves.
There is a culture war and one side is
refusing to recognize it and trying to
make peace and withdrawing step by
step, while the other side keeps going
forward without a majority of the people.
The time has come that you should know
that the period is over, this ideal
period for you we are putting to an end.

Miriam Glasser-Tussia: What are you threatening?
Granot: This ideal has ended.
Glasser-Tussia: Now to fight?
Granot: Now to fight.
Glasser-Tussia: Steel with steel?
Granot: Steel with steel.
Glasser-Tussia: Missile against missile?
Granot: Missile against missile.[16]

The Implications of Polarization Among Jews for the Political Role of Israeli Arabs

If the votes received in 1984 by the political parties most closely associated with Likud and Labor are added together the totals are nearly identical. Likud, Tehiya, the National Religious Party, Morasha, and Ometz together received 875,001 votes. The Labor Party, Yahad, Shinui, and the Civil Rights Movement together received 874,821 votes. Only 180 votes separated these two blocs, so radically opposed on so many issues! It is a commonplace of Israeli political reporting that such divisions have given disproportionate clout to the ultra-orthodox parties—Shas and Agudat Israel. But the extraordinarily deep and even split within the Jewish sector, compounded by increasing alienation between "secular" left of center voters and the Haredim,[17] affects the incentive structure of Jewish politicians in several ways that suggest the likelihood of enhanced bargaining opportunities for Arab voters and Arab political entrepreneurs.

Under conditions of polarization the floating vote between Labor, Likud, and their respective allies has dropped as a proportion of the total Jewish vote.[18] In contrast, dramatic swings of large numbers of Arab votes, from Labor and its Arab Affiliates in 1977 to Rakah's "Democratic Front for Peace and Equality," from Rakah to Labor in 1981, and from Labor affiliated lists and Rakah to the Progressive List for Peace and left-center parties (Yahad, Shinui, and Ratz) in 1984, indicate that the floating vote among Arabs is rising in both absolute and relative terms. Because of higher population growth rates and a sharp rise in Arab participation rates, the Arab vote rose by 23 percent between 1981 and 1984 compared to less than 7 percent among Jewish voters. If these 33,000 new voters are added to the 20,000 Arabs who had previously voted for the Labor Affiliated Arab lists (none of which appeared in 1984) and to the 5,000 fewer Arab votes that Rakah received in 1984 compared to 1981, the total Arab "floating vote" in 1984 can be roughly but conservatively estimated as between 55,000 and 60,000 (out of a total Arab vote in 1984 of 225,000, of which 207,000 were valid). This is the equivalent of 3–4 Knesset seats.

Even if the effects of Jewish polarization are ignored, the increasing size of the Arab vote would make it considerably more important than in the past for Jewish politicians to cater to the preferences of Arab voters. In fact, not only are the incentives to campaign for Arab votes higher, but the risks to doing so are lower. The polarization I have discussed can be assumed to reduce the likelihood that many Jewish voters on the hawkish-right would vote for Labor or Labor leaning parties under any circumstances. Accordingly, Jewish politicians in these parties can be expected to perceive that they have substantially less to lose by making effective appeals for Arab votes—appeals that they may have avoided in the past for fear of alienating potential Jewish supporters. These same politicians can also be expected to calculate that their own supporters will be less likely to desert their parties in reaction to solicitousness toward Arabs since the political and ideological costs of voting for the Likud or a Likud-leaning party have become so high.

None of this would be relevant to political outcomes, of course, if Arabs in Israel had become so alienated from Jewish-Zionist politics as to refuse to play the enlivened political game by bargaining, individually and collectively, with their votes. But polls showing that Arabs identify themselves as "Israeli," even as they also embrace "Palestinian" and "Arab" identities, and the apparent failure of campaigns by radical Arabs to boycott Knesset elections, suggest the opposite.[19] The impressive response of Arabs throughout Israel in 1980 to an effort to organize a country-wide political party, and the important role which the Council of Arab Mayors has played in representing Arab sentiment and demands, both suggest that the younger, better educated Arab voters of the 1980s, if more "Palestinian," are also pragmatic in their search for opportunities within the Israeli political arena to improve their situation.

Evidence is mounting that the logic of polarized political competition among Jews, and the presence of increasing numbers of strategic Arab voters, are changing the calculations and behavior of Jewish politicians. I shall consider this evidence under three categories: (1) increasing solicitousness by Jewish politicians for Arab concerns that is unprecedented in its substantiveness and consistency; (2) trends in Arab voting that are consistent with increasingly strategic political behavior and which impacted consequentially on recent elections; (3) explicit recognition by Israeli politicans and observers of the growing significance of the Arab vote and the changing rules of the political game.

Increasing Solicitousness

Jewish politicians have traditionally solicited Arab votes for their parties or for "Affiliated Arab Lists" created by Jewish parties specifically for the purpose of attracting Arab votes. As described elsewhere,[20] Arab citizens have traditionally been vulnerable to pressure by parties within the government who control ministries and other resources vital to their life and livelihood. In this context of Arab economic and political weakness, mainstream parties seldom, if ever, addressed the Arab population as a whole during election campaigns or worked consistently between elections to establish a record of supportiveness for Arab concerns. With the passage of time visits to Arab villages by party workers immediately prior to elections, and the grand promises they traditionally made at that time to religious notables and clan leaders, were treated with increasing cynicism.[21]

Polarization within the Jewish sector sharpened considerably in early 1983, boiling over into violence when one Jewish peace demonstrator was killed by a grenade thrown by a Jewish counter-demonstrator. Since approximately that time, and in sharp contrast to the historical pattern of Jewish-Arab political relations, Jewish politicians, not only, but especially, representing center-left and liberal parties, have exhibited unusual sensitivity and responsiveness to Arab economic, social, cultural, and political demands.

In the 1984 election campaign several parties invested a great deal of time and energy in the solicitation of Arab votes. These parties also expanded opportunities for their members to participate in the design of the lists of candidates presented to the public. For the first time, Arab members of the Labor Party were permitted to choose who among them would appear on a "realistic" place on the Labor Alignment (Labor and Mapam) list. Abdel Wahab Daroushe appeared on the thirty-sixth place on the Alignment list and, along with Muhammad Watad of Mapam, was elected. It is instructive that, to accommodate Daroushe, the Labor Party was willing to move Eliahu Navi, the prominent Sephardi Mayor of Beersheva, from a realistic to an unrealistic place on the ticket.[22] The leaders of Labor, Shinui, the Civil Rights Movement, and Ezer Weizman's new party—Yahad, made repeated visits to Arab communities. Shinui included Zeidan Attashe (who was elected) in the third place on its list. While Shinui paid particular attention to the Druse community, the CRM, building on its active defense of Beduin land claims in the Negev, focused its campaign there. Yahad included a Muslim Arab mayor in the sixth place on its list and featured a detailed list of Israeli Arab concerns very prominently in its official platform. Yahad's platform tried hard to convey the sense of its break with past practice of promises that would be ignored after the election was over.

> Israel's Arabs hitherto divided their votes between the various parties on the basis of promises that generally were never kept. It is time that these votes were given to a party whose promises have credibility and will be kept, a party with an unquestionable commitment to friendly and good neighborly relations with the Arabs. Israel's Arabs are citizens of the State of Israel, and their rights and obligations are equal to those of the other citizens of the State.[23]

Following the elections the National Unity Government was formed and Shinui's leader, Amnon Rubinstein, was appointed as Minister of Communications. One symbolic, but highly significant action he took was to issue a stamp in honor of Muslim citizens of Israel. Rubinstein cited this stamp, the first Israeli stamp to depict themes pertaining to Arab Israelis, as evidence of Shinui's effectiveness as an ideological party intent on making substantial changes in Israeli society.

> In these two years Shinui has put a strong mark on the government's decisions . . . I believe that Shinui is an ideological party whose every action reflects its ideology. At the Communication Ministry each step, beginning with staff cutbacks and down to stamp issues, is based on ideology. For the first time in this country I issued a stamp in honor of the Muslims, on the occasion of 'Id al-Fitr.' Now, at Christmas, we will issue a stamp in honor of the Christian community. It is all a matter of ideology. Shinui reflects our desire to work changes in Israeli society.[24]

More than any other figure in the new government, Ezer Weizman sought ways to demonstrate his good faith to Israeli Arabs, establishing thereby a reputation for sensitivity to their demands unequalled by any mainstream Jewish politician since the creation of Israel in 1948. It is not unusual for a Minister without portfolio, such as Ezer Weizman, to be assigned overall responsibility in the government for monitoring affairs in the Arab sector. But Weizman, true to Yahad's platform and his own clear sense of the political potential of Israeli Arab voters, broke from tradition by taking his assignment in this area very seriously. First he fired Benjamin Gur-Aryeh, the tough security services veteran who had served for five years as "Adviser to the Prime Minister on Arab Affairs." As noted earlier, the "Office of the Adviser," had been, from the abolition of the military government in Arab areas in 1966 until 1985, the bureaucratic apparatus directly responsible for the supervision of policy in the Arab sector. Heavily influenced by "Arabists" within the security services, and working closely with them, this office, and the "Arab Departments" of the various ministries whose work it coordinated, were resented by most Israeli Arabs as symbolizing discrimination against them and their effective exclusion from Israeli society. Having fired Gur-Aryeh, Weizman then made the startling proposal that the office itself be abolished and that Arab affairs become, essentially, a Cabinet level responsibility. His proposal was accepted by Prime Minister Shimon Peres. He then chose Yosef Ginat, whose moderate, integration oriented views toward Israeli Arabs were well known, as his chief assistant in the development and implementation of policies toward the Arab population.

Weizman and Ginat, with consistent support from Avraham Tamir in the Prime Minister's office, also took action on a wide range of specific issues of great practical and symbolic importance to Israeli Arabs. Um el Fahm's long stalled application for municipal status was approved, making it the second Arab city in Israel. A virtual freeze on the implementation of demolition orders against thousands of "illegal" structures in Arab villages was implemented, precipitating the resignation of Israel Koenig, a veteran Interior Ministry official intensely disliked by Galilee Arabs for his explicitly hostile stance toward them. Repeated meetings between the Prime Minister and/or Weizman and the Council of Arab Mayors seemed to signal an acceptance of that body by the government as a quasi-official representative of Israeli Arabs—a status which the previous Labor government, under Yitzhak Rabin, had categorically refused to accord it. When the government announced the formation of a Jewish-Arab advisory committee, to be registered as a foundation authorized to raise funds abroad for projects in the Arab sector, the head of the National Committee of Arab Local Council Heads, Shefar'am mayor Ibrahim Nimr Hussein was named as one of its eight members. The semi-official Arabic newspaper, Al-Anba, associated in

Israeli Arab minds with traditional government policies toward the Arab sector, was closed. Finally, and perhaps most meaningfully, Weizman declared that "Area Nine," a substantial tract of land effectively expropriated from Arab villages in the central Galilee, would be returned to its Arab owners.

Weizman made no attempt to conceal from Jewish audiences his efforts to respond positively to Arab concerns. In an interview published in Haaretz in February 1985, Weizman was asked for his reaction to the idea that "Because of your activity in the Arab sector . . . you've forgotten about the Jews." Weizman responded:

> People can say what they want. At the moment there are twenty-four ministers in the government whose job is to worry about the Jews. My job is to worry about the Arabs. Twenty-four to one, that isn't a bad proportion.[25]

Some saw Weizman as a stalking horse for Shimon Peres and the Labor Party; as an experiment to see if Arab political support could be mobilized by responding substantially to Arab demands without alienating Jewish voters. The integration of Weizman and his Yahad movement into the Labor Party, Weizman's informal designation as Foreign Minister in the next Labor run government, and Peres' own efforts are evidence that Labor in general, and Peres in particular, believed the experiment was a success. Indeed Prime Minister Peres spoke to Arab Israelis and behaved toward them in ways that were strikingly different from Begin and Shamir in the previous two Israeli governments. While the latter had, at best, ignored Israeli Arabs, Prime Minister Peres visited Arab localities and declared often, to both Arab and Jewish audiences, his belief that fundamental changes in government policy toward Israeli Arabs, and in Arab-Jewish relations in Israel, were in the offing.[26] To Jewish audiences he explained Israel's "new policy" toward Israeli Arabs as follows:

> I would say we have all witnessed a stage in the maturing of relations between Jews and Arabs. We have all matured. Some of us have even become old and we cannot behave like small children. The intention is not only to eliminate the post of Adviser on Arab Affairs, but to incorporate Arabs and Druse in the decisionmaking establishment, so that they can express their views before decisions are made and I am certain this is a development in the right direction.[27]

The general change in the attitude of high echelons within the Labor Party toward Israeli Arabs has been apparent in a variety of spheres. After decades of unfulfilled promises some substantial joint industrial ventures in Arab localities have been or are being implemented by the Histadrut.[28] Labor Party Members of Knesset have also sharply attacked officials in

Likud controlled ministries for their lack of knowledge and apparent unconcern for the economic problems of the Beduin.

One of the most dramatic indications of Peres' belief that non-Jewish Israelis can and should be courted, even at the risk of alienating rightward leaning Jews, is his response to an unprecedentedly violent attack by Druse villagers in the upper Galilee on Israeli policemen. Early in July 1987, Druse from Beit Jann set up a "settlement" in the nature reserve that surrounds their village to protest land expropriation and land shortages for housing and agriculture. When police and border guards were sent to evacuate the settlement, they were attacked by several hundred Druse, wielding chains and knives. Eighteen policemen and Green Patrol officers were injured. One hundred villagers then pitched their tents again on the site.[29]

Pro-Likud journalists, such as Shmuel Schnitzer, saw the incident as raising questions about the loyalty of the Druse and the possible need to disband the heavily Druse Border Partol. Even the liberal Haaretz editorialized about "the shameful pogrom which the residents of Beit Jann unleashed against the police." But undeterred by accusations of Arab vote-mongering, Shimon Peres led a delegation of five Labor Ministers, including Minister of Agriculture Aryeh Nehemkin. They promised the local council of Beit Jann that Agriculture Ministry regulations would changed so as to permit villagers unrestricted access to their land. Peres personally promised to introduce legislation in the Knesset to remove all Beit Jann land from the nature reserve in question.[30]

The center and left of center parties have been most visible and vigorous in their response to the growing importance of Arab votes. But despite the protests it has made with increasing frequency against Labor Party pandering to the Arabs, the Likud itself has manifested a sensitivity to Israeli Arab concerns which contrasts greatly with its own previous record. When the Labor led version of the national unity government implemented Weizman's proposals to abolish the Office of the Adviser on Arab Affairs and return Area 9 to its original owners, Likud members of the government protested vigorously. They characterized the moves as craven attempts to attract Arab votes at the expense of Jewish national and Zionist imperatives. Various Likud Members of Knesset condemned the return of expropriated land as "creating the nucleus of a Palestinian state in the Galilee," "a process of selling national interests for political gains," "reeking of partisan politics," "the beginning of the Arab struggle to liberate the Galilee of Jewish hands," and "liable to revive Arab extremism within the Green Line."[31] Weizman, said MK Ronnie Milo, a Herut Member of Knesset known for his acid tongue and militantly anti-Arab stance, was acting as "the Yehoshua Hankin of the Arabs."[32] When the Likud took charge of the national unity government, Milo warned, these decisions would be reversed. Indeed Ronnie Milo's name was prominently advanced as the Likud's candidate to take charge of Arab affairs.[33]

But it would appear that the Likud chose not to abandon tbe general change in policy toward the Arab sector initiated under Peres and Weizman. Those Likud Members of Knesset who so vociferously opposed Weizman's policies also accused most Likud ministers of ignoring the problem. In May 1986, Ginat met in a closed session with Herut activists, to whom he explained the general lines of the government's new policy toward Israeli Arabs. In response to sharp attacks on that policy and on his personal reliability Ginat observed that "from neither Shamir nor Arens have I heard the intolerance toward Israeli Arabs expressed by rank and file Herutniks."[34] In the fall of 1986, when the rotation did take place and responsibility for Arab affairs was taken away from Weizman, the Office of the Advisor to the Prime Minister on Arab Affairs was not re-created. Instead of Ronnie Milo, Moshe Arens was delegated with overall responsibility for Arab affairs. Arens, like Weizman, was a former Minister of Defense serving in the National Unity Government as a Minister without Portfolio. Significantly, Arens is the only leading Likud minister with a reputation for speaking and thinking about Israel as a "pluralist" society.[35] Though Arens had personally opposed the return of Area 9 to its Arab owners, once put in charge, he decided against reversing the decision. Though many in Likud had expressed their support for Benjamin Gur-Aryeh, when he was fired by Weizman, Arens chose not to re-hire Gur-Aryeh as his special assistant for Arab affairs. Although treated warily at first, Arens was soon receiving praise from Israeli Arabs for the seriousness with which he viewed the affairs of the Arab minority and his reasoned, moderate approach. Like his predecessor, Arens has met, albeit informally, with the Council on Arab Mayors.[36] Under his tenure the Cabinet approved the Markowitz Commission recommendations concerning the effective cancellation of thousands of demolition orders. During Weizman's term of responsibility, plans were under way finally to allow Arab villagers from Biram and Ikrit, evacuated in 1948, to return to their villages. Under Arens, those plans are being put into effect.

To be sure, the Likud has not shown as much energy, sensitivity, or imagination in responding to Arab concerns, such as increased financial support for Arab local council budgets, as the Labor Party. Amos Gilboa, appointed by Arens as his special assistant for minority affairs, is a military man specializing on the Arab world as a whole and has no specific background in Israeli Arab affairs. Placing more positive emphasis on Druse and Circassians, who are conscripted into the Israeli army, as opposed to Muslim and Christian Arabs, who serve in the army only rarely and on a volunteer basis, Arens echoes the sentiments of many others in the Likud that "equal rights" must be conditional on "equal obligations." Over the negative votes of each Labor Party minister in the national unity government, the Likud and religious party ministers passed a resolution raising university tuition fees for non-veterans (that is, effectively, for non-Jews). Although Israeli governments have traditionally used the non-veteran status of most non-Jews to discriminate in the distribution of various benefits, the Likud's attempt to continue this tradition reflects its relative lack of sensitivity to the changing political role of Arabs in Israel.

In this context, the result of the decision is highly instructive, and supports the general argument I have advanced. Not only was it made over strong objections by the Labor Party against such blantant "discrimination," the decision was also greeted by a storm of protest from Arab and Jewish students and by the refusal of several universities to implement the order. Some months later, the government reversed itself on the measure in favor of a more moderate increase in tuition fees for all students.

Strategic Arab Voting

Analysis of Arab voting patterns in the last two Knesset elections, as well as the political bargaining and maneuvering which Arab Knesset Members and others have engaged in to advance demands on behalf of the general Israeli Arab population, suggest that the new solicitousness of Jewish politicians reflects a rational response to an incentive structure changing in ways discussed earlier.

In the nine Israeli parliamentary elections held between 1949 and 1977 Arab voting behavior can largely be described in terms of two distinct but related patterns. Depending on which election one examines, anywhere from 35 percent to 67 percent of Arab votes were given to Zionist parties (or lists affiliated to those parties) whose control of various ministries and other official and quasi-official institutions (such as the Histadrut) offered Arabs the hope of direct, personal, material sanctions if their votes were not forthcoming. During that same period from 11 percent to 51 percent of Arab votes went to the Communist Party. Arab political support for the Communist Party meant gaining access to the considerable resources (including educational opportunities in eastern bloc countries) that Rakah controls.

The point is that whether an Arab cast his vote for the Communists or for the Labor party, its Affiliated Lists, or the National Religious Party, his vote was not a strategic act designed to affect outcomes in the Israeli political arena in a way that might protect or enhance the interests of the Arab minority as a whole. One factor discouraging strategic voting behavior by Arabs, aside from their dependence on the resources controlled by the established political parties, was the widespread conviction that no matter how they voted the Labor Party organized government that would follow the elections would not be perceptibly different from that which preceded it. In 1977 the Communist Party's share of the Arab vote peaked at 50.6 percent. But Likud's surprise victory in 1977, and its relatively harsh policies toward Israeli Arabs between 1977 and 1981, encouraged many Arabs to vote strategically for the first time in 1981.[37] In that year many of those Arabs who in 1977 had voted for Rakah out of frustration and protest, seem to have switched to Labor as the "lesser of the two evils," hoping to assist the Labor Party in regaining power. The proportion of Arabs voting for the Labor party or its affiliated list increased for the first time since 1951, jumping from 30 percent in 1977 to 39 percent in 1981. At the same time Rakah's share of the Arab vote dropped for the first time in twenty years, from 51 percent in 1977 to 38 percent in 1981.[38]

To a great extent the pattern of Arab voting in 1984 was an extension and accentuation of the emergence of Arab strategic voting in 1981. But in 1984 the trend was expressed, not so much as increased votes for the Labor Party, but as increased support for small liberal-dovish parties whose commitment to Arab interests was relatively clear, for whom the Arab votes were of comparatively greater importance, and who could therefore be trusted to carry out their commitment to Arab voters in the context of a Labor led coalition government in which they would participate. "The desire to influence the political system has now become," according to Raanan Cohen, "one of the factors determining the distribution of Arab votes, though in comparison with others, not the decisive factor."[39]

Cohen's is the most comprehensive analysis of Arab voting patterns that has yet been published. He provides specific data for the last four parliamentary elections, divided into Arab votes for the Labor Party, its Affiliated Lists, the Communist Party, the Progressive List for Peace (Meari-Peled, 1984), Gahal/Likud, the religious parties, and "others." The last category is made up almost entirely of small liberal or left-leaning dovish parties such as Shelli/Moked, Shulamit Aloni's Civil Rights Movement, Shinui, Yahad (1984), and Lova Eliav's list (1984). Increasing proportions of the Arab vote cast for parties in the "others" category is thus a fairly good indicator of increases in the extent of Arab strategic voting. In 1973 only 3 percent of Israeli Arab votes went to the parties in this category, in 1977, 10 percent. In 1981 11 percent of Arab votes were delivered to these parties. In 1984 30,000 Arab votes went to these parties, equalling approximately 17 percent of the total Arab vote.[40]

Analysis of Arab votes within the "others" category shows that approximately 35 percent went to Weizman's Yahad Party (which thus received 6 percent of the total Arab vote) while 29 percent went to Shinui (5 percent of the total Arab vote). To be sure, personal interests and parochial loyalties still play a key role in Arab voting. Shinui received many Druse votes as a direct result of Zeidan Attashe's appearance in a realistic place on its list. But those Arabs who have voted for these small left-leaning "coalitionable" parties, or who can be expected to vote for them in the future, can have a disproportionate impact on the behavior of those parties, and thus on the political system as a whole. The 10,500 Arab votes which Yahad received was fully 23 percent of its total vote. Sixteen percent of Shinui votes in 1984 were Arab. By comparison, five and a half percent of Labor Party votes came from the Arab sector.

The Knesset elections of 1984 were the first in which no "affiliated Arab lists" competed. In 1981 some 13 percent of Arab votes went to a list affiliated to the Labor Party, or to one of two other lists, headed by Arab notables with close previous ties to the Labor Party. Village by village analysis of where these votes went in 1984 shows that they did not flow to the Labor Party.[41] Nor, in large measure, did they go to the Communist Party. Instead they gravitated toward the Progressive List for Peace and to Shinui, Yahad, and the other parties included in the "others" category. This strongly suggests that these votes, and perhaps others among the 18 percent of the Arab vote that went to the PLP, are "up for grabs" in the next election, especially if the PLP does not (or is not allowed to) compete. Add to this the rapidly growing pool of eligible Arab voters and the relatively low participation rates of Arabs in the last two elections, and one can clearly understand the political rationality of Jewish politicians who manifest the kind of increasing solicitiousness for Arab concerns that I have described above.[42]

Aside from the voting behavior of Israeli Arabs, the increased bargaining power of Arab elites in Israel's polarized political system is evidenced in subtle but important ways. Space permits only three examples.

The Progressive List for Peace does not conceal its support for the PLO. It is represented in the Knesset by a former member of the outlawed "El-Ard" Arab nationalist organization and by the Jewish leader of the Israel Committee for Israeli-Palestinian Peace. But instead of being categorically excluded from Labor Party calculations about possible coalitions or successful votes of no-confidence in the Likud version of the national unity government, its two votes have repeatedly figured in major decisions by Labor Party strategists. Indeed, unlike the Communist Party, the PLP's explicit purpose is to effect significant changes in government policy toward Israeli Arabs and in the overall complexion of Israeli politics by using the parliamentary strength its votes have given it.[43] A most significant episode occurred shortly after the 1984 elections when Shlomo Hillel, the Labor Party's candidate, was elected Speaker of the Knesset over the Likud candidate—Meir Cohen-Avidov, known for his stridently anti-Arab rhetoric. The difference between victory and defeat were the two votes cast by the PLP for Hillel. This support was delivered to the Labor Party in return for promises guaranteeing PLP representation on certain key Knesset committees. The negotiations that resulted in this arrangement, and the successful vote, helped establish the PLP as a usable political resource—thereby setting a potentially important precedent.[44]

In recent years the International Center for Peace in the Middle East, with which are associated leading doves in the Labor Party, Shinui, and the CRM, as well as Mapam and Peace Now, has considerably broadened its activities to emphasize Israeli Arab issues—coexistence, education, civil liberties, etc. Apparently believing that under current circumstances more is to be gained politically than lost by publicizing Israeli Arab support and involvement in its activities, the Center published an appeal in February 1987 calling for a peace agreement based on territorial compromise and mutual recognition of rights to self-determination between Israel and the Palestinian people. In addition to its Executive Committee Members and Knesset Members, the names of 201 public figures were attached to the announcement. Fully ten per cent of those listed were Israeli Arabs.[45]

On June 24, 1987, the Council of Arab Mayors called an unprecedentedly successful general strike of Israeli Arabs under the slogan of "Equality." The Jerusalem Post described the strike as almost totally effective. Demanding an end to discrimination in government aid to Arab municipalities, more support for economic development in the Arab sector, and the construction of 1500 new classrooms in Arab villages, the organizers were reported to be delighted with the peacefulness of the protest and the virtual halt they were able to bring to the operation of schools, stores, businesses, and local government in Arab areas. Aside from the impressiveness of the strike itself, and the promise by its organizers that it would only mark the beginning of an intensified, but legal and peaceful struggle for equality, what was most instructive about the event was the government's toleration of it and the absence of provocative police actions that in 1976 and 1982 had turned similar events into violent confrontations. Arens' own measured comments about the strike, and the absence of elaborate security precautions, reflect a de facto acceptance of the right of the Arab minority to engage in mass political activity without being attacked for attempting to undermine the security of the state.[46]

Observer Comment on Arab Political Clout

Both the rising solicitousness of Jewish politicians toward Arabs and the increasing political clout of Israeli Arabs, have been explicitly recognized by Jewish leaders and commentators. Analyzing the results of the 1981 elections, Daniel Elazar commented that Israeli Arabs "came close to succeeding in putting the Ma'arach over the top in number of seats."[47] Prior to the 1984 elections New York Times correspondent Thomas Friedman observed that:

more than ever before, Jewish politicans are looking to Israel's 250,000 Arab, Druse and Bedouin voters to get them elected to the next Parliament. Arab voters have the strength to elect roughly 12 of the 120 members of the Israeli Parliament and in a close election, as this one is expected to be, their choices could be decisive.[48]

Immediately after the 1984 election results were tallied pollster Hanoch Smith ascribed in part the Likud-religious bloc's loss of its majority to the Arab vote.[49] While Gush Emunim and other right-wing elements attempted to delegitimize the election outcome by arguing that "the majority of the Jewish public voted for a Likud-led government," one left-wing Jewish journalist called for a "declared willingness" to rely on Arab support to form a government "even if there were no practical need for such support."[50] But as Boaz Evron has explained, from the point of view of the left side of the Israeli political spectrum, there *is* a "practical need."

> If it were not for the Arab vote, the Likud might well have been able to form a government in the last elections, leaving Labor in the opposition. Israeli Arabs wield a major weight in Israeli politics, and they exercise it intelligently in their own behalf.[51]

Almost from the installation of the national unity government speculation began as to how soon it would fall apart and what the outcome of new elections would be. With the evenness in the split among Jews that I described earlier, attention was quickly focused on prospective Arab voters. Yosef Goell, a journalist with long experience covering the Arab sector, described in late 1985 how:

> in the super-heated political atmosphere of the national unity government, Labor's Police Minister Haim Bar-Lev is also lumped in with the 'terrible trio'—Weizman, Ginat, and Director-General of the Prime Minister's Office Avraham Tamir—as carrying favor with the Arabs for narrow electoral purposes.[52]

Adding substance to these accusations, Goell remarked that despite Interior Ministry threats to demolish illegal Arab structures, "it's a good bet that none of the threatened homes will actually be razed in an election year."[53]

Commenting on the political interest of parties in power to help resolve problems besetting education in the Arab sector, Aharon Geva reminded his (mostly) Labor Party readers that

> Even a purely egotistical electoral interest requires us to reduce this historical inequality insofar as possible. Arab pupils constitute 17 percent of Israel's school population, and today's pupil is tomorrow's voter.[54]

Nahum Barnea, editor of Koteret Rashit, traced the Likud's decision finally to allow Arabs from Ikrit and Biram to return to their villages, as a product of hard-headed political calculations, outweighing old fears that dangerous precedents might be set for other Arab refugees.

> The two largest parties have come to understand that the Arabs of Israel have substantial electoral power that will grow steadily with the years. On matters of opinion there can be arguments, but not on votes in the ballot box: if the two parties want to break out of the stalemate between them the only way will be to court Arab voters.[55]

Indeed, looking forward to the next election, pollster Hanoch Smith asserts that Arab voters "can potentially play spoilers for the Likud . . . if not for the Arab vote, the Likud-religious bloc would be able to form a solid government."[56]

There have been reports that the differential ability of individual Labor Party politicians to appeal effectively to Arab voters has become an important factor in determining who will lead the party in the next election. In Ezer Weizman's campaign to place himself in contention as Labor's candidate for the Premiership, his special ties to Israeli Arabs are being touted as an valuable resource. According to sources described as "close to Weizman,"

> the support he is gaining in the Arab sector could bring the party 75,000 votes from this sector, if Weizman heads the list. "I do not think the Labor Party will rush to give up three or four seats."[57]

Conclusion: Binationalism on the Way

Such observations and analyses are most important, not as evidence that Israeli Arabs have become, or are soon to become, the decisive factor in Israeli politics, but that the context of Jewish Arab relations in Israel have been powerfully affected by the deep and even split among Jews over fundamental issues. Though many scholars and analysts have noted the trend toward the increasingly strategic and meaningful political behavior of Israel's Arab citizens, its profound implications have generally been ignored. Operating within the assumptions of a mononational paradigm of Israeli society, most interpret it as indicating that Arabs are finally becoming "integrated" into and accepting of the Jewish-Zionist political system. My analysis suggests that continued polarization among Jews, and the growing numbers and sophistication of Arab voters, is actually in the process of transforming that political system. Though binationalism will not be used to describe the changes thereby brought about until well after those changes have occurred, it is already more accurate to conceive of Israel as a binational than as a mononational society. In other words, Israel may be "the Jewish state" in ideological and, to an extent, in legal terms, but empirically its existence as such is increasingly problematic. The absorption of the West Bank and Gaza will accelerate processes of transition, not trigger them.

Recent discussions by West Bank Arabs of strategies entailing the mobilization of Palestinians within the Jerusalem municipality or the broader Israeli political arena are evidence that the logic of de facto annexation is not lost on those who suffer its consequences most directly. For although ideologies, and abstract political identities, can guide and structure political competition, in the end they can be sustained only if they do not systematically contradict the perceived interests of those who must sacrifice to implement and honor them. As divisions within both the Jewish and Arab Palestinian communities deepen, elements within each camp will be driven toward alliances with one another. Binational outcomes that are not the first choice of either side can thus emerge. While making the choices that will hasten or slow this process between the Jordan River and the Mediterranean Sea, both Arabs and Jews will watch closely what is happening between the two peoples within the Green Line.

I am pleased to acknowledge the contribution of my honors student, Leslie Newman, Dartmouth Class of '87, to the research upon which this article is based.

Notes

1. These figures are based in part on estimates by Israel's Central Bureau of Statistics for November 1987.

2. For an excellent example of the analytical and prescriptive implications of this expectation see the collection of essays on deeply divided societies in Africa edited by Donald Rothchild and Victor A. Olorunsola, *State Versus Ethnic Claims: African Policy Dilemmas*, (Boulder: Westview Press, 1983). David Laitin's essay in this volume "The Ogadeen Question and Changes in Somali Identity," is an important exception to this collection and the literture as a whole.

3. For a well-documented study of this phenomenon in scores of different countries see Donald E. Horowitz, *Ethnic Groups in Conflict*, (Berkeley: University of California Press, 1985). Horowitz's description of inter and intra-communal politics in Sri Lanka, in the 1960s is, however, suggestive of how polarization within a dominant segment (the Sinhalese) can lead to political alliances that span the communal divide (between Sinhalese and Tamils). See especially pp. 342–369.

4. Without suggesting anything about emergent binationalism, some scholars have noted the relationship between the polarization of the Jewish sector and increasing political opportunities for Israeli Arabs. See Shlomo Aronson and Nathan Yanai, "Critical Aspects of the Elections and their Implications," in *The Roots of Begin's Success: The1981 Israeli Elections*, (London: Croom Helm, 1984), p. 13; and Avner Yaniv and Majid el-Haj, "Voting Behavior of the Arabs," in Asher Arian

(ed.), *The Elections in Israel—1981*, (Tel-Avia: Ramot Publishing Company, 1983), p. 162.

5. For analysis of the "system of control" over Arabs in Israel see Ian Lustick, *Arabs in the Jewish State: Israel's Control of a National Minority*, (Austin: University of Texas Press, 1980).

6. Ze'ev Tsur, *From the Partition Dispute to the Allon Plan*, (Ramat Ephal: Tabenkin Institute, 1982), p. 9.

7. Charles S. Liebman and Eliezer Don-Yehiya, *Civil Religion in Israel*, (Berkeley: University of California Press, 1985).

8. Concerning the polarization of Israeli society over this and related issues see Myron J. Aronoff, "Political Polarization: Contradictory Interpretations of Israeli Reality," in *The Begin Era*, Steven Heydemann (ed.), (Boulder: Westview Press, 1984), pp. 53–77; Ian Lustick, "The West Bank and Gaza Strip in Israeli Politics," Heydemann (ed.), op. cit., pp. 73–98; and Giora Goldberg and Efraim Ben-Zadok, "Gush Emunim in the West Bank," *Middle Eastern Studies*, Vol. 22, no. 1, (January 1986), pp. 52–73.

9. See Michal Shamir and Asher Arian, "The Ethnic Vote in Israel's 1981 Elections," in *The Elections in Israel—1981*, (Tel-Aviv: Ramot Publishing Company, 1983), pp. 91–111.

10. For a discussion of the extent to which ideological and emotional attachments to the territories acquired in the 1967 war, particularly those perceived as parts of the Biblical "Land of Israel," i.e. the West Bank and the Gaza Strip, have gradually replaced tactical or security based rationales for their retention in the minds of wide strata within Israel, see Ofira Seliktar, *New Zionism and the Foreign Policy System of Israel*, (Carbondale: Southern Illinois University Press, 1986), pp. 154–162.

11. Polls conducted by the Modi'in Ezrahi Institute, reported in Ma'ariv, May 12, 1987, translated by the Foreign Broadcast Information Service, Daily Report: Near East and Africa (After June 1, 1987, renamed Daily Report: Near East and South Asia hereafter FBIS), May 15, 1987, pp. I7–18.

12. Asher Arian, "What the Israeli Election Portends," *Public Opinion*, (August/ September 1984), p.55.

13. Amnon Sella, "Custodians and Redeemers: Israeli Leaders' Perceptions of Peace, 1967–79," *Middle Eastern Studies*, Vol. 22, no. 2, (April 1986), pp. 247–248.

14. Dahaf, for *Koteret Raashit*, March 9, 1983.

15. Reprinted from *Proceedings of the Knesset in Nekuda*, #70, (March 2, 1984), p. 25.

16. Ibid.

17. According to a poll conducted in June 1986 twice as many Israeli Jews found Arabs "acceptable" as found ultra-orthodox Jews. Fifty percent said they felt "distant" from the ultra-orthodox compared to 35 percent who said they felt "distant" from Israeli Arabs. Poll conducted by Hanoch Smith, reported in *New Outlook*, Vol.29, no. 7, (July 1986), p. 31. See also the comments of Knesset Education Committee Chairman Nahman Raz, reported by Lea Levavi in *The Jerusalem Post International Edition*, week ending October 25, 1986.

18. Asher Arian, *Politics in Israel: The Second Generation*, (Chatham, New Jersey: Chatham House, 1985), pp. 148–151.

19. For differing interpretations of polls dealing with Arab self-identification in Israel, which yet agree on the fact that substantial numbers embrace both Palestinian and Israeli identities see Sammy Smooha, *The Orientation and Politicization of the Arab Minority in Israel*, (Haifa: University of Haifa Institute of Middle Eastern Studies, 1984), Monograph #2, pp. 48–50; and Murad A'si, *Israeli and Palestian Public Opinion*, (Kingston, Canada: Near East Cultural and Educational Foundation of Canada, 1986), Occasional Paper #5, pp. 16–17.

20. Ian Lustick, *Arabs in the Jewish State: Israel's Control of a National Minority*, op. cit., pp.136–137; 150–197; 208–209.

21. Concerning the lack of serious interest in Arab issues displayed by political parties in the campaign preceding the 1981 elections, and the cynicism in the Arab sector with which their efforts were greeted see *Ha'aretz*, December 2, 1980, and Meir Hareuveni, "Parties Open Race for Arab Votes," *Ma'ariv*, August 28, 1980.

22. Navi immediately left the Party in protest, but regardless of its desire to recruit attractive Sephardi politicians, the Labor Party held firm.

23. *Yahad: The Platform*, (Tel-Aviv, 1984), p. 22.

24. Ayal Erlich, "Once Upon a Time There were Two Friends," *Ha'aretz*, supplement, translated by the Joint Publications Research Service, JPRS Report: Near East and South Asia (hereafter "JPRS"), NEA-86-151, (December12, 1986), p. 17. For Rubinstein's analysis of the Arab minority issue as an important element in the larger political struggle between left and right in Israel see Amnon Rubinstein, "Anti-Semitism in Reverse," *Ha'aretz*, September 2, 1984.

25. *Ha'aretz*, February 1, 1985.

26. At the first of these meetings even Rakah Member of Knesset and Mayor of Nazareth Tawfik Zayyad acknowledged the historic change in attitude and policy which Peres' move represented. Asher Wallfish, "8 Arab Mayors Meet Peres," *Jerusalem Post*, November 21, 1984. See the text of Peres' interviews on Israel's Arabic radio station, where he stressed his aspiration for an Israel in which "all citizens will be equal before the law and in terms of opportunities granted to them." *Jerusalem in Arabic*, April 25, 1985, transcribed by FBIS, April 25,1987, p. I1.

27. Television interview, transcribed by FBIS, April 1, 1985, p. I2.

28. *Jerusalem Post*, July 7, 1986. In December 1984, three days after Prime Minister Peres promised Arab municipal officials that the government would try to equalize services in Arab and Jewish localities, the Interior Ministry announced a series of large grants to Arab local authorities. A good deal of support from the Labor Party was forthcoming for a proposal discussed in early 1987 to eliminate the category of "nationality" from Israeli Identity Cards. With the Foreign Ministry in Peres' hands, the first Israeli Muslim Arab was appointed to head a consulate abroad—Mohammed Massarwi, who appeared in the sixth place on Ezer Weizman's Yahad list in the 1984 elections, was named Israel's Consul-General in Atlanta, Georgia.

29. *Jerusalem Domestic Service*, July 6, 1987, transcribed in FBIS, (July 7, 1987), p. L9.

30. "Rifts in the Druse-Jewish Alliance," *Israeli Press Highlights*, Harry Milkman (ed.), (American Jewish Committee), July 20, 1987.

31. Yehoshua Beytzur and Yehudah Goren, "Area 9 Is the Nucleus of a Palestinian State," *Ma'ariv*, August 13, 1986, JPRS, NEA-86-121, (September 24, 1986), pp. 20-22; and Robert Rosenberg, "Area 9 Decision Puts Emphasis on Internal Arab Relations," *Jerusalem Post*, August 8, 1986.

32. Interview with Ronnie Milo, *Koteret Rashit*, #124, (April 17, 1985), p. 9. The reference is to one of the agents of the Jewish National Fund active, before 1948, in the acquisition of Arab land and its transfer to Jewish ownership.

33. Benny Morris, "Ronnie Milo Expects to Take Over Weizman's Arab Job," *Jerusalem Post*, July 29,1986; and Robert Rosenberg, "Area 9 Decision Puts Emphasis on Internal Arab Relations," *Jerusalem Post*,August 8, 1986. Concerning expectations that the Likud would reverse the Labor/Weizman/Ginat policy toward Israeli Arabs see Tom Segev, "The Two Years of Ginat," *Koteret Rashit*, #199, September 24, 1986, p. 20.

34. *Ma'ariv*, May 5, 1986.

35. For an early and illuminating statement of Arens' views on the Arab minority and Israel as a potentially "pluralistic" society, see Moshe Arens, "The Dilemma of Israel's Arabs," *Jerusalem Post Weekly Edition*,October 18-24, 1981. As of this writing (December 1987) Arens has resigned and Milo has been appointed to take his place. Milo's surprisingly restrained, and even solicitous behavior toward Israeli Arabs since he assumed the post, adds further support to my general argument.

36. David Rudge, "Arab Local Leaders Happy after Meeting with Arens," *Jerusalem Post International Edition*, week ending January 24, 1987. See the interview with Arens by Yehuda Litani and Elaine Fletcher, "A Liberal Hardliner Sees a 'Road to Peace'," *Jerusalem Post International Edition*, week ending November 8, 1986.

37. See Ian Lustick, "Israel's Arab Minority in the Begin Era," in *Israel in the Begin Era*, Robert Freedman (ed.), (New York: Praeger, 1982), pp. 143-146.

38. These figures are from Raanan Cohen, Processes of Political Organization and Patterns of Voting among the Arabs of Israel (Masters Thesis: University of Tel-Aviv, Social Science Faculty), June 1985, Part 2.

39. Raanan Cohen, *Processes of Political Organization and Patterns of Voting among the Arabs of Israel*, op. cit., Part 1, p. 102. The figures provided by Cohen for the percentages of the Arab vote cast for these parties differ slightly from those used to calculate the above percentages, provided by Avner Regov. See Yosef Goell, "Minority Majority," *Jerusalem Post*, August 10, 1984.

40. Ibid., pp. 10, 24, 38, and 52. Cohen's figure of 176,000 Arab votes does not appear to include the 20,000-30,000 votes cast by Arabs living in the "mixed cities" (Haifa, Tel-Aviv-Jaffa, Acre, etc.)

41. I conducted this analysis on village by village data provided by Raanan Cohen in *Processes of Political Organization* . . ., op. cit., Part 2.

42. Concerning the potential for a substantial increase in strategic Arab voting that could attend a rise in the rate of voter participation in the Arab sector see Cohen, op. cit., Part 1, p. 132.

43. Interview with Muhammed Miari, "The Making of a Political Movement," *Journal of Palestine Studies*, Vol. XIV, no. 1, (Fall 1984), pp. 36-44. For examples of the demands advanced by the PLP as conditions of its support for a narrow Labor led government see transcribed broadcasts of the *Jerusalem Domestic Service*, August 21, 1984, in FBIS, August 21, 1984, pp. 11-13.

44. On the PLP's potential as a maker and breaker of governments see Allan E. Shapiro, *The Jerusalem Post*, September 4, 1984.

45. *The Jerusalem Post International Edition*, week ending February 28, 1987.

46. On the success of the strike see articles by Yehuda Litani, and David Rudge and Elaine Fletcher in *The Jerusalem Post*, June 25, 1987. For Shulamit Aloni's defense of Israeli Arab rights to conduct a "political strike" see "So What's Wrong with a Political Strike," Yediot Acharonot, June 30, 1987, translated in *Israel Press Briefs*, #54, (July 1987), pp. 16–17.

47. Daniel J. Elazar, "The 1981 Elections: Into the Second Generation of Statehood," in *Israel at the Polls, 1981*, Howard R. Penninman and Daniel J. Elazar (eds.), (Bloomington: Indiana University Press, 1986), p.14.

48. Thomas L. Friedman, "Israeli Politicans Court Long-Ignored Arab Voters," *New York Times*, July 9, 1984.

49. *The Jerusalem Post*, August 3, 1984.

50. Yehuda Lahav, in *Al-Hamishmar*, August 24, 1984.

51. Boaz Evron, "Where We Stand," *New Outlook*, Vol. 29, no. 7, (July 1986), p.17.

52. Yosef Goell, "Demolition Disorders," *The Jerusalem Post*, December 20, 1985.

53. Ibid.

54. Davar, November 10, 1986. Translated in *Israel Press Briefs*, No. 49, (December 1986), p.19.

55. Nahum Barnea, "And Again, Ikrit and Biram," *Koteret Rashit*, #237, June 17, 1987, p. 3. As of this writing this decision has not yet been implemented.

56. *The Israeli Economist*, No. 43, (April-May 1987).

57. *Hadashot*, April 8, 1987.

6

The People's View on the Resolution of the Israeli-Arab Conflict

Michael Inbar and Ephraim Yuchtman-Yaar

Introduction

Among the voluminous writing on the Arab-Israeli conflict, survey attitude literature is the exception rather than the rule. Most of our ideas about the attitudes of the people involved in the Middle East conflict are based on the perception and intuition of politicians, diplomats, journalists and cultural scholars. These perceptions may reflect the views of some circles of elites rather than those of the masses.

Yet understanding the sentiments of the grass-roots in the Arab-Israeli conflict is extremely important. First, political leaders, whether Arab or Israeli, are influenced by the sentiments and commitments of their constituents. Second, when political issues are bitterly disputed in a society, and when political leadership finds it necessary or expedient to mobilize public support for some course of action, knowledge of the true distribution of attitudes is of theoretical interest as well as of practical import for contending political camps. Whether the society is democratic or not, it is ultimately the grass root sentiment that sets limits and possible directions for conflict resolution.

The few extant survey studies of public opinion on the Arab Israeli conflict are typically limited to one population, making inter-group comparisons an exercise in speculation. The present study seeks to address this shortcoming by providing a systematic and synchronous comparison of the attitudes of Israeli Jews, Israeli Arabs and the West Bank Palestinians. To the best of our knowledge, this is the first research of its kind.[1]

The major advantage of the study is that the same battery of questions are used to compare the views of three central protagonists in the conflict and that the study was carried out simultaneously. Synchronous comparisons are especially important in the Middle East, where events often evolve in rapid and dramatic succession.

The study, carried out in the spring of 1985, covered a broad variety of issues including the cognitive mapping of the Arab-Israeli conflict, interpersonal relations, and socioeconomic factors. In the present chapter, however, we shall restrict ourselves to the analysis of the political solutions that the respondents would ideally desire and those that they would find acceptable. The continuum of solutions presented and actually selected runs the entire gamut of political choices advocated in the Palestinian and Israeli camps, ranging from the creation of Greater Palestine from which the Jews would be expelled to Greater Israel from which the Palestinians would be expelled.

All respondents were presented with the same set of ten alternative solutions (see Appendix A). This procedure provides the basis for detailed inter- and intra-group comparisons which would otherwise not be possible.

As the focus of our analysis implies, the major question that we wish to clarify is the extent to which the people hold competing or indeed unbridgeable ideas about how to solve the conflict. To probe this question in more depth, we propose to analyze the preferences at two levels: ideal (desired) solution and realistic (acceptable) one. Analysis of these two levels of preference, enables us to compare the usefulness of the distinction between the affective and cognitive dimensions and clarifies the attitudinal dynamics associated with the Israeli-Arab conflict.

Design of the Study

The data on which our analysis is based were gathered in the late spring of 1985. They were obtained by means of standardized questionnaires administered in the home of the respondents by trained interviewers. The samples were drawn from three populations: Israeli Jews, Israeli Arabs, and West Bank Arabs. The sampling procedure in each of these populations differed according to various constraints, yielding a combination of sampling procedures which may be summarized as follows.

The Israeli Jewish and Israeli Arab samples are generally representative samples of their corresponding adult populations (18 years of age and above). They were interviewed by native speaking Israelis of Jewish and Arab origin respectively. Together, these two samples include some 1800 inter-viewees, of whom approximately ⅔ are Jewish[2] and ⅓ Arab in a stratified design, adopted in order to increase the member of Israeli Arab respondents whose group constitute only some 17 percent of the Israeli population.[3]

In contrast, the West Bank sample is quite different in scope and composition. First in terms of size, it includes only some two hundred respondents. Second, it is limited to young (18–35 years old) urban males living in the cities of Nablus and Hebron.

These characteristics are the result of both practical and substantive considerations. Practically, we felt it necessary to limit the sample of West Bank respondents to a manageable number of respondents within the limits of what we conceived of as a preliminary study. The reason for this approach was the then prevalent image that a survey touching on political attitudes could probably not be carried out in a reasonably scientific manner on the West Bank, certainly not by social scientists associated with the Israeli Jewish academic establishment.[4] This consideration, coupled with severe budgetary constraints, led to the relatively small size of the sample of West Bank respondents at our disposal. Based on these considerations, the choice of the segment of the West Bank population that we have elected to interview reflects our view of the importance that the attitudes of young urban males have for the understanding of the political climate of national groups.

In retrospect, it is worth noting that the West Bank survey turned out to have been easier to carry out than anticipated, and that its interpretation does not appear to pose special problems. The result of the debriefings of our interviewers, the similarity of some of our findings with the Al Fajr survey (1986), combined with their consistency with theoretically expected differences between Israeli Jews and the two Palestinian samples on the one hand and differences between the latter two samples on the other, all suggest that the data at our disposal are fairly valid.

Static Images of Conflict Resolution:
The Ideal and the Acceptable Solutions

In light of the ongoing political debate about possible solutions to the conflict, it is instructive to see how actual preferences are distributed across the three national groups of our respondents.

Bearing in mind the theoretical distinction between the affective and cognitive dimensions of people's attitudes, on examination of the ideal (desired) solutions as opposed to the acceptable (practical) one is of interest. Views about ideal solutions are shaped by such intangibles as a sense of moral imperative, personal and national justice, or even wishful thinking. On the other hand, perceptions of acceptable solutions involve more instrumental considerations such as balance of power, military strength, and the influence of major powers.

Ideal Solutions

Table 6.1 presents a comparison among Palestinians, Israeli Jews and Israeli Arabs with regard to ideal solutions. Out of the ten alternative

TABLE 6.1

Ideal Solutions in the Israeli-Arab Conflict (percentages)

	(1) Palestinians	(2) Israeli- Arabs	(3) Israeli- Jews
1. Greater Palestine (a) (expulsion of Jews)	034.6	010.9	000.0
2. Binational Greater Palestine (a) (without expulsion of Jews)	034.6	033.3	002.6
3. Independent Palestine (b)	024.0	027.9	000.4
4. Jordanian-Palestine State (c)	003.9	005.4	002.6
5. Independent Palestine (d) with border modifications	001.7	017.8	006.0
6. Jordanian-Palestine State (d) with border modifications	000.6	000.8	024.1
7. Palestinian autonomy in the occupied territories	000.6	003.1	010.0
8. Continuation of the Status Quo	000.0	000.0	008.2

9. Binational Greater Israel (e)
   (without expulsion of
   Palestinians)
	000.0	000.8	016.4

10. Greater Israel (e)
   (with expulsion of
   Palestinians)
	000.0	000.0	029.7

Total	100.0	100.0	100.0

Note: The percentage distribution reflects the respondents' choice of the most desirable solution of the ten solutions described above.

(a) in the territory of West Bank and Gaza and pre-1967 Israel
(b) in the pre-1967 West Bank and Gaza territory
(c) in the territory of pre-1967 Jordan
(d) the border modifications are designed to accommodate Israel's security needs
(e) in the territory of West Bank and Gaza and pre-1967 Israel

options presented to the respondents, the overwhelming majority of the Palestinians split their choices among the first three alternatives. Some 34.6 percent opted for a uninational Greater Palestinian state entailing the expulsion of Jews, 34.6 percent indicated their desire for the binational Greater Palestinian state, and 24.0 percent for an independent Palestinian state along Israel. It should be noted that, in fact, the two first and most extreme solutions, which are tantanamous to the abolition of the Jewish state, account for over two-thirds of all the choices expressed.

Two other findings are noteworthy. The first pertains to the much discussed "Jordanian option," that is, some type of a Palestinian-Jordanian federation. As indicated in Table 6.1, this option, with or without territorial modification, is for all intents and purposes totally rejected. The second finding is that an independent Palestinian state becomes a significantly supported political solution only when it includes the pre-1967 borders of the occupied territories.

While it is not surprising that the Palestinians virtually ignore all the more Israeli-oriented options, it is significant that only a miniscule minority (0.6 percent) supported an autonomy proposal.

The pattern of ideal preference for Israeli Jews shows a much greater spread than in the Palestinian case. As seen in Table 6.1, column 3, six options account for 95 percent of the Jewish choice. However, there is one important similarity with the Palestinian preference pattern. Two out of the three most desired Jewish solutions are also the most extreme: 16.4 percent support annexation without expulsion, i.e. a binational Greater Israel, and 29.7 percent support annexation with expulsion, i.e. a uninational Greater Israel. The difference in the pattern of spread of the two national groups is that the second most desirable Jewish solution is a relatively moderate one from an Israeli perspective. A Jordanian-Palestinian state with border modification is supported by 24.1 percent of the sample.

These two findings may be compared with those discussed for the Palestinian sample by juxtaposing two figures. Among the Palestinians the two most popular solutions are the two most radical ones, and, as already noted, are supported by over two-thirds of the sample. Among the Jews, on the other hand, less than half of the respondents chose the equivalent solutions. In operational terms, this means that whereas for the Palestinians there exists a politically dominant solution, no similar statement can be made in the case of the Jews.

It is also interesting that the Jews differ from the Palestinians with regard to the "Jordanian option." Specifically, if we compare their preference for a purely Palestinian state, and the similar pair of solutions involving Jordan, we find an interaction effect. An independent Jordanian-Palestinian state, combined with territorial changes, stands out as a relatively desirable solution in the Jewish eyes—in fact the second most popular. On the other hand, neither a Jordanian-Palestinian settlement without border modifications, nor a Palestinian state with or without such modifications, are particularly desirable to the Jewish sample.

From the standpoint of conflict-resolution, the comparison of the preferences of the Israeli Jews and the Palestinians with regard to the entire set of alternatives, indicates no similarity in the degree of support given to any of the solutions by the two groups. Thus the most moderate solution desired by a significant proportion of Palestinians (e.g., a Palestinian state in the pre-1967 West Bank/Gaza) is almost completely rejected by the Jews (24.0 percent versus 0.4 percent, respectively). Interestingly, though the Palestinians are more supportive of a binational state. Whereas 34.6 percent of the Palestinians chose as their preferred solution a Greater Palestine without expelling the Jews, only 16.4 percent of the Jews indicated that they would support a Greater Israel without expelling the Palestinians.

By virtue of their minority position, the Israeli Arabs have a dual identity, a fact which has been repeatedly documented in previous research. Whether this duality affects their attitudes towards the ideal solution is an issue of both theoretical and practical interest.

Table 6.1 column 2 shows that, on the whole, the views of the Israeli Arabs are closer to the Palestinians then to the Jews. Most notably, their two first preferences overlap with two of the three first choices of Palestinians. Some 33.3 percent of the Israeli Arabs chose a binational Greater Palestinian state (e.g., without the expulsion of the Jews), followed by 27.3 percent who opted for a Palestinian state alongside Israel within the pre-1967 West Bank/Gaza borders. In addition, the Israeli Arabs totally reject five of the solutions (6 through 10) which were also rejected by the Palestinians. It is especially noteworthy that the Israeli Arabs, like the Palestinians also strongly rejected the option of a Jordanian-Palestinian state, regardless of its territorial shape.

On the other hand, there are two significant differences between the two Arab groups. The most salient one is the reluctance of Israeli Arabs to support the creation of a Greater Palestinian state including expulsion of Jews (only about 10 percent supported this option). In contrast, this solution was chosen by the Palestinians as one of the more preferred ones, gaining the support of over one third of them. The second and complementary difference is the relative high support for the creation of an independent Palestinian state with border modifications in accordance with Israel's security needs. Nearly 18 percent of Israeli Arabs found this option as the most desirable, as opposed to only about 2 percent of the Palestinians.

In terms of conflict resolution the trends which emerge from the comparison of the three samples are not encouraging. The two national ethnic groups are deeply fragmented, and there is virtually no agreement between them. No overlapping solution on which both a majority of Israeli

Arabs or Palestinians on the one hand, and Israeli Jews on the other, agree emerged. There is not even a single solution on which a plurality of them agree as a common denominator. Thus, the most moderate solution that a significant number of Israeli's find desirable—a Jordanian-Palestinian state (chosen by 24.1 percent of the respondents), is supported by less than one percent of both the Palestinians and the Israeli Arabs. Similarly, the relatively moderate (from a Palestinian viewpoint) option of an independent Palestinian state in all of the pre-1967 West Bank and Gaza Strip (found desirable by 24 percent of Palestinians and 27.9 percent of Israeli Arabs), is supported by less than half of a percent of Israeli Jews. In short, at the level of effective ideological preferences, the prospects for conflict resolution are not presently encouraging.

Acceptable Solutions

In order to analyze the dimension of acceptable solutions we also asked each respondent which solutions he/she could live with in practice. Two issues are of special interest here. The first is whether the respondents show evidence of an ideal versus more practical level of thinking in relating to the conflict. Obviously, when intensely held idealviews obfuscate the difference between the two conceptual levels in individuals' attitudes, conflict resolution is difficult to achieve. Conversely, a distinction between the ideal and the practical levels is likely to facilitate the process of conflict resolution. The second issue is whether this cognitive differentiation, or lack thereof, is a characteristic trait of the entire population or is restricted to some national subsamples and/or segments of respondents within each of them. Identifying potential loci of pragmatic attitudes may be of great practical importance in creating a conflict resolution dialogue among the actors.

The acceptability ranking of solutions for the entire sample is presented in Table 6.2. As column 1 of this table indicates, the acceptability ranking of the Palestinians follows closely the pattern of their ideal preference. Thus the three most acceptable solutions are as follows: binational Greater Palestine, without expulsion of the Jews, independent Palestinian state in the entire West Bank and Gaza Strip, and uninational Greater Palestine, with the expulsion of the Jews (supported by 64.4, 54.4 and 53.4 percent respectively).

The same pattern prevails with regard to all other solutions, including the two which involve Jordan. The only notable exception is the independent Palestinian state with border modifications. This solution was found acceptable by about 45 percent as compared with 1.7 percent who found it desirable. Another contrast is noteworthy. It will be recalled that at the level of ideal solutions the two most radical solutions are virtually indistinguishable in terms of the support they receive (34 percent in both cases).

TABLE 6.2
Acceptable Solutions in the Israeli-Arab Conflict (percentages)

	(1) Palestinians	(2) Israeli-Arabs	(3) Israeli-Jews
1. Greater Palestine (a) (expulsion of Jews)	053.4	023.1	001.2[xx]
2. Binational Greater Palestine (a) (without expulsion of Jews)	064.4	059.5	009.5
3. Independent Palestine (b)	054.4	078.1	007.7
4. Jordanian-Palestinian State (c)	019.1	023.0	010.6
5. Independent Palestine with (d) border modifications	045.3	063.0	019.2
6. Jordanian-Palestinian State (d) with border modifications	012.9	020.7	037.6
7. Palestinian autonomy in the occupied territories	009.4	034.1	019.6
8. Continuation of the Status Quo	000.5	003.1	023.9
9. Binational Greater Israel (e) (without expulsion of Palestinians)	001.5	005.3	033.2
10. Greater Israel (e) (with expulsion of Palestinians)	000.5[xx]	000.0	042.9

Note: The percentage distributions are of the respondents' answers to the following question: "To what extent is each of the following solutions for peaceful relations between the Palestinians and Isrealis, within the framework of a general peace agreement in the Middle-East, acceptable or unacceptable to you?" The answering scale ranged from (1) - not acceptable at all, to (5) - very acceptable. The percentage presented represented the collapsed 4 and 5 categories (acceptable and very acceptable).

[xx] - These anomolous results are undoubtedly the results of misunderstanding of the options on the part of a tiny minority of respondents.

(a) in the territory of West Bank and Gaza and pre-1967 Israel
(b) in the pre-1967 West Bank and Gaza territory
(c) in the territory of pre-1967 Jordan
(d) the border modifications are designed to accommodate Israeli's security needs
(e) in the territory of West Bank and Gaza and pre-1967 Israel

However at the acceptability level a clear distancing occurs. Thus, the binational Greater Palestinian State without expulsion is supported by about 64 percent and opposed by 27 percent of the respondents, thus making it the dominant one. Uninational Greater Palestine with expulsion comes in at a second with about 53 percent supporting it and 40 percent opposing it.

Theoretically speaking, these findings indicate that the Palestinians tend to make a distinction between the desirable and the acceptable. Practically, though, even their pragmatically more moderate solution of a binational Greater Palestine without expulsion, falls drastically short of an option which might be accepted by Israel.

The Israeli Jews, like the Palestinians, show a high degree of correspondence between their ideal and acceptable solutions. The rank ordering of the three most desirable solutions—uninational Greater Israel with expulsion, Jordanian-Palestinian state with border modifications, and binational Greater Israel without expulsion—42.9, 37.6 and 33.2 percent of choices, respectively is the same in terms of acceptability (Table 6.2, column 3).

The most noticable feature of this distribution is that, again, no solution is supported by even a simple majority of respondents. Moreover, the only option which comes closest to meeting this criterion, that is Greater Israel with expulsion, is still opposed by a large plurality (43 percent vs 76 percent repectively). In short, the Israeli Jews have not evolved any acceptable solution which is consensually attractive. In contrast with the Palestinians, the pattern here is rejection and fragmentation.

At first glance the Israeli Arabs, like the other two national groups exhibit a high degree of similarity between the two levels of choice (see Table 6.2, column 2). However, a closer look reveals that there are also interesting differences in the ordering of solutions. For instance, while the binational solution of Greater Palestine comes first at the level of preference, the option of an independent Palestinian state without modified borders emerges as the dominant choice at the level of acceptability. Furthermore, the option of an independent Palestinian state with border modifications which was chosen as an ideal by only about 18 percent of the subsample, gains the support of 63 percent when considered from the standpoint of acceptability. In fact, at the acceptability level, this option is somewhat more attractive than the more extreme binational solution. Consistent with this trend we find that the autonomy solution which was desired by a mere 3.1 percent of the Israeli Arabs is considered acceptable by 34.1 percent.

In summing up the comparison between the ideal and acceptable levels for all national subsamples a number of conclusions emerge. First we find support for the theoretically expected differentiation between the ideally desired and the acceptable solutions. This differentiation is greatest among the Israeli Arabs and smallest among the Israeli Jews. The apparent lack of differentiation among Jews takes the concrete form of a pattern of rejection for all solutions. This attitude contrasts sharply with the trends in the two Arab subsamples where some solutions are attractive to a majority of respondents. In other words, at this stage of the Arab-Israeli conflict, the Israeli Jews are apparently in the psychological situation known as an "avoidance-approach"; they find *all* solutions discussed unappealing in theory as well as in practice.

Another conclusion is the pronounced absence of an overlap between relatively moderate solutions simultaneously supported by pluralities of both Jews and Palestinians. The most moderate solution acceptable to a sizeable proportion of the Jewish respondents, that is, the Jordanian-Palestinian state with border modification which was supported by about 38 percent, gained only 20.7 percent of support among the Israeli Arabs and 12.9 percent among Palestinians. Similarly, the most moderate solution from an Arab perspective—an independent Palestinian state with border modification, which obtained the support of 63 percent of Israeli Arabs and 45.3 percent of the Palestinians, was endorsed by a mere 19.2 percent of Israeli Jews. The gap is of course much greater when the first choice of the Palestinians (binational Greater Palestine with 64.4 percent) and of the Israeli Arabs (independent Palestinian state/no border modifications with 78.1 percent) are considered.

The third conclusion is that no solution involving Jordan enjoys any substantial support among the Arabs, even at the acceptability level. Thus, the support for these alternatives reached a maximum of 23 percent among the Israeli Arabs and of 19 percent among the Palestinians.

Finally, comparing the Israeli Arabs to the other respondents, it is clear that on the whole their choices are closer to the Palestinians than to the Jews. At the same time it is significant that both at the desirability and acceptability level, they endorse less extreme solutions than the Palestinian Arabs.

Dynamic Images of Conflict Resolution: Trends over Time

The foregoing findings provide a picture of the situation in the spring of 1985, when the survey was carried out. As with any one-shot survey, the question emerges of the representativeness of the cross-sectional images of conflict resolution. The question is particularly relevant in a volatile situation like the one which prevails in the Middle East. Events like peace with Egypt, on the one hand, and the war in Lebanon, on the other, are likely to substantially modify the attitudes of people.

TABLE 6.3
Ideal Solutions for the Israeli-Arab Conflict: A Longitudinal Comparison

	Israeli-Arabs	
	1982	1985
1. Greater Palestine (expulsion of Jews)	09.2	10.9
2. Binational Greater Palestine (without expulsion of Jews)	16.1	33.3
	Israeli-Jews	
	1982	1985
9. Greater Israel (expulsion of Palestinians)	22.4	29.7
10. Binational Greater Israel (without expulsion of Palestinians)	17.8	16.4

To address the temporal issue we shall use a set of data collected in an earlier round of interviews in April 1982, shortly before Israel's withdrawal from the Sinai. Unfortunately, the earlier interviews did not include the Palestinians.[5] The samples of Israeli Jews and the Israeli Arabs we did interview in the 1982 survey were essentially asked the same type of questions as in the 1985 survey. We shall focus, in the analysis below, on the sets of identical questions in the two surveys. In particular, we shall consider the two mirror image pairs of most extreme solutions from either the Israeli or the Israeli Arab point of view.

Ideal Solutions

Table 6.3 presents the paired comparisons of solutions selected for the analysis between 1982 and 1985. Beginning with ideal solutions of Israeli Arabs, the pattern obtained is one of clear radicalization. Thus, the two radical solutions gained in support. A Greater Palestinian state without expulsion of Jews increased its support from 9.2 percent to 10.9 percent and even more dramatically a Greater Palestine without expulsion went up from 16.1 percent to 33.3 percent. Together, these two options garnered 44 percent of support in 1985 as opposed to only 25 percent in 1982.

The Israeli Jews, who were already quite radical in 1982 also exhibit an increase in extremism, albeit a smaller one. Support for Greater Israel with expulsion of the Arabs went up from 22.4 percent to 29.7 percent, whereas support for a Greater Israel without expulsion decreased from 17.8 percent to 16.4 percent.

The net result of the different degrees of extremism of the Israeli-Jewish population in 1982 in comparison with the Israeli-Arab one, and of the dramatic radicalization of the latter since 1982, is that presently the two populations are almost equally radicalized. Thus, in 1985, 44 percent and 46 percent of the Israeli-Arab and of Israeli-Jewish populations, respectively, support their camp's most radical solutions. This is to be contrasted with the figures of 25 percent and 40 percent in 1982, respectively.

Acceptable Solutions

Turning now to the acceptability of this set of solutions, Table 6.4 shows the relevant data. In the Israeli-Arab sample only one of the two solutions— the less radical of them—changed over time by a notable amount (more than 5 percent), according to our arbitrary definition. Similarly, in the Israeli-Jewish sample only one solution, Greater Israel with expulsion, shifted in popularity by more than this percentage. In this case, though, it is the more extreme of the two solutions which significantly gained in popularity.

Juxtaposing the findings which emerge from the analysis of solutions at the levels of desirability and acceptability, a double trend stands out. On the one hand, we observe that among the Israeli Jews, the pattern of shift, or lack of it, in support of the two solutions is identical at both levels of expression. Thus, between 1982 and 1985 there is no significant change in support for the less radical of the two solutions, while the more radical one clearly gains in support at both levels. Among the Israeli-Arabs, on the other hand, the temporal consistency between the two levels is limited to the less radical of the two solutions. It is endorsed at both levels by more respondents in 1985 than in 1982. However, this does not hold true for the more extreme solutions. The radicalization found at the ideal level does not find a corresponding expression at the level of acceptability. One could speculate that this discrepancy reflects the position of relative powerlessness of the Israeli-Arab population.[6] Indeed in conflict situations it is not uncommon that the discrepancy between desired goals and those which are acceptable is greater for the subordinate than for the superordinate groups.

Be this as it may, the overall finding which stands out from the above analysis is that at this point in time the Israeli Jews and the Israeli Arabs

TABLE 6.4
Acceptable Solutions for the Israeli-Arab Conflict: A Longitudinal Analysis

		Israeli-Arabs	
		1982	1985
1.	Greater Palestine (expulsion of Jews)	26.4	23.1
2.	Binational Greater Palestine (without expulsion of Jews)	35.1	59.5
		Israeli-Jews	
		1982	1985
9.	Greater Israel (expulsion of Palestinians)	30.3	42.9
10.	Binational Greater Israel (without expulsion of Palestinians)	37.6	33.2

have converged at a similar level of radicalization, both in terms of acceptable and desirable solutions.

Internal Variations in Attitudes Towards Conflict Resolutions

In the above analyses we have treated the national subsamples as whole units. However, it is of theoretical and empirical importance to find out whether socioeconomic characteristics of respondents within each national group effect the kind of solutions supported. Our previous studies indicate that such differences do exist, both within and across samples.[7]

In order to examine whether any particular set of socioeconomic characteristics is related to choices of solutions, we shall present the multiple regression analysis performed on the most extreme of the two solutions discussed in the previous section (the reasons for this choice are noted in Inbar and Yuchtman-Yaar, 1989). This solution, Greater Palestine with expulsion, was regressed in each sample according to age, education, religiosity and economic status.

Table 6.5 which contains the standardized regression coefficients (betas), exhibits some interesting patterns. In particular, we see that in the Israeli

TABLE 6.5

Multiple Regression Analysis of the Most Radical Solution by
Socio-Demographic Characteristics of the Respondents

	(1) Palestinians	(2) Israeli-Arabs	(3) Israeli-Jews
Age	-.13	-.14	-.02
Economic status	.23*	-.11	.02
Religiosity	.03	-.18*	-.23*
Education	.10	-.10	-.28*
Adjusted R^2	.06	.05	.12

*p .05

Index:

Age - natural scale ranging from 18 to 35.

Economic status - based on respondent's report of family's economic
expenditure according to a scale ranging from 1-5.

Religiosity - self defined according to a scale ranging from: very religious (1)
to secular (4).

Educational level - this variable was coded according to number of years of
schooling (natural scale) in the Jewish sample and according to level of school
completed in the Israeli-Arab and Palestinian samples, ranging from (1)
elementary school to (7) university.

Jewish sample two of the four socioeconomic characteristic—education and
religiosity—exert some influence on the choice. Specifically, it is the more
religious and less educated respondents who tend to endorse this radical
solution. On the other hand, in the case of the Israeli Arabs only religiosity
seems to effect the choice. It is noteworthy that this variable operates
similarly in both samples; for the Israeli Jews, also, the more religious the
respondent, the more extreme the response.

Finally, in the Palestinian case economic status is the only background
variable which significantly influences political extremism. The form of the
relationship indicates that the more well-to-do Palestinians (and by implication
the more educated) are the more radical ones. However, in contrast to both
the Israeli Jews and the Israeli Arabs, the political choice of the Palestinians
cannot be predicted from their religiosity. The limitation of the Palestinian

subsample at our disposal precludes a data-based analysis of this difference, but we may venture a tentative hypothesis.

As other students of the West Bank have noted, for historical reasons religious Arabs in the occupied territories are more prone to a Pan Arab or Pan Islamic outlook than Israeli Arabs.[8] One reason is that the political mobilization of the religious Muslims in the West Bank took place earlier than the crystalization of Palestinian nationalism as expressed by the PLO. As a result, a religious inclination does not automatically lead an individual to chose the radical political option of Greater Palestine with expulsion of Jews. In fact, devout West Bank Palestinians may well distribute their choices along the entire scale of options. Conversely, among the Israeli Arabs religious radicalization has been a much more recent phenomenon, coinciding with the emergence of Palestinian radical nationalism. Finally, in the case of the Jews a religious outlook may easily lead to the Greater Israel option, as it embodies the vision of Redemption.

Conclusions: Binationalism by Default and by Design

The analyses that we have reported can be summerized in a few conclusions. First, we have seen that the Palestinians, the Israeli Jews and the Israeli Arabs do not hold monolithic views among themselves concerning any one solution to the conflict. The amount of divergence varies among the national subsamples. In the case of the Palestinians and the Israeli Arabs, we find at least one solution which enjoys the support of a majority of respondents. Among the Israeli Jews the picture is one of dissent concerning the solution to the conflict. Indeed, in this case the image which emerges is one of grass root division about the desirable as well the acceptable solution to end the Arab-Israeli dispute.

Second, we have found evidence that people do distinguish between ideal or ideological aspiration, and practical goals constrained by power politics. This distinction is found in all the three national subsamples, with ideal solutions being consistently more extreme than the acceptable ones. The ability to distinguish between the ideal and the acceptable is greatest among the Israeli Arabs and smallest among the Israeli Jews.

This difference may have as its explanation the fact that more dominant groups tend to be less constrained by power considerations, having the ability to convert their ideological goals into policies. On the other hand, dominated groups are by definition more constrained by political realities and thus may have to make a clearer distinction between the ideal and the acceptable. In this connection it is interesting to note that the Palestinians occupy an intermediate structural position which may explain the size of the difference we find for them between ideal and acceptable solutions. While not totally matching the Israeli Jews in sovereignty of will, they are more independent in their political asperations, and paradoxically may feel freer to express these than do the larger dominated Israeli Arabs. Needless to say, conflict resolution is more difficult to achieve among actors who rigidly hold on to ideal goals.

Third, we have found that both at the ideal and acceptable level, there are great national differences. In particular, there is no single solution that both a plurality of Israeli Jews on the one hand, and Israeli and West Banker Arabs, on the other hand, are simultaneously willing to live with, i.e. accept, let alone one that both sides to the conflict desire at the ideal level. The greatest gap is found, as one might have expected, between the Palestinians and the Israeli Jews. By far, the Palestinians are the more extreme in both their ideal and acceptable solutions. At both levels the solutions call for establishing a Greater Palestinian state, which is coterminous with the abolition of Israel. The Israeli Jews split their ideal and acceptable preference between the extremity of a Greater Israel, (involving the annexation of the territories), and a Jordanian-Palestinian state with border modifications. The Israeli Arabs who fall in between are nonetheless much closer in their views to the Palestinians than to the Israeli Jews.

Fourth, the longitudinal data, albeit limited to Israeli Jews and Israeli Arabs, indicate that both groups have undergone a process of radicalization. However, generalizing across the two most extreme solutions taken together, this trend is more marked among the Israeli Arabs then among the Israeli Jews. Yet the end result in 1985 is that both populations have converged to a same level of radicalization.

Fifth, the analysis of individual attributes (education, age, economic status, and religiosity) reveals that these have a relatively limited impact compared to national identity. Still, it is of some interest that lower economic status and religiosity correlates with extreme attitudes among Israeli Jews, and religiosity explains radical sentiments among Israeli Arabs. In the case of the Palestinians religiosity is bound with traditionalism and modernity. On the whole, however, religion, long at the heart of the Arab-Israeli conflict, remains a factor in its perpetuation and radicalization.

Authors' Note

The authors share equal responsibility for all aspects of the ongoing research project of which the present article is a part, a cooperation that finds its expression in the order of authorship that is transposed in each successive report. We gratefully acknowledge the support provided for the preparation of this chapter by a grant from the Ford Foundation (no. 13) received through the Israel Foundations Trustees, as well as the facilities provided within the framework of the Barbara and Morton Mandell Chair in Cognitive Social Psychology and Education at the Hebrew University of Jerusalem. We are also indebted to Aida Dynia for her assistance in the library research, for the time consuming and skillful help in making the computer runs necessary for data analysis, and for her active participation in several of our discussions.

Notes

1. The Study published by the El Fajr West Bank weekly (September 12, 1986; pp. 1, 5–6, 16) was limited to West Bank Arab respondents. In terms of comparability it has therefore the same kind of limitation as our previous research has.

2. The survey of the Jewish population was carried out by "Dahaf," a leading Israeli public opinion firm.

3. This figure includes the three major Arab religious denominations, namely the Muslims, Christians and Druzes. The latter are a minority amounting to about 10 percent of the Israeli Arab population (see Statistical Abstract of Israel, 1986). They enjoy a politically unique status in the Israeli society, and have not been included in the analysis that we herewith report. The sampling and interview of the Israeli Arabs was conducted in cooperation with Professor Sammy Smooha of Haifa University. Drawing on his techniques and experience for selecting probability samples among Israeli Arabs, and mindful of the variety of communities among which the population is distributed, it was decided upon the number of respondents which would be obtained in an unstratified probability sample of the Israeli population as a whole. The field work was carried out by a joint team of Israeli Arab students recruited and trained at the Universities of Tel Aviv and Haifa. Professor Sasson Someh of Tel-Aviv University supervised the translation of the Hebrew questionnaire into Arabic to ensure linguistic accuracy and semantic faithfulness.

4. The El Fajr Weekly (1986) notes the same problem in discussing its own public opinion poll of the West Bank. We should also add that we should consider carrying out our survey as speedily as possible to avoid a possible contamination of the answers or a refusal to respond in the wake of conceivable interferences from the PLO. Heeding this advice we organized the data collection in a manner which permitted concluding the bulk of this part of the study within a week.

5. For details see Michael Inbar and Ephraim Yuchtman-Yaar, "Some Cognitive Dimensions of the Israeli-Arab Conflict," *Journal of Conflict Resolution*, Vol. 29, no. 4, 1985, pp. 699–725 and Ephraim Yuchtman-Yaar and Michael Inbar, "Social Distance in the Israeli-Arab Conflict: A Resource-Dependency Analysis," *Comparative Psychological Analysis*, Vol. 19, no. 3, 1986, pp. 283–316.

6. Yuchtman-Yaar and Inbar, "Social Distances."

7. Inbar and Yuchtman-Yaar, "Some Cognitive Dimensions " and Yuchtman-Yaar and Inbar, "Social Distances."

8. The limitations of the data set at our disposal preclude our doing so in the present analysis. We may note, however, that the anomalous asymmetry observed between the Israeli and Palestinian Arabs fits the implications of the analysis of certain students of the Arab scene. They note that for historical reasons religious Arabs in the West Bank are more prone to a Pan-Arabic or Pan-Islamic outlook— within which political preferences may vary. Futhermore, the political radicalization of the religious Muslims in the West Bank took place earlier than the crystalization

of Palestinian nationalism as expressed by the PLO. In the case of the Israeli Arabs, however, religious radicalization developed more recently (since the early 1970s) and coincided with the emergence of the Palestinian radical nationalism. Eliazer Be'eri, *The Palestinains Under Jordanian Rule: Three Issues*, (Jerusalem: The Magnes Press, 1978), Hebrew; Amnon Cohen, *Political parties in the West Bank under the Jordainian Regime (1948–1967)*, (Jerusalem: The Magnes Press, 1980); Shaul Mishal, *West Bank/ East Bank: The Palestiniansin Jordan 1949–1967*, (New Haven: Yale University Press, 1978).

7

The Impact of Occupation on the Military: The Case of the IDF, 1967–1987

Yoram Peri

Introduction

On June 10, 1967, the Israel Defense Force (IDF) found itself facing a situation which it had never previously encountered. After six days of battle, and the defeat of the armies of three Arab states, the IDF found itself in control of an area of 70,000 square kilometers, three and a half times the size of the State of Israel, with a population of more than one million Palestinians. It soon became apparent that the IDF would, for quite a while, not only be responsible for security in the areas, but would have to assume the duties of civil government as well.

The main reason for the immediate establishment of the Military Government (MG) was the political situation that prevailed immediately after the war. The IDF, spread out in the field, was the only body which possessed the ability to fill the governmental vacuum then existing in the territories. The political prestige of the Defense Minister, Moshe Dayan, enabled him to overcome the opposition of other ministers in the government, who wanted the various governmental departments to operate directly in the territories, just as they operate within the boundaries of the State of Israel, leaving only security affairs to the IDF.[1]

Later, it became apparent that the establishment of the MG was also necessitated by legal and international considerations. Israel was opposed to defining the West Bank and the Gaza Strip as areas to which international law regarding occupation rulings applied. This was because such a definition presupposes Israeli recognition of Jordanian sovereignty on the West Bank, and Egyptian sovereignty on the Gaza Strip.

In spite of this, Israel announced that "it would conduct itself in these areas in accordance with the humanitarian directives determined at the

Fourth Geneva Convention regarding the protection of citizens in times of war, and with the Hague directives of 1907." Accordingly, "the commander of the IDF is the supreme authority in the conquered area."[2]

During the summer of 1967, the feeling prevailed that the occupation was only temporary. However, it soon became clear that this "temporariness" was going to continue for a long time. By 1988, the IDF had occupied the territories for 21 years. By now, most IDF officers and soldiers are more familiar with duties in the territories than they are with the functions that they were intended to carry out before 1967.

In fact, Israel is the only example of a democratic state maintaining a military government in a continuous occupied territory. How does a nation in arms deal with such a role? What happens to a professional army which is compelled, over a long period of time, to perform duties which deviate sharply from its basic goals?[3]

The literature has rarely dealt with this problem. Ever since France left Algeria, there has been no historical example that is similar to that facing the Israeli Military Government in the territories. The Algerian case is quite different. Both comparative and theoretical studies deal at great length with military regimes but not with a military government subservient to a democratic government in an occupied territory. Related cases, such as that of the Allied forces during World War II, were of a temporary nature and of short duration.[4] Thus, the Israeli case is especially interesting, both in its own context and because of the theoretical problems it raises: What happens to the army of a democratic state which, over a long period of time, performs the tasks of a military government in an occupied area?

The Problem

Any occupation army is faced with three potential crises, all of which can stem from the harm done to its professional character. They are: (1) the loss of its political neutrality; (2) a crisis of self-image and self-identity, and (3) damage to its relationship with the civil society. All of these factors could bring about a crisis of legitimacy.

Occupation armies tend to develop a military-political doctrine, often causing them to lose their neutral political character. Dealing with internal security problems and conducting counter-insurgency warfare of a political nature, and attending to the needs of the local population, may well contribute to the development of a political doctrine.[5]

Adopting a political doctrine could change the traditional relationships that prevailed between the military and political systems in the occupying state. The army then becomes increasingly involved in the political process itself, as an independent special interest group, and could also be identified with one specific school of political thought, be it of the government or of the opposition.

A telling example is that of the French army in Algeria after General de Gaulle came to power. As a result of the deep identification that they developed with the political doctrine, the French generals in Algeria decided not only to oppose the President's policies but also to bring about by force a change of the legitimate authority in Paris. This was one of the few examples of an attempted military coup in a developed democratic state.[6]

The self-image and identity crises arise from the fact that the occupation army is unfamiliar with and unprepared for two sets of functions. Professional officers do not have the experience of Praetorian, political armies. Problems arising from the needs of the civilian population, health services, education, employment and welfare are unfamiliar tasks for soldiers and are considered undesirable by an army that trains for a totally different purpose: to deter war and to be victorious should one break out.

Nor are the security functions expected of an occupation army familiar to a professional one. Assigned the responsibility for internal security in the occupied areas, such an army maintains public order, prevents sabotage, terror and subversion, disperses demonstrations and enforces curfews, all in order to minimize civilian unrest. Policing and pacification functions such as these are not attractive to professional officers. Being compelled to carry them out can lead to crises of self-image and identity.

These crises develop dramatically if there is a difference between the commonly accepted norms prevailing in the occupying state and those held in the occupied areas. Social control methods, interrogation rules and judicial procedures employed in the occupied areas differ from those used in the occupying state, a fact that intensifies the moral problems facing the occupiers. In addition to these potential crises, there exists the danger of corruption in the ranks and deterioration of morale, something to which every occupying military force is susceptible, stemming from the unlimited power it has over a defenseless civilian population.

An occupying military force faces a third crisis, that of its relationship with the civilian population. The first crisis, its loss of neutral-political character can bring about a crisis at the elite level between the upper ranks of the army and the upper political echelon. The crises of self-image and self-identity are an internal problem within the military organization. The third crisis stems from civil-military relations. The army's identification with a specific world view; its involvement in political warfare, pacification and civic action programs; and the adoption of previously unacceptable behavioral norms, may well result in sharp criticism from various groups in the occupying society. In a citizens' army, this danger or crisis is far greater and can result in antagonism between the various social groups and the army, leading to a bitter crisis of legitimacy.

These three hypotheses of what could develop within the IDF were the focal points of a research project that was undertaken between 1984–1987. The study made use of three primary sources:

1. Archival materials dating from 1967, which are located in the offices of the Military Government, the General Staff of the IDF and Israel's Defense Ministry.
2. Interviews with 120 people who filled various senior roles dealing with all facets of MG, including: defense ministers, coordinators of the territories, military governors and other functionaries in the MG, senior IDF officers who dealt with the MG, chiefs of staff, regional commanders and officers of various ranks; officials such as Cabinet officers, members of parliament, officials of the judiciary, government functionaries and security service personnel.
3. A survey involved interviews with 100 colonels and brigadier generals which placed the emphasis on their values and belief system.

The study also made use of many secondary sources such as newspapers, magazines, documents and research material on this subject. It is worth mentioning that, to date, no academic study has dealt with the IDF in relation to the MG and the presence of the military in the territories. The research is supported by a grant from the Ford Foundation, via the Israel Association for Research Funds and Education (Ford Foundation grant number 12, 1984, Research No.1—"Israel-Arab Relations").

Since its establishment in 1967 and until 1987, the MG has undergone many changes, both in structure and in policy. In addition, the political environment in which it operated has changed. A detailed analysis of the MG necessitates a historical discussion which is not feasible within the framework of this article. Nevertheless, there are sufficient grounds for the conclusive answer to the three hypotheses presented above.

Despite 20 years of MG, the IDF did not develop an exclusive political-military doctrine; it did not suffer from a self-image or self-identity crisis; and there was no crisis in the relations between the IDF and Israeli civil society. The IDF did not suffer a crisis of legitimacy. However, on the 21st year, a radical change took place. On December 9, 1987, the *Intifadeh*, the Palestinian uprising against the Israeli occupation was launched on the West Bank and Gaza Strip. The uprising brought a radical change in the nature of the Israeli rule, creating a new reality for the IDF. Indeed, 1988 can be defined as the beginning of a new chapter in the history of the IDF in the territories.

For those who research the impact of the occupation on the IDF, the events of 1988 were of major significance. They demonstrated that the crises anticipated for an occupation army can be prevented only under certain conditions, as was the case in the first 20 years. The removal of these conditions, as occurred in 1988, rendered the crises inevitable.

This paper will deal mainly with the first 20 years of occupation. The last year will be used as basis for comparison. What follows is an argument that the developments which were expected to effect the IDF did not, in fact, take place. This is followed by the analysis of the conditions that prevented the crises, a description of the changes in 1988, and the predicted consequences in the near future as a result of the new situation.

Political Doctrine

During the 20 years preceding 1967, the IDF did not develop an exclusive political doctrine regarding either general or security issues. While the IDF does play a very active role in the national decision-making process and, while its level of involvement in the political process must be defined as a military-political partnership, this was also the situation prior to 1967.[7]

Both before and after 1967, the involvement of the IDF in the Israeli society did not take on an exclusive, specific political character; the IDF continued to reflect the range of political opinions that existed in Israel. The issues in the defense sphere include the question of the future of the territories and Israel's willingness to make territorial concessions in exchange for peace; attitudes toward Jewish settlement in the territories and the policy regarding the Palestinians there.

Over the period of 20 years, the upper echelon of the IDF has expressed a very wide range of opinions on these subjects. Among the generals and also among the lower ranking officers, there are those who support annexation of the territories (e.g. Major General Rafael Eitan, Lt. Generals Ariel Sharon and Rehavam Ze'evi), and those who support a territorial compromise in exchange for a peace treaty with Jordan (e.g. Major Generals Haim Bar-Lev and Mordechai Gur).

Regarding the Palestinians and PLO, there are, among the generals, those who represent the most dovish position in Israel and are willing, under certain conditions, to negotiate with the PLO (Lt. Generals Ezer Weizman, Aharon Yariv and Yehoshafat Harkabi), and there are those who oppose negotiations with the Palestinians and demand that Israel dictate a political arrangement to the Arab states, even if that should lead to an Israeli-initiated war (Major General Benni Peled).

The same is true regarding the Jewish settlements in the territories. The military elite includes those who believe in establishing Jewish settlements throughout the territories, those who support restricted Jewish settlement, guided only by security considerations, and those who vehemently oppose the continuation of settlement in the territories.

In addition, IDF officers hold a wide variety of opinions regarding the treatment of the local population in the territories. On the one hand, those who believe in the "kid gloves" approach support an improvement in the quality of life, encouragement of local leadership, fostering self-management and opposing collective punishment in order to encourage peaceful co-existence between Jews and Arabs. On the other hand, believers in the "iron fist" approach support pressuring the population, severely limiting Palestinian freedom of action, restricting economic development and enacting harsh supervisory and punishment measures. The goal for these is maximal Arab emigration and total submission for those who choose to remain in the area. Between these two extremes, various nuances, opinions and positions can be found.

An examination of the political positions of the IDF officers who chose to enter political life after their retirement and who were elected to the 11th Knesset in 1984, clearly demonstrates this wide range of opinions. Major General Rafael Eitan is an MK belonging to the hawkish party, 'Ha-Tehiyah,' while Lt. General Matti Peled is one of two MKs who support the establishment of a PLO-lead independent Palestinian state in the West Bank.

This ideological pluralism appears not only among officers who have retired from the army and became politicians, but also among senior officers in the army today. In a study which was carried out in 1985, involving 100 colonels and brigadier generals, a question was asked regarding their willingness to make territorial concessions in the territories in exchange for a peace agreement. The majority were in favor of concessions.[8]

Naturally, the positions of a few key officers, such as the Chief of Staff, the Coordinator in the Territories or the commander of the Central Command, could create the impression that the IDF has a political doctrine. For example, when Rafael Eitan was the Chief of Staff, he aided and assisted the Gush Emunim settlers because of his ideological identification with them. Also, during this time, soldiers serving in the territories were granted far greater leeway than previously in the use of live ammunition against the local Palestinian population.[9]

On the other hand, during the summer of 1987, soon after Chief of Staff Dan Shomrom and OC Central Command Lt. General Amram Mitzna took office, it became apparent that the settlers would be taken to task for any harm they inflicted on the Palestinian residents. Consequently, both generals, particularly General Mitzna, were labelled 'doves' and even 'pro-PLO.'

Thus, over the course of 20 years, it has been possible to observe that the two opposing political camps in Israel criticize the upper echelon of the IDF, occasionally simultaneously. This demonstrates that the IDF did not have a single, uniform and continuous policy regarding this issue.

Self-Image and Self-Identity

Over the last 20 years, there have been times when questions have arisen, both in the IDF and in the civilian society, regarding the role of the IDF. This has been the case particularly when violence increased in the territories. However, doubts regarding self-image or identity which stemmed from the occupation did not reach crisis proportions.

As has been previously mentioned, two factors can bring about a crisis: role expansion into the civil sector and the policing and counter-insurgency role. While the establishment of the MG added a great number of civilian roles, penetration into the civil sector was not a new experience for the IDF. Since its establishment, the IDF has held a wide-ranging and flexible view of its duties and was inclined to cross over into the civilian domain in matters other than exclusively security ones.[10]

Futhermore, the high level of interactions IDF officers maintain with civilians, combined with widespread reserve duty of civilian professionals, eased the IDF's acclimatization to civil roles. During the whole period, there were, as a result, very few expressions of dissatisfaction by army personnel with the civil duties thrust upon them.

Police duties, pacification and counter-insurgency warfare evinced more than a few reactions from the upper echelon of the army, particularly during periods of unrest. One analyst has written:

> Every wave of violence that spreads through the West Bank raises the question of how this sort of operation affects IDF soldiers. Should the IDF disperse demonstrations, or should another body take over the responsibility? These questions became more pointed when faced with television reports showing IDF soldiers severely beating school children. The answer is not simple. By law, the defense establishment is charged with maintaining security and order. Bearing that in mind, the side effects of these missions are not healthy for the IDF. Soldiers and officers have long and pointed discussions regarding these moral questions . . . And the more selective the fighting unit, the more questions are raised. In the words of an officer who deals with security matters in the area: We have a serious problem here. The army places the conscripts in situations for which they were not trained. You take a paratrooper who trains all year to attack and kill the enemy and you bring him to the streets of the West Bank and confront him with children aged 10-12. Therefore it is necessary to tread carefully. It should be borne in mind that during basic training, the soldiers are not taught how to disperse demonstrations. I don't think it would be healthy to do so. One needs a lot of wisdom and compassion to work in the territories.[11]

These attitudes show the difficulties and the problems that the army has to deal with, particularly when violence flares up in the West Bank.

Nevertheless, it is impossible to speak of an identity or self-image crisis. Even these expressions describe fears of what *could* happen in the future rather than the current situation.

A useful way to illustrate and prove the claim that the West Bank situation has not led to a crisis is to compare the effect of the Lebanon War on the IDF, particularly during its occupation there from the summer of 1982 until the summer of 1985. During that period, opinions were expressed in the press almost daily, not only by columnists and reservists but also by career officers and conscripts, on the role of the IDF.

More can be learned about the crisis by examining the number of pathological phenomena that were exposed in the IDF during this period. There was an increase in the number of suicides in units stationed in Lebanon, an increase in the level of drug abuse in the army (particularly among units stationed in Lebanon), an increase in criminal offenses resulting from illegal trade with the local residents, and even the selling of IDF weapons by soldiers to local citizens in Lebanon or criminals in Israel. At the same time there was a decrease in the willingness of civilians to serve in the reserves and a dramatic increase in the number of conscientious objectors.[12]

The fear of the crisis engulfing the army, and the destructive consequences it faced by remaining in Lebanon, was one of the main factors that led the upper echelon of the IDF to put extremely heavy pressure on the government to advance and accelerate its evacuation of Lebanon.

The various developments that occurred within the IDF and in its relationship to the civilian population, against the background and occupation of Lebanon, illustrate what could have been the character of the self-image crisis, the identity crisis and, ultimately, the crisis of legitimacy resulting from remaining in the territories. The rapidity and acuteness in which the crisis developed in Lebanon illustrates the absence of similar phenomena in the occupation of the territories.

Civil-Military Relations

The occupation of the territories did not bring about a crisis in the areas of civil-military relations. This fact is surprising since Israeli society is deeply divided in its opinions regarding the territories and their inhabitants, while the IDF is identified with the occupation and the military government. Nevertheless, in spite of the breakdown of the national consensus regarding security, the IDF itself did not become a subject of dispute.

Since the establishment of Israel, the IDF has enjoyed a very high level of admiration in the Israeli society. It remains the public institution receiving the most trust, even after 20 years of occupation. In a public opinion survey that was undertaken in January, 1987, and which encompassed a representative sample of the adult Jewish population in Israel, the respondents were asked to what degree they had trust in the various national institution.[13]

Public attitudes towards the IDF can also be seen by examining the level of conscientious objection. During the period of the war in Lebanon, this phenomenon took on new and heretofore unknown proportions. Between the years 1982 and 1985, 150 soldiers and officers were sentenced to jail for refusing to serve in Lebanon. While the number not brought to trial is estimated in the thousands, although cannot be ascertained since many reached various arrangements with their commanders.[14]

While the phenomenon was sharply attacked by both the military and civilian sectors, public sentiment against serving in Lebanon was on the increase. A representative case is that of an open letter written in the summer of 1982, by a group of reservists to the Prime Minister, Menachem Begin:

> We are 15 officers and 17 soldiers who ask you not to send us to Lebanon since we cannot bear it. We have killed and been killed too much in this war. We conquered, we bombed, we destroyed. Why? To what end?[15]

Compared with the level of conscientious objection in the wake of the Lebanon War, the number of objectors in the territories since 1967 is insignificant. All told, there have been between 20 and 30 cases. Prior to the Lebanon War, the IDF had no need to deal with this problem on any significant level.[16]

Futhermore, the motivation of the young people to be drafted into the IDF continues to be high. In research that was undertaken by the Dahaf Institute in May, 1986, among 599 high school students, 86% of the boys declared that they would volunteer to serve in the army, even if there were no compulsory service. The results of similar, earlier surveys were very much the same.[17]

In addition, the percentage of young men volunteering for elite units in the IDF has not perceptibly changed over the years. While there were understandably periodic ups and downs in the percentage of volunteers to certain corps, commanders of these units state that throughout the whole period, there has been a surplus of volunteers in relation to the number of places available.[18]

The same is true of the officer corps:

> The desire to be an officer represents a sensitive sensor which responds to changes in the positions and treatment regarding army service among the civilian population in Israel . . . The IDF never lacked for officer candidates. In contrast, during the Lebanon War there was a decrease in motivation to serve as an officer or to take on combat duties.[19]

During the 1980s, there was a decrease in the number of junior officers who were willing to sign on for longer periods of duty, especially in the technical services. One view is that this situation resulted from the incentives offered to technical people in the civilian market. Another view sees this as a change in motivation from that of a calling to a career-oriented one. However, it is generally conceded that this phenomenon is not related to the occupation in any way.

In conclusion, in spite of the potential dangers that have confronted the IDF since 1967, its neutral political character remained unchanged, its self-image and identity were not harmed, and it suffered no crisis in its relations with the civil society. The IDF did not go through a crisis of legitimacy. It continued to reflect the image held both by civilians and by soldiers prior to 1967 of an a-political, professional military body, and the West Bank occupation did not change this attitude.

How were the expected phenomena and potential crises averted? Crises in the military deriving from occupation can be prevented only when certain conditions in the occupying society and the military are fulfilled:

1. A high level of consensus within the occupying society regarding the need of continuing occupation would reduce the probability of the crises.
2. A relatively low level of resistance of the occupied society towards the military government will reduce potential crises.
3. The use of certain institutional mechanisms by the occupying military, might reduce the negative consequences of the occupation.

A close examination of the first 20 years of the Israeli occupation of the territories demonstrates that all three conditions were met. First, there was a national consensus in the Israeli society concerning the need for the IDF to remain in the occupied territories. Similarly to the traditional two aspects of the "Just War"—*jus ad bellum* and *jus in bello*—the occupation is perceived to be legitimate because it is the result of a just war, and because of the way it is conducted. Wrote General Gazit:

> Israel did not enter into the Six-Day War because it had aggressive, expansionist intentions, and not because it had any inclination to rule over the Arabs of the territories. Israel entered into military battle because it was faced with a dire security-defense problem and was forced to find a solution. This explains the reason for the occupation. As for the continued occupation, the territories must be retained because of their defensive-topographical significance, and not because of the population residing there.[20]

The first coordinator in the occupied territories, Lt. General Shlomo Gazit, along with others of the political-military hierarchy, believed that these reasons comprised a sufficient basis to legitimize the occupation to such a degree that they thought that the residents of the territories themselves would concur with it. Accordingly, Gazit continues in the same article: "On the assumption that it is difficult, if not impossible, to shift the population's affections from the terrorist organizations to the Israeli Military Government, it is possible, at least, to cause those affections to be passive . . ."

There are additional mechanisms for the legitimization of the occupation. One is to emphasize its temporary nature: "Israel will retain the territories until a political solution is found."[21] Perhaps the occupation is not a positive situation but it is necessary for security reasons and, in addition, serves a positive purpose: it will bring about a political solution. Of course, this claim serves those who favor a territorial compromise well, for they say explicitly that the territories represent a bargaining chip which Israel can exchange for a peace agreement.

In order to avoid taking sides between the two political groups—those who favor a territorial compromise and those who favor annexation—"the IDF's position is that it must hold the territories in order to provide the government with options for political settlements when the time comes."[22]

However, not only the condition that relates to the occupying society was met, but the second condition, the reaction of the occupied society to the occupiers was also fulfilled. Contrary to the impression which might have been created by international press coverage of the Israeli occupation, the Palestinian level of resistance towards the Israeli military government was very low.

Immediately after the occupation, in 1967, an attempt was made by the PLO to organize the indigenous population to resist occupation. It failed. Since then, and until the *Intifadeh*, political and violent resistance continued mainly outside the territories and was actively supported inside the territories by a very small part of the population. The vast majority, although it did not accept the Israeli occupation, cooperated with the military administration in the running of everyday life.

Thousands of local civil servants worked in the occupying administration's offices, including the elected councils. More than 100,000 workers commuted to Israel daily. The population at large paid taxes and fulfilled other civil duties and daily life flowed without the interference of subversive activities, either military or political. No wonder Israelis travelled in the territories unhindered and the military Israeli presence in the territories was negligible, as will be explained later.

All these created the feeling that though the Palestinain inhabitants are not interested in the continuation of the Israeli presence, they did not plan to act in a subversive way to terminate it. Instead, they were pinning their hopes on outside elements, the Arab states and first and foremost, the PLO, to rescue them from their predicament.

This enabled Israel to maintain the occupation at a low cost, in what was locally referred to as "deluxe occupation." In other words, a political structure that did not suffer from the symptoms of a government lacking defacto legitimacy.[23]

Lastly, there was the third factor that significantly reduced the disfunctional ramifications of the occupation on the IDF and its relations with Israeli civil society. This was the various mechanisms implemented by the military, some planned and intentional, others unintentional.

Five such mechanisms can be delineated.

Legitimizing the Occupation and the Military Government

The IDF was an active partner in creating national consensus about the necessity to maintain control of the territories until a political settlement could be reached. It used several methods to establish this legitimacy. Another legitmization device is to administer the territories at the lowest cost possible. "It should be the lowest from a budgetary point of view, to Israeli economy, low at the administrative level and inexpensive in terms of Israel's public relations and low in terms of casualties of Israelis and residents of the territories."[24]

According to this approach, maintaining stability and order in the territories is the most important condition to achieving legitimization.

> The world of today finds it politically difficult to come to terms with the continuing retention of occupied areas . . . As the disquiet increases in such an area . . . the political, international, Islamic and Arab opposition to the occupation will increase . . . From a moral point of view, it is difficult to suppose that the Israeli society could come to terms with the need to implement cruel, repressive measures to maintain order in the territories. The Israeli society has become used to the widest support of public opinion regarding the policies and operations of the security forces; in light of this, the repression of civilian unrest . . . would be most difficult to come to terms with . . . If public opinion in Israel doesn't come to terms with what is being done in the territories, we will not be able to remain there for one additional day.

The principles that were developed by Defense Minister Moshe Dayan during the first years of occupation were termed the 'benign occupation' and were intended to legitimize the occupation.

Another important mechanism used to achieve legitimization is the strict enforcement of the legal foundation of MG operations. Naturally, there are those who claim that Israeli operations in the territories lack any legal basis. For the purposes of this discussion, the legal debate is irrelevant. What matters is the IDF's subjective approach: to what degree does the MG see itself as being obligated to base its operations on a legal foundation, and to what degree does it justify its policy based on its legality?

Examination of the MG's *modus operandi*, as well as an examination of many documents, reveals an intense effort to demonstrate that these operations stand on the firmest of legal grounds. This is apparent not only from materials intended for the general public, but also materials intended for the IDF's own internal use.[25]

The desire to base the military government on a solid legal footing created a special cadre of legal advisors for the IDF in MG headquarters, in the territories and in the Defense Ministry. These legal advisors keep tabs on the MG's operations in the closest manner possible.[26] The Israeli government even agreed that the Supreme Court, which serves as a High Court of Justice, would hear cases by residents of the territories against the military authorities. This is a uniquely Israeli phenomenon—there is no precedent for a situation in which the residents of an occupied territory are able to turn to the courts of the occupying state—and is viewed by the IDF as further proof of the legal and enlightened nature of the occupation, granting it legitimacy.[27]

During the first years after the occupation, an additional mechanism of legitimization came into play. This was the perception of an Israeli 'sense of mission' in the territories. Similar to classical colonial regimes, the belief was nurtured that the Israeli occupation would bring about economic and social development in the area, that it would raise the standard of living of the population, and lead to democratization. Many embraced this belief, not only political groups but also academicians and various professionals hired during these years to work on various development projects. This belief was further strengthened by the fact that during the first decade of conquest, the GNP in the territories increased by an average of 12 percent a year.[28]

Along with the 'developing occupation' concept, another perception, of which Moshe Dayan was the primary shaper, was fostered and that was that the occupation would create a basis for cooperation between Jews and Arabs in the future, regardless of the final political status of the territories. The belief that ongoing mutual contact would eliminate prejudices, that it would ease the conflicts, and that it would bring about greater understanding and closeness between Israelis and Palestinians, is repeated over and over in the statements of the framers of the occupation policy.

Looking back over the past 20 years, or even less, this approach seems naive at best and possibly delusive. Nevertheless, the enthusiasm and deep confidence of the people who developed it bear witness to the function of legitimization which it fulfilled. Such a lofty goal is likely, in the final analysis, to justify even the unpleasantness of occupation.

The Incorporation of the Civil System into the Military Government

Although the IDF represented the highest authority in the territories, wielding authority over legislative, administrative and judicial functions, it has not been the only governmental body there. As early as October 11, 1968, a ministerial committee determined that the various civil operations in the areas would be carried out by representatives of governmental ministries coordinated by the MG. Only security matters were to be the sole responsibility of the military.

The structure of the MG unit is such that both at the regional level and at the local level, civilians who represent various ministries, such as education, health, transporation, etc., work as staff officers of the Military Governor. While maintaining their professional link with the Israeli civil ministries they are officially subordinate to the Military Governor.

Futhermore, while ministerial responsibility for the territories is in the hands of the Defense Minister, it was already determined in the summer of 1967 that their senior administrative body—a sort of unofficial 'territories government'—would be a civilian body, a committee which would include the directors of the various government ministries, headed by the Minister of Finance. This committee issued several thousand directives regarding all aspects of life in the territories.

The relationship between the IDF and the Ministry of Defense, on the one hand, and government ministries headed by their director-generals on the other, underwent various changes that warrant amplification. It is sufficient to state that, even during the periods when the former were dominant, they never acted alone. Thus, the difficulty facing the professional military body that has to perform civil functions was not as severe, due to the fact that the IDF had civilian partners in the territories who fulfilled these functions. While it is entirely understandable that the local population may not differentiate between the representative of an Israeli civil office serving as a staff officer and between a man in uniform, for the Israelis, and particularly for the IDF itself, this was an important distinction.

The involvement of the civilian ministries in the territories increased after the Yom Kippur War, when de facto annexation proceedings were accelerated and the various ministries increased their direct operations there. Between March, 1979, and March, 1981, the standing of the Jewish settlements in the territories also changed. Regional and municipal councils, similar to those operating in Israel proper, were established. These councils were under direct Israeli authority, as though they were part of the public administration system of Israel, within the boundaries of the Green Line. The councils were removed from the jurisdiction of the MG.[29] Accordingly, the civil duties of the MG in the territories were further decreased, particularly in the one sensitive area that could cause friction, Jewish settlement in the territories.

In conclusion, the military government has not been the central actor administering civil functions in the territories and it is certainly has not been the only one. A researcher who has followed the military government went so far as to define the situation as "a process by which the IDF abdicates from dealing with civil functions."[30]

The Shin Bet—The Central Control Apparatus

The IDF's desire to retain the territories at the lowest possible cost has been realized to a considerable extent in at least one area: control functions in the territories have involved a very small number of IDF personnel and only a few dozen Israelis have been employed on the West Bank by the MG. Security has been maintained by a brigade of several hundred conscripted and reserve soldiers; this in an area of 2,100 square miles which contains a population of more than 760,000 residents. Maintaining public order in the territories—apart from those times of crisis when there is an increase in the number of forces deployed—has not prevented the IDF from following its normal routine.

This fact is due to the nature of the control structure employed by Israel in the territories. It is not an overtone deploying many army units, but rather involves covert, preventative and deterent measures by security forces. In order to conserve army manpower allocations for policing purposes, and at the same time to demonstrate a military presence in the area, the Minister of Defense, shortly after the occupation, decided to transfer IDF training bases from Israel to the West Bank. After the Sinai was evacuated in the early 1980s, the IDF moved additional bases from there to the West Bank. Although these units do not perform security duties, their presence in the territories acts as a deterrent. More important, though the army is the ultimate authority in political, social and security control in the territories, this function if not confined to the IDF. To a great extent it is carried out by the Shin Bet, the Security Services.

Until 1967, the Shin Bet has fulfilled two roles, one of which was to deal with counter-intelligence against foreign agents (generally from the Eastern bloc), and the other to prevent sabotage by Arab residents of the State of Israel. Following the commencement of Palestinian terrorist operations in the territories and in Israel in the fall of 1967, the Shin Bet came to deal increasingly with the West Bank.

Back in 1967, the Shin Bet was a small, ambitious organization that burst
into the governmental vaccuum which became apparent with the appearance
of terrorism. It was given responsibility for research, intelligence and interrogation of prisoners. It participated in the actual preparation of cases that
were sent to the military courts. All this was undertaken in an atmosphere
new to the service: foreign territory, a hostile population under military
government, enemy command posts that were established on the other side
of the border and terrorist operations against institutions and Israeli citizens
abroad. For the first time, the Shin Bet suffered casualties and was forced to
deal with thousands of prisoners a year. During the 70s, the Shin Bet brought,
on the average, approximately 1,500 prisoners a month to trial. Today, on
the average, about twenty terrorist rings are uncovered each month, most of
them before they go into action.[31]

The Shin Bet's role is not only to gather information about organizations
or sabotage operations, to expose them and prevent them, or to capture
their executors after the fact. In fact, the Shin Bet has succeeded in
spreading a dense net of Israeli agents (their number is said to be more
than one hundred) and hundreds, perhaps thousands, of Palestinian col-
laborators in the West Bank, virtually permeating the local population.
The Shin Bet's success in preventing about 90% of attempted terrorist
actions attests to the degree to which the population is exposed to the
wary gaze of the Shin Bet.
Exposure of the deeds, opinions, beliefs and thoughts of the population
is a useful tool in controlling daily life. Because local residents, due to the
nature of the occupation, require many permits and licenses from the
authorities, the military government, equipped with information supplied
by the Shin Bet, can use the stick and carrot method, without resorting
to physical, violent control.
Because the Shin Bet is not only an intelligence tool but also an apparatus
for social control, the military role is reduced to one of physical suppression,
crowd control, curfew enforcement, punitive measures and capturing terrorist
rings and suspects. Accordingly, the army is released from having to perform
certain aspects of counter-insurgency warfare, aspects that generally arouse
critical reactions not only among the occupied population but also among
the occupying society.
The matter of interrogations are a good example. After a suspect has
been arrested by a joint unit of the army, the Shin Bet and the police, he
is interrogated generally late at night, not by army intelligence but by Shin
Bet interrogators, who have achieved an 80% confession rate. They prepare
the case which is then passed along to the military prosecutor who brings
the suspect before a military court.
The initial part of the process—the interrogation—is performed by the
Shin Bet. Even if an estimate of close to 200,000 detentions and interrogations

of the residents of the territories during 20 years is exaggerated, the harshest encounter between the occupier and the occupied is with the Shin Bet and not with the soldiers of the IDF.[32]

During Shin Bet interrogations, there is no small measure of intimidation and threats by means of emotional and physical pressure, which differs from the accepted norms of Shin Bet interrogation in Israel proper. From the point of view of the Palestinian residents, it makes no difference whether they face an IDF soldier or a civilian Shin Bet interrogator. However, from the IDF point of view, the fact that the Shin Bet attends to these interrogations prevents it from having to fulfill these roles. It also eliminates the need for the soul-searching which it raises, and the public criticism. Thus, the interrogation norms employed against detainees in the territories caused a public outcry in Israel and led to the establishment of a judicial committee of inquiry in 1987, the Shin Bet was at the center of the public storm while the military was untouched by the affair.

The Depoliticization of the Military Government

The fourth apparatus that the IDF used to protect itself from the dysfunctional results that stem from the occupation is particularly interesting since it is based on self-deception. Since June, 1967, and to the same extent 20 years later, the IDF continues to foster the belief that the military government fulfills an administrative, non-political function.

Ministers of defense, chiefs of staff, heads of the MG and IDF officers have frequently demonstrated the perception that the role of the military government is not to establish political facts. Accordingly, policy in the territories is determined solely by the political echelon and is merely executed by the military. The goals of the MG are to normalize and guarantee stability and order in the territories, to provide public services and to improve economic conditions. The purpose of this activity regarding the widest political area is "to keep all policy options open for the political echelon until such time that it shall render a decision regarding a political solution for the territories."[33]

In the summer of 1967, in an attempt to limit the military government's presence as much as possible, Moshe Dayan established several principles which were reaffirmed by those who succeeded him. One of these is that of 'non-presence':

> Any presence by the Israeli military rule—the military government's buildings, the Israeli flag, security patrols, the sign of military headquarters—all contain elements of provocation and create points of friction and conflict between the authorities and the residents. Therefore, they must be removed. The headquarters of the MG must be removed from the centers of the cities— except for the physical presence of IDF soldiers on the streets of the cities—

as well as every other Israeli trace . . . The less a foreign military government is seen and heard, the more tolerable its presence becomes.

The second principle is that of non-intervention:

All areas of the economy and administration have been placed entirely in Arab hands while the MG limits itself to providing the budget for the various operations. The population will be administered by its own people, in the way that it see fit . . . except for those areas which could have a direct effect on Israel. . . The military governmental apparatus does not interfere with what is done and does not attempt to force development on the population against its will.

These principles demonstrate the approach of indirect rule which is similar to the colonial experience of the British and in contrast to the French experience of direct rule. Furthermore, they express the deep desire of the framers of the MG to disengage it from politics, thus making it purely administrative.

As could be expected, even during the formulation of these guidelines there were deep inherent contradictions. Thus, for example, on November 21, 1967, at a meeting between the Coordinating Committee and the Minister of Defense, it was decided to have "minimal interference in the actual administration of the territories." Two months previously, the same committee had taken the exact opposite position when it decided on the "creation of dependence and cooperation with the local administrations as a means of preventing unrest."[34]

Over the course of 20 years, there were times when the principles of indirect rule changed. Such, for example, was the case when Ariel Sharon was Minister of Defense and Menachem Milson was the highest authority in the MG in the territories. They promulgated direct rule which included appointing military officers as mayors. Nevertheless, even when the principle of indirect rule was in effect, there was a significant gap between doctrine and reality.

The approximately 1,200 ordinances that were issued by the MG during this period completely changed daily life in the territories. These ordinances did not deal solely with administrative aspects, but brought about deep institutional change, which was intended to achieve explicit political goals. The MG greatly interferes with political life in the territories; it encourages elections (1972, 1976) or prevents them (the mid 80s); opposes some political groups (The Committee of National Guidance or the PLO) and promotes others (The Village Leagues); it encourages anti-Jordanian Palestinian leadership (Dayan during the late 60s) and cooperates with King Hussein to strengthen pro-Jordanian elements in the West Bank (Rabin, 1984–1987).

The MG's deep level of involvement in all areas of life, especially in administrative matters such as water, agriculture, housing, banking and the roads system, had a far-reaching political significance for the future of the territories.[35]

Therefore, those supporters of direct rule who criticize the principle of non-intervention, miss the point. The more significant issue concerning Dayan's doctrine is not the question of direct or indirect intervention but rather the attempt to create an a-political military government, and the belief that this is possible.[36]

The belief that the functions of the military government can be removed from the political sphere and be made administrative has two aims: first, to reduce the repressive effect of the occupation on the residents in order to achieve normalization; and, secondly, to prevent any damage to the a-political image of the IDF. If efforts to achieve the first goal failed, the same cannot be said for the second. The existence of the MG did not harm the IDF's a-political image, neither in its own view nor in that of the rest of the Israeli society.

The Structural Mechanism of the IDF

In addition to doctrinal mechanisms, structural mechanisms helped to reduce the effect of the occupation on the army. These mechanisms caused the military to have only a partial share in the MG and turned the MG into a secondary and minor factor to the IDF.

Immediately upon the conclusion of the Six-Day War, Moshe Dayan developed a command structure that would grant him centralized power and greatly reduce the power that could have been wielded by the Chief of Staff and the General Staff. This was accomplished by creating the position of the Coordinator in the Territories, a person who has two duties. While he serves as the department head of the military government in the IDF's operations branch, subordinate to the branch head and through him to the Chief of Staff, he also serves as head of the civil unit in the Defense Ministry that coordinates operations in the territories and thus reports directly to the Defense Minister. Gazit clarifies Dayan's intentions:

> The fact that an aide for the territories to the Minister of Defense is also in charge of the military government within the General Staff, enabled the Minister of Defense to circumvent the IDF bureaucracy and to ensure the almost immediate execution of his instructions. Not only did the Minister of Defense by-passed at least two levels—the Chief of Staff and the Head of the Operations Branch, who are above the Coordinator—but he also prevented the General Staff from formulating a position of its own.[37]

The General Staff, which like any bureaucratic body did not wish to relinquish potential areas of operation or influence, opposed the Minister's policy. Although the General Staff

> wanted to protect its areas of responsibility and operations, and to prevent the Minister of Defense from 'getting carried away', it was forced to give in and to retreat from the positions in which it was entrenched. Accordingly, throughout the course of the whole period, the General Staff did not deal with, nor did it take any interest in the goings-on in the territories.

This state of affairs continued, and occasionally deteriorated, even after the first years, following the formation of the MG. The territories constitute a minor matter on the Chief of Staff's daily agenda, except in times of crisis. When the General Staff convened for its regular weekly meeting, it also rarely dealt with the subject of the territories.

Among IDF officers, the MG constituted an insignificant body. There were very few officers involved in its operations and, after 20 years, only a few hundred have served there. Serving in the MG unit was considered unrespectable and, accordingly, it was unpopular. During the 1960s, Dayan tried to send outstanding officers to these posts because of his belief in their mission. He, therefore, interviewed each candidate for an officer posting to the MG, including the junior ranks. But this policy was discontinued. During the 1980s, most of those who have served in the MG are not likely to have a promising future in the IDF. Thus began the vicious cycle of the decline of the unit's status and prestige.

The influence of the MG on the IDF was insignificant. This can be discerned by examining the career patterns of officers who served in the MG, be they of low or high rank. Very few, after several years of service in the MG, reached key positions in the IDF, and most did not embark on the primary career track of the IDF. As a result, the MG can be seen as an insignificant extension of the IDF. If any officers were negatively influenced by their service in the MG, these influences did not penetrate into the main body of the IDF itself.

The influence of veterans of the MG on the high command levels was prevented by the relative isolation of MG officers, a reverse policy was enacted regarding soldiers performing guard duty. Instead of establishing permanent units who would specialize in this task, the IDF preferred to send conscripts and reservists to the territories for short periods.

This naturally harmed the professional ability of such units, trained to fill policing and counter-insurgency roles. On the other hand, it eliminated the necessity of establishing a specialized occupational military framework. The possiblity of establishing such units became a matter of public debate during periods of tension, and was quickly forgotten afterwards without any policies being changed.[38] The only constant professional body in the territories was the Border Guard. This unit functioned in a military context under the supervision of the military commander in the area. However, it was a police unit which consisted primarily of several Israeli minorities, such as Druzes, Circassians and others.

Conclusion

For twenty years since the establishment of the military government, the IDF did not suffer a crisis of legitimacy. The hypothesis that the functions of a military government cannot be compatible with the professional character of a military like the IDF is unsubstantiated. The IDF did not develop an exclusive political doctrine; it did not become involved in the internal political process in Israel any more than it previously had; it did not suffer from self-image or self-identity crises, and no schism was created between the IDF and Israel's civil society, or any part thereof.

All of these anticipated results were prevented due to two extra-military conditions: a consensus for the occupation within the Israeli society, a low level of resistance to the occupation by the Palestinian society, and, in addition the establishment of various mechanisms in the areas of the doctrine, structure and operations of the military government. What characterizes the IDF's reactions to its new situation following 1967 is the awareness of the potential dangers that stem from its occupation of the territories. It can be stated that the IDF's institutional fears of damage to its internal cohesiveness, to its effectiveness, its corporate and professional values, and its standing in Israeli society, all resulted from the fact that the senior command and, during most periods, the political level, worked to prevent change in the IDF's traditional character.

Towards the end of 1987, within a few weeks, these achievements of the military were jeopardized. For the first time since the summer of 1967 a widespread civilian uprising swept the entire West Bank encompassing every social sector. The second condition the low level of resistance to the occupying power collapsed.

The army, like the civilians, were taken by surprise by the scope of the uprising and estimated that it was a passing spate which would decline soon. But the estimate proved false.

Demonstrations of thousands swept the villages and townships of the West Bank and Gaza; shops, businesses and schools shut down, local policemen, teachers and administration officials resigned; violent attacks, although without live ammunition, against the army, occurred daily; inhabitants who collaborated with the occupation were lynched; and residents stopped paying taxes and created alternative organizations to the occupying administration.[39]

The IDF reacted harshly to the uprising. In order to restore law and order on the West Bank and to re-establish the crumbling Israeli rule, it used violent measures, including live ammunition. From dozens of dead Palestinians in the first few weeks, the figures rose during the year to hundreds. The few hundred Israeli soldiers posted in the territories increased to over 7,000. Special military equipment for riot control including truncheions, tear-gas grenades, rubber bullets and other anti-riot weapons were air-lifted from the United States to Israel. The IDF has developed new techniques and methods to disperse demonstrators, including the use of helicopters, pebble-shooting cannons, and tear-gas bombs.

The army's daily routine changed overnight. Policing and pacification tasks became the main military activity in the territories. As a result, the entire annual work program of the military was changed. Instead of undergoing routine training, regular units were transferred to patrol the streets of the West Bank. The mobilization of reserve units was increased. Police and border police units were enlarged and the structure of the army's field commands in the territories was changed. While until 1988, law and order was maintained by a brigade under the command of a colonel, responsible to the central command, O/C, in 1988 three field headquarters were created, under the command of four brigadier-generals. A similar structure was established in the Gaza Strip.[40]

The increased use of physical oppression against uprisers, the large number of casualties, the detention without trial of many thousands and the beating of demonstrators, raised a public storm in Israel. Overnight, the IDF became an army of occupation.

The three conditions which existed for 20 years changed and as a result the symptoms which had been avoided so far, began to emerge. The necessity to conduct counter-insurgency warfare against the Palestinians, forced the army to develop a political-military doctrine. (For example, a decision was reached to limit the freedom of the press in the troubled areas, to use collective punishment, to penalize parents for their children's actions, to institute speedy expulsion procedures against riot mongers, etc.) This doctrine was commended by certain circles in Israel, but was denounced by others.

The result placed the army at the forefront of the political argument in an unprecedented manner. Demands by Knesset members and ministers to dismiss the military Chief of Staff and Central Command Officer-in-Charge for not using harsh enough measures to quell the riots, were one example.

The need to maintain policing and pacification functions in the civilian population, consisting mainly of children and women, brought a flood of self-criticism in the army. The newspapers filled with descriptions of reserve soldiers and officers who had difficulties coping with their activities. These

The Case of the IDF

were the first indications of the crisis of self-identity and self-image threatening the IDF.

The emergence of a crisis in civil-military relations can be demonstrated by the fact that during the first six months of 1988 the number of conscientious objectors to military service in the territories was roughly similar to the number of objectors in the 20 years before that (excluding Lebanon).[41]

The transformation in the nature of the roles of the military government, and in particular the increased level of violence, eliminated the "deluxe occupation." Consequently, particularly out of concern to the moral damage caused to the soldiers, the need for continuing occupation was cast into serious doubt for the first time since 1967. The majority of the Israeli population and professional army still believed in the need for occupation, but expressions of doubt and questioning were becoming louder.

The official policy of the IDF was defined as restoring law and order, to enable the government to reach a political solution without external pressure. However, for the first time, a new assumption was implied: the government's time was not unlimited.

The *Intifadeh* had brought about one major change: the feeling that the status quo in the territories could continue indefinitely made way for the conception that something must be done to change it, and that if it would not change, the continuing occupation would extoll a new, much heavier price than it did until 1988.

The purpose of this paper is not to analyze the events of 1988 but the first 20 years of occupation. Therefore, the brief mention of the events in 1988 may serve to illustrate the thesis presented in the opening of this chapter. Twenty years of occupation did not infect the army with the malaise of an occupying force. This is because the conditions that prevented the emergence of crises in its relation with the Israeli political establishment, the civil society and with itself.

With the changing of these conditions, the IDF entered a new era in 1988. In every one of these three areas, it now faces the dangers plaguing other occupation armies: the politicization of the army; confrontation with the government; the creation of a rift between the military and the civil society and the development of an identity and self-image crisis, which will bring, ultimately, to a crisis of legitimacy. These consequences are not inevitable, but the probability of their developing in the near future is higher than ever since Israel's victory in the Six Day War.

Notes

1. See Shlomo Gazit, *Crystallization of Policies and Organizational Molds in the Administered Territories, 1967–1968*. M.A. thesis, Tel Aviv University, 1983, (Hebrew).

This work was the basis for Gazit's book: *The Stick and the Carrot*, (Tel Aviv: Zemorah, Bitan 1985), (also Hebrew).

2. *Judaea and Shomron*, an official publication of the IDF spokesman, March, 1984. pp. 74–75. For the legal position concerning Israel's status in the territories, see Moshe Drori, *The Legislation in the Area of Judea and Samaria*, (Jerusalem: Hebrew University, 1975), (in Hebrew).

3. See the classic analysis of Samuel P. Huntington in: *The Soldier and the State: The Theory and Politics of Civil-Military Relations*, (Cambridge, Mass: Belknap Press of Harvard University Press, 1957).

4. See, for example, *The Annals of the American Academy of Political and Social Science*, January, 1950. An issue on "Military Government."

5. A. R. Luckman, "A Comparative Typology of Civil-Military Relations," *Government and Opposition*, Vol. 6, no. 1, 1971.

6. See, for example, J. S. Ambler, *The French Army in Politics, 1945–62*, (Ohio: Ohio University Press, 1966).

7. An analysis of the term 'military political partnership' can be seen in Yoram Peri, *Between Battles and Ballots: Israeli Military in Politics*, (Cambridge: Cambridge University Press, 1983).

8. Yoram Peri: "*The Professional Ethics of the Military*." Unpublished paper, 1986.

9. This is done by differentiating between "procedures for opening fire" and "procedures for detaining suspects." In the first case, an IDF soldier is permitted to use his weapon only in self-defense when his life appears to be in danger. In the second case, he may shoot at any suspect who refuses to stop and identify himself. The increase in the number of killings in the territories when Eitan was Chief of Staff caused one of the largest public storms on the subject.

10. Moshe Lissak, "The Israeli Defense Forces as an Agent of Socialization and Education, A study of Role Expansion in a Democratic Society" in Van Gils (ed.), *The Perceived Role of the Military*, (Rotterdam: Rotterdam University, 1971), pp. 325–340.

11. Joseph Walter, "Violence in the West Bank," *Ma'ariv*, February 20, 1987.

12. The Israeli press followed these events in depth. See, for example, Tzvi Har-El, "An Officer and Drug Dealing," *Ha'aretz*, December 26, 1986.

13. *Israeli Democracy*. An Israel-Diaspora Institute publication, Tel Aviv University, Vol. 1, February, 1987, p.16.

14. See Ruth Linn, "The Moral Judgement of Lebanon War Draft Resisters," *Research in Education*, no. 42, November, 1985, pp. 19–32.

15. For the Reservist Soldier's letter see *Ha-Ir*, July 9, 1982. For a treatment of the subject of draft resistance during the Lebanon War, see Ruth Linn, "Conscious Objection in Israel During the War in Lebanon," *Armed Forces and Society*, Vol. 12, no. 4, 1986, pp. 489–511.

16. An interview with the former head of the Personnel Branch, Lt. Gen. Moshe Nativ, in 1985. In 1970 a letter was sent by 35 high school students to the Prime Minister in which they announced that, in the event of a future war, they would not be able to defend the Jewish settlements on the West Bank. In spite of the lively public reaction, it should be noted that the text of the letter is quite gentle. It discussed intent to the future and is drafted with restraint compared to the

expressions of resistance to the Lebanon War. Subsequently, all the signatories on the letter were drafted and even served in the territories.

17. *Davar*, 12 May, 1986.

18. *Ma'ariv*, 24 July, 1987.

19. For a wider discussion, see Reuven Gal, *A Portrait of the Israeli Soldier*, (Westport Conn: Greenwood Press, 1986), p. 68.

20. Shlomo Gazit, *The Administered Territories—Five Years*. Information sheets published by the Center for the Office of Education and Culture, Jerusalem, August, 1972, p.13.

21. This was the official policy of the Israeli Government until 1977 and has been the policy of the Labor camp since.

22. An interview with the Coordinator, Lt. General Raphael Vardi, 1985

23. See for example S. Gazit, 1985, pp. 320–324.

24. S. Gazit, 1982, pp. 287–288.

25. For example, the basic book of the General Staff on the subject *The Military Government*, no. 3. This is classified material.

26. The headquarters of the Chief Military Advocate periodically publishes legal opinions on issues relating to the territories which are brought to the attention of the staff of the military government.

27. Regarding this matter, see Moshe Ha-Negbi, *Bondage of Justice*, (Jerusalem: American Jewish Congressional Commission on International Affairs, 1982). (Hebrew)

28. *Judaea, Samaria and the Gaza District Since 1967*, (Jerusalem: Publication of the Israeli Information Center, 1986).

29. Myron Benvenisti, *Israel and the Administered Territories*, Data Collection Project, special report no. 1, The West Bank and Gaza Strip, Jerusalem. Undated, p. 22.

30. An interview with Myron Benvenisti, 1985.

31. Rananit Vardi, "The Shin Bet," *Yediot Aharonot*, June 6, 1987.

32. Ibrahim Matar, "The New Sultans," *Israel and Palestine*, August, 1986.

33. Regarding the non-political character of the Military Government, see article by Shlomo Gazit, "The Administered Territories and the Policy," *Ma'arahot*, 1970, p. 19. The following two quotations are taken from page 14 of this article.

34. A letter of the Ministry of Defense dated November 12, 1967 gm/148, summarizing a meeting of the coordinating committee of November 17, 1967. Also Ministry of Defense letter gm/72, dated October 13,˙ 1967, operating principles in the administered territories, a summary of the meeting of the coordinating committee with the Minister of Defense of September 29, 1967.

35. It was these decisions that caused deep integration between the State of Israel and the West Bank and led to the claim that Israel has de facto annexed the territories and that retreat from them is impossible. This is the central thesis of Myron Benvenisti, *The West Bank Data Project, A Survey of Israel's Politics*, American Enterprise Institute for Public Policy, Washington, 1984, pp. 64–69. See also the series of articles by Danny Rubinstein, "Construction in the Territories," *Davar*, July 27–29, 1987.

36. Prof. Menachem Milson, who published articles on this subject, was the most aggressive critic and tried to implement the policy of direct intervention when he served in the West Bank.

37. Gazit, S. 1982, pp. 80–81

38. General Yisrael Tal, a founder of Israel's security policy, supports having special units outside of the IDF to handle operations in the territories. The purpose of this is to remove the IDF completely from this area.

39. See a detailed description of the *Intifadeh* in Yoram Peri, "The Seventh War," *Davar*, 11–16 March, 1988.

40. These developments were extensively described in the Israeli press in March–May 1988. Information was also received by interviews with commanders of the Central Command on March 1988.

41. Yizhar Be'er, "This is not Vietnam," *Hadashot*, May 20, 1988.

8

The Economy of Binational Israel

Simcha Bahiri

Introduction

The West Bank and Gaza Strip were occupied by Israel in the Six Day War of 1967. Initially, Israel called for an exchange of these territories in return for peace. This was rejected by the Arab states, hardening the Israeli position. A process of creeping annexation began which twenty years later has transformed Israel into a de facto binational state. Nowhere has this transformation been more visible than in the realm of economic realities. Yet the debate about the scope, permanence and the degree of reversability of the binational economy has never been settled. Part of the confusion stems from the fact that both proponents and opponents of annexation have used economic arguments to bolster their case. Yet there also exists a general theoretical problem of identifying the characteristics of a binational economy and defining the ways in which such a construct differs from other forms of economic integration. While there is no formal definition of a binational economy in the literature for the purpose of this chapter, we must formalize this concept.

An international economy usually refers to a world economy in which units of different sizes are characterized by a variable degree of integration. By its nature, a small economy is more integrated or dependent on a larger world or regional economy than a larger unit. The heterogeneity of internal subsystems gives the larger unit or system a higher degree of autarchy and larger domestic market.

The smaller economy is more dependent on external trade. This does not necessarily lead to its exploitation by the other units large and small, as the smaller system may be fully developed and enjoy favorable terms of trade. External trade however, represents a large degree of its output and consumption. Smaller economies are therefore more dependent and more intensely integrated within a greater economic framework.

The same analogue can be used in describing a binational economy, except that the system involves only two contiguous national units. This pattern should be distinguished from two separate national unitary economies. A unitary economy is so fully integrated that the *economic subsystems* cannot survive without constant interaction. In a binational economy separate, identifiable, semiautonomous national economies still exist as a subsystems in a fairly integrated overall system. A binational economy is an integrated economy with a high degree of economic interdependence between the two ethnonational units involved. Obviously, the degree and effect of integration is unequal for each of the natural entities and depends on the level of their development. If the larger unit is economically more developed, then its degree of dependence on the smaller, less developed unit is more limited. Clearly, this type of relationship prevails between the developed economy of Israel and the underdeveloped West Bank and Gaza Strip, abbreviated as the WB/GS.

More developed economies, whether small or large, tend to enjoy more favorable terms of trade in economic transactions with less developed countries. Some analysts have developed the concept of dependency (whether investment, resource or trade) to describe those relations which are characterized by unequal exchange between nations. This dependency is said to be the result of either formal imperialism (political control and/or military occupation by a dominant power) colonialism (control plus settlements by nationals of the dominant power) or informal imperialism (economic control through multinational corporations or other means).

Dependency can be a useful conceptual tool to understand the nature of a national economy. Though there are political and legal ambiguities to nonstatutory binationalism, economically speaking this relationship may be viewed in terms of core and periphery units. Core territories economically dominate their peripheral areas and may or may not be contiguous. The most pronounced feature of this binational economy is the developmental disparity between the two units. The Israeli economy is over twenty times the size of the WB/GS economy with a per capita income approaching five times the size of the WB/GS unit.

These disparities explain why the pattern of effects on each of the national units is radically different. The WB/GS, as we will subsequently demonstrate, is overwhelmingly dependent on the Israeli economy, i.e., involving over half of their total employment (in both Israel and the territories) and consumption, and over a quarter of direct output. The impact of WB/GS on the Israeli economy is more limited and mostly confined to providing labor for the agriculture, construction, and some industrial manufacturing.

Historical Background

In order to understand the present patterns of the binational economy, a short historical background is in order. Economic integration of the territories into Israel was originally spontaneous and unplanned and was largely a creeping annexation process. Because Labor's policy of Jewish uninationalism did not view territories as a permanent part of the state, economic integration developed slowly and almost randomly. Some economic collaboration stemmed from strategic realities after the 1967 war. The large Palestinian labor force had to find an Israeli substitute for vanished local employment and opportunities in other Arab countries. Likewise, Israel became a major trade partner of the territories in lieu of links with Arab states severed after the occupation. The process of integration intensified after Begin's Second Republic and became planned.

In looking for some functional means of economic cooperation Begin's Israel drew on the prestate experience. Even in the mandatory period there was a degree of economic "Jewish-Arab dualism" or cooporation despite the existence of two separate economies, Jewish and the Arab. During the Mandate, Zionist authorities, following a policy of the "conquest of labor," did not welcome Arab labor in the Jewish sector. Nonetheless there were areas of economic exchange. The total output of these informal exchanges was marginal compared to the separate economic activity in the Arab and Jewish sectors, but even so, it mitigated their autarkic nature.

After the establishment of the state, the Israeli economy was divorced from that of the WB/GS, through a small Arab population of some 175,000 remained within its borders. Most of the Arab minority in the early years were under military government. The degree of their economic integration, i.e, labor, trade and services was initially limited. However, because Arab agricultural land was expropriated, many Arab farmers were reduced to wage earners in the often physically distant Jewish sector. Labor migration functionally integrated Arabs into the Israeli economy, a trend accelerated after the relaxation of military government in the late 1950s.

It was through this process of integration that the economy of Israel became progressively a unitary national economy. The Arabs lost most of the prestate remnants of an independent economic sector and become fully, albeit dependently integrated in the national economy. For instance, the 4 percent increase in per capita consumption of the Arabs matched the level of Jewish consumption increase until 1967. At the same time, the increase of private consumption among the Arabs was more dependent on their employment in the Jewish sector than on real economic or industrial development in the Arab sector. Likewise, the distribution of the Arab labor force was significantly different from the Jewish labor force, with

Arabs predominating in lower unskilled and semiskilled professions (Table 8.1.)

In spite of many problems, the integrated Israeli economy has performed quite well during the first two decades of independence. Between 1949 and 1967 the Israeli Gross National Product grew at an annual rate of 9 percent, the 1966–1967 recession notwithstanding. Investment grew at an annual rate of 6 percent and other indicators of economic well being showed a promising start. However, this initial impressive rate of development was never equalled in later years.

As opposed to the economic success of Israel, the WB/GS enjoyed a less spectacular fate. The West Bank was occupied by Jordan in 1948 and shortly thereafter annexed by the Hashemite Emirate of Trans-Jordan, thus becoming part of the kingdom of Jordan. Although the Arab sector of Palestine lagged considerably behind the Jewish sector, it had reached a higher level of social and economic development, than that of the East Bank (Trans-Jordan) prior to 1948.[1]

During and after the first war between the Arabs and Israelis, perhaps 450,000 of the roughly 750,000 Palestinian refugees fled eastward. Three fourths settled in the West Bank, joining the already existing population of 400,000, while more than 100,000 went to the East Bank of the Jordan River, which had had a 1946 population of 430,000. The annexation of the West Bank meant that two thirds of the population of Jordan was now of Palestinian origin.[2] While causing a severe strain on the economy of Jordan, the influx of the more skilled Palestinian population contributed to economic growth, particularly in the commerce and service sectors. Because much of the infrastructure (railroads, ports, etc.) was concentrated in coastal areas, the formation of Israel cut off West Bank and East Bank hinterlands from their traditional routes of trade and commerce. After an initial period of investment in infrastructure, most notably, the East hor Canal, Jordan attained an annual growth rate of 10–11 percent in the ten years prior to the 1967 war, although admittedly this was from a small initial base.[3] However, despite the fact that all Palestinians were granted Jordanian citizenship, the West Bank was discriminated against in the allocation of economic projects.

As a result, the rate of economic development of the West Bank lagged behind the level of the East Bank between 1948 and 1967. This was particularly noticeable with regard to manufacturing as the central Jordanian authority did less to promote the industrialization of the West Bank. According to some reports of the Jordanian Central Bank, the West Bank accounted for only some 20 percent of Jordan's total industrial output.[4] Others maintain that the value added of the industrial sector in the East Bank was almost triple that of the West Bank.[5] These factors contributed

TABLE 8.1
1985 WB/GS and Israeli Sectional and Ethnic Employment Analysis(1)

	Agriculture Number	%	Industry(3) Number	%	Construction Number	%	Services(4) Number	%	Total Number	%
WB/GS										
1. WB/GS Residents Employed in WB/GS	37.9	24.4	24.6	16.1	37.9	11.1	73.9	48.4	152.7	100
2. WB/GS Residents Employed in Israel	13.9	15.6	15.9	17.8	42.4	47.0	17.0	19.1	89.2	100
3. Total WB/GS Employment	51.1	21.1	40.5	16.8	59.3	24.5	90.0	37.6	241.8	100
4. Percentage of WB/GS Labor Employed In Israel (2/3)	-	27.2	-	39.3	-	71.5	-	18.7	-	36.9
5. Percentage of Israel's Labor from WB/GS (2/10)	-	15.1	-	4.7	-	37.0	-	1.9	-	6.1
Israel(2)										
6. Jewish Labor in Israel	62.5	5.1	293.0	24.2	43.2	3.6	814.9	67.1	1213.6	100
7. Israeli-Arab Labor in Israel	15.6	10.1	31.3	20.2	29.1	18.8	78.7	50.9	154.7	100
8. Total Israeli Labor in Israel (6/7)	78.1	5.7	324.3	23.7	72.3	5.3	893.6	65.3	1368.3	100
9. Arab Labor in Israel (2/7)	29.5	12.1	47.2	19.4	71.5	29.3	95.7	39.2	243.9	100
10. Total Employment in Israel (6/9)	92.0	6.3	340.2	23.3	114.7	7.9	910.6	62.5	1457.5	100
11. Arab Labor in Israel as Percentage of Labor in Israel (9/10)	-	29.5	-	13.9	-	62.3	-	10.5	-	16.7

(1) Source: Central Bureau of Statistics, Jerusalem
(2) Jewish Labor in WB/GS is only included in data on Israel
(3) Industry includes manufacturing, handicrafts, electricity, and mining
(4) Services include all categories not covered elsewhere - both public and private

to a migration of West Bank residents to East Bank positions in government, commerce and services.

Moreover, the West Bank viewed as a separate economic entity from the East Bank, had a highly adverse trade balance in commodities. West Bankers tried to balance this deficit by trade in services, tourism and remittances from guest workers abroad and transfer payments.[6]

The Gaza Strip was occupied by Egypt in 1948. Its original population of some 190,000 Palestinians was augmented by 210,000 refugees from what became Israel. Because of the vast influx of refugees and the separation from the rest of Palestine the Gazan economy was virtually on the point of collapse. The economic marginality of Gaza was further enhanced by the realities of the Egyptian administration, which treated the region as a distinct political entity separated from the Egyptian heartland by the Sinai desert.

The structural features of the Gaza Strip economy reflected this political and geographic separation. The main economic activity was agriculture which provided employment to 40 percent of the inhabitants and contributed about one third of the gross national product. Due to the presence of military forces—Egyptian, the Palestinian Liberation Army, UN observers as well as UNRWA personnel, part of the service sector developed more rapidly than other sectors. Even so, the dynamic of the service sector, based on the transitory nature of a garrison society, was not sufficient to introduce many long lasting structural changes into the economy. Most significantly, with the exception of citrus processing activities, there was little industrial development. Largely agricultural and stagnant, with a high level of unemployment, the Gaza Strip economy was even less developed than the West Bank economy. Ultimately though, both economies were most unsuited to face the challenge of the highly industrialized and technological economy of Israel after 1967.[7]

Integration Without Design: 1967–1977

The extremely rapid chain of events which led to the Six Day War and the occupation of the densely populated WB/GS areas left the Israeli Goverment without any coherent policy towards the territories beyond the hope that would be exchanged for a peace treaty. When Arab states rejected the official Israeli peace plan during the Khartoum Conference of 1967, Labor settled for what amounted to a negative policy of no annexation and no withdrawal. Whatever economic philosophy was involved in this position, it was underlaid by the concern that the territories should not become a "net economic burden."[8]

The concept of "net economic burden" was never clearly or officially defined by Israel, but Labor policies in the WB/GS indicate that the

government was anxious to offset some of the considerable costs of administering the territories by promoting local economic activities while
protecting the Israeli economy from Palestinian competition. To this end,
Israel devised the "open bridges" policy which allowed relative free movement
between the West Bank, Gaza Strip and Jordan. At the same time, those
products such as cement or agricultural produce which could compete with
Israeli goods at home or abroad were curtailed. Conversely, Israeli exports
into the territories were encouraged.

This political framework served as a backdrop for the initial stage of
integration of the Israeli and WB/GS economy. Any assessment of the true
scope of the economic interaction is necessarily hampered by the nature
of statistical information. Most of the information is based on data compiled
by Israel's Central Bureau of Statistics. However, as Benvenisti and other
analysts point out, information may at times be misleading or even biased,
especially when for statistical purposes the territories are considered to be
an independent unit. Such an accounting system does not reflect complex
economic interaction over the defunct Green Line or the activity of the
Jewish settlers which is included in the Israeli economy. One cannot describe
the economic interaction between two adjacent localities, such as Kiryat
Arba and Hebron, as "international trade."[9] Furthermore, in the absence
of an official census of WS/GS, the last of which was conducted by Israel
in 1967, the analysis rests on noncensus official population and demographic
statistics conducted by the Central Bureau of Statistics and the Bank of
Israel. Nevertheless, the data provides some indication of the broad patterns
of integration.

The major form of economic integration was based on *direct trade*—
particularly exports of Israeli goods to the territories. With the occupation,
the general direction of WB/GS trade switched from Jordan and Egypt to
Israel, especially with regard to imports. By 1977, 90 percent of the imports
came from Israel. The bulk of imports from Israel, (over two thirds of the
total) consisted of industrial products. By contrast, the imports from Jordan
and the rest of the world reached only 10 percent of Israel's. The export
pattern of the WB/GS was less lopsided, with Israel and Jordan providing
the major markets. Even so, exports to Jordan were less then half of that
going to Israel.

The trends in trade clearly demonstrate the emerging dependent economic
integration. While the WB/GS was almost totally dependent on Israel for
imports and exports, Israel's exports to the WB/GS represented only some
7 percent of its total commodity exports. Imports from the territories
represented just about 3 percent of total Israel's commoditites imports.
With commodity imports from Israel being roughly three times exports,
the WB/GS developed a large negative trade balance, offset by the "export"
of labor to Israel.

In fact, the "export" of WB/GS labor to Israel and the subcontracting for Israel become the second major form of economic integration. After the initial disarray of the war, the number of Palestinian laborers crossing the Green Line daily reached some 10,000 laborers in 1968. Until 1971 most Palestinian workers were employed under a system of official work permits, but the system soon became inadequate as the number of workers burgeoned. Already by the end of that year, 45,000 Palestinians worked in Israel. By 1977, the number with work permits remained constant but total employed reached some 66,000. The rapid growth of the Israeli economy between the 1967 and 1973 wars created a labor shortage at a time when there was high unemployment in the West Bank (12 percent) and Gaza Strip (20 percent.) Higher wages in Israel as well as traditional "hidden unemployment" in the Territories also enhanced this trend.

As in the case of trade, labor based integration showed a markedly one sided dependency. While one third of the West Bank and 40 percent in the Gaza Strip labor force was employed in Israel, Palestinians accounted for only some 5-6 percent of the employed Israeli labor force. However, in some sectors of the Israeli economy and most notably the construction industry Palestinians accounted for over one third of the work force. Overall, cheap and unskilled Palestinian labor has tended to replace Jewish workers in low level positions.

In spite of dependency, economic integration has benefited the WB/GS. While Israel's annual rate of growth between 1967-77 in terms of GNP and gross investment did not exceed 6 percent, the comparable figures for the territories were 13 percent and 26 percent. Part of this high growth rate is explained by the fact that the territories started at an exceptionally low level of development. In addition, the Palestinian labor force employed in Israel generated a high volume of transfer funds which spurred construction and services in WB/GS. However, the high growth rate of the territories was unevenly distributed. Agriculture, construction and services grew at a faster rate than industry. The spectacular level of growth lead to a rapid improvement in the standards of living and a reduction of unemployment.

Overall, though, integration had little impact on Israel. In 1977 the territories represented less than 4 percent of the combined GNP of Israel and the WB/GS. As a result, in the first decade of the occupation, the integration both interms of intensity and scope was easily reversable.

The Emergence of a Binational Economy: 1977–1987

With the ascendance of Likud to power in 1977 new policies aimed at integrating the territories more fully into Israel began to take effect. This was especially true with regard to the West Bank. It should be noted that although up to now we have been treating the West Bank and Gaza Strip as a single unit, they are of course separate economic entities. There is very little trade between the two territories nor much labor movement from one to another. Aside from some products such as cigarettes and cultural items, both economies are oriented towards an exchange with Israel. Jewish settlements in the West Bank were the major form of integration. By 1985, the Israeli state and the Jewish bodies, private and public, had expropriated some 52 percent of all land in the area.[10] The number of settlers in the WB/GS at the end of that year reached 52,000, which is 1.5 percent of the total Jewish population and 4 percent of the population of the territories (excluding Jerusalem.) For legal and statistical purposes these settlers and settlements are treated as if they are part of Israel. This factor makes it difficult to estimate the true scope of integration. For instance, Jewish investors, benefitting from government subsidies, have established economic enterprises in the WB/GS which employ Arab labor. Other settlers commute daily across the Green Line to work in Israel but their earnings support the local economy.

For a variety of reasons, the new wave of integration has not resulted in a rapid rate of growth for the GNP compared to the Labor Period of 1968–1977. The previous 12 percent rate of GNP growth has declined in the 1977–84 period to around 4 percent annually.[11] In the past three years, GNP growth has further declined to 2 percent, slightly above the *Israeli rate of 1.5 percent*. Investment declined and official unemployment reached 3 percent compared to the earlier level of 1 percent. One reason is that in the previous decade growth was disproportionally fast because of the low starting point of the WB/GS economy and its recovery from the war. This growth peaked at a time when the Israeli economy has slowed down considerably. Palestinians also attribute their low growth to government controls over water use and restrictions on crops which compete with Israeli agriculture. Whatever the reasons, statistics suggest a stagnant provincial underdeveloped economy. Its greatest "developmental" factor is the large migratory labor force, standing at 37 .percent in the West Bank and approaching half of the labor force in Gaza.

Thus, in 1985 the GNP of the territories was around $1.6 billion while the Gross Domestic Product (GDP = GNP − Net Transfers) was only $1.12 billion—the difference being largely due to labor earnings in Israel and to a lesser extent in the Gulf. Table 8.2 which compares the sectoral GDP, shows that employment and productivity (GDP/employment) for the WB/GS is relatively small compared to that of Israel. Overall, in 1985 it stood just about 4 percent of that of Israel's, but in certain sectors like manufacturing WB/GS' GNP amounted only to 2 percent of Israel's.

Nearly 90 percent of the WB/GS imports in 1985 came from Israel (see Table 8.3.) These imports to the Territories were utilized as resources for

TABLE 8.2
1985 GDP, Employment, and Productivity in Israel and WB/GS*

	Israel		WB/GS		WB/GS as T of Israel
	$ million	%	$ million	%	
Gross Domestic Product	22,000	100	1,050	100	5
Agriculture	1,320	6	189	18	14
Min., Manuf. & Elec.	5,500	25	95	9	2
Construction	1,760	8	178	17	10
Services	13,420	61	588	56	4
	thousand	%	thousand	%	%
Employed	1,368	100	153	100	11
Agriculture	82	6	37	24	45
Min., Manuf. & Elec.	315	23	25	16	8
Construction	96	7	17	11	18
Services	875	64	74	49	8
	$	%	$	%	%
GDP/Employed (Pry)	16,081	100	6,863	100	43
Agriculture	16,098	100	5,108	75	32
Min., Manuf. & Elec.	17,460	109	3,800	56	22
Construction	18,333	114	10,470	152	57
Services	15,337	95	7,946	115	52

*Source: Adapted from Central Bureau of Statistics (Jerusalem).

consumption and investment. The $602 million in imports represented nearly 36 percent of resources utilized in the WB/GS and the trend intensified in 1986. As in the previous decade WB/GS is dependent in large measure on Israel for its exports. These exports including subcontracting for Israeli industry were over two thirds of the WB/GS exports, with most of the balance going to Jordan. The Israeli economy is less dependent on exports to the WB/GS, which constituted less than 9 percent of the overall total. Nonetheless, the relationship has some significance. Excluding the diamond and defense industries exports, exports to the WB/GS accounted for 22 percent of Israel's exports. The territories are second only to the United States as Israel's main overall market and exceed Israeli exports to the rest of Asia and Oceania.

The emerging binational character of the economy is most pronounced in the labor market. This binationality is best reflected in the very significant difference between the distribution of Jewish and Arab labor including Israeli Arabs (see Table 8.1.) In the productive sectors of the Israeli economy—agriculture, industry and construction, Jewish labor constituted less than one third of the total. In contrast, Arab labor in those sectors accounted for over three fifths of total Arab labor in the Israeli economy. In other words, Arab labor accounted for over 27 percent of production labor in Israel.

TABLE 8.3
1985 Foreign Trade in Goods: The West Bank and Gaza Strip* (millions US $)

	WB	GS	WB+GS	% of Israel's** Trade
Imports: Grand Total	392.4	279.9	672.3	8.1
Agricultural	60.8	41.2	102.0	11.7
Industrial	331.6	238.7	570.3	7.7
From Israel: Total	345.4	257.0	601.9	9.6
Agricultural	54.0	33.7	87.7	18.7
Industrial	291.4	223.3	514.7	8.9
From Jordan: Total	8.7	–	8.7	–
Agricultural	0.3	–	0.3	–
Industrial	8.4	–	8.4	–
From Other Countries: Total	38.3	22.9	61.2	–
Agricultural	6.5	7.9	14.0	–
Industrial	31.8	15.4	47.2	–
Exports: Grand Total	166.4	102.5	268.9	4.3
Agricultural	47.4	30.9	78.3	16.7
Industrial	119.0	71.6	190.6	3.3
To Israel: Total	96.1	81.7	177.8	2.1
Agricultural	14.9	10.1	25.0	2.9
Industrial	81.2	71.6	152.8	2.0
To Jordan: Total	89.3	16.1	85.4	–
Agricultural	32.5	16.1	48.6	–
Industrial	36.8	–	36.8	–
To Other Countries: Total	1.0	4.7	5.7	–
Agricultural	–	4.7	4.7	–
Industrial	1.0	–	1.0	–

*Source: Central Bureau of Statistics Jerusalem
**For Import or Export total – straight comparison of the Israeli date; For Imports from Israel % refers to total Israel Exports and for Exports % refers to total Israel Imports.

Table 8.1 illustrates the structure of Arab labor in Israel. While one sixteenth of the Israeli labor force comes from the territories, where Israeli Arabs are included, Arabs comprise more than one sixth of the total. In construction this proportion reaches five eights, although only one tenth of Arab labor force is in the service sector, mainly in menial positions. It should be noted that over two thirds of the Jewish labor is employed in this sector.

In the combined binational economy nearly one quarter involves Arab workers; in industry one fifth, in construction two thirds and in services only one sixth. Although the Arab sector involves a smaller percentage of the population in employment, that is one fifth as compared to the Jewish employment of one thirds. Arab labor is especially significant in Israeli agriculture and construction.

The dependence of detailed Arab industry on the Jewish sector, of Arab labor on the Jewish sector and Arab trade on the Jewish sector makes it clear that towards the end of the second decade Israel and the WB/GS

moved towards a binational economy with an increasing amount of integration. Nevertheless, the different scale of the two economies and the
different stages of their development means that the WB/GS economy is
more dependent on the Israeli economy than vice versa. Despite this
dependence, the WB/GS economy can still function as a separate unit in
the event of political separation. This dichotomy constitutes the major
characteristic of a binational economy. That is, the WB/GS is simultaneously
an integral part of the larger (Israeli dominated) binational economy and
economic subsystem identifiably separate from that of Israel.

Another interesting conclusion is that the present pattern of economic
relations is unlikely to increase the degree of integration of the two semi-
separate economies, even if the political stalemate should continue in the
next decade. In other words, in the absence of political design specifically
aimed at economic integration, the mere political co-existence of Israel and
the territories would not result in a unitary economy in the next decade.
The political implication of the economic realities detailed above are
extremely important. Since the binational economy is fully reversable, the
economic factor should play a fairly negligible role in the decision to either
relinquish or annex the territories. However, there are different economic
costs attached to the two major alternatives of peacefully giving up the
territories or forcibly annexing West Bank and Gaza.

Alternative Scenarios to 1997

One of the most difficult tasks in discussing the various options for
solving the present political impress with regard to the territories involves
calculating the economic cost of various scenarios. In the absence of an
objective economic projection, the discussion about various solution tends
to be politicized along ideological lines. Proponents of a peaceful withdrawal
from the territories argue that cheap Arab labor and a captive market
hampered the introduction of high technology necessary for Israel's global
competition. Added to the price of continuous war and occupation, this
cost makes the Territories an overall economic burden. Advocates of
annexation point out that in addition to strategic advantages, the territories
are a major economic advantage, especially for Jewish settlement. The
following analysis would provide a projection based on two scenarios—a
peaceful relinquishment and a forceful retention of the territories. There
are scenarios which fall in between these two outcomes, although the
number of variations to consider makes the results of such plans difficult
to assess. Nonetheless, some possible permutations will also be discussed.

As stated, the two major scenarios are basically an Israeli-dominated,
forced "unity," or seperate development, with possible economic cooperation

on more equal terms (see Appendix A for forecasting methods and as-sumptions used).

The first scenario is basically a continuation of present government policies aimed at continued Jewish settlement in the area and integration of the WB/GS economy with that of Israel, also known as the "Greater Israel" option. Possible variations of the scenario range from complete annexation with full civil rights for the occupied areas and their inhabitants, to some form of "local autonomy." At the other end of the spectrum of the "Greater Israel" option is the establishment of WB/GS autonomy for Arab inhabitants with an economy fully integrated into that of Israel. However, the inhabitants would enjoy only a limited degree of self-rule and no integration into the Israeli political process. Economic transactions with Jordan and the rest of the Arab world would be minimized. Realistically speaking, few if any other countries in the world would recognize or approve of such an entity, which might adversely affect Israel's relations with her major aid and trading partners.

The alternative scenario involves separation of Israel from the territories, resulting in separate economic development. In essence, the plan envisions two national economies, Israel and the territories. This might range from a (relatively) demilitarized, independent Palestinian state in the WB/GS to a confederation or union of a dimilitarized WB/GS with Jordan. There could be close cooperation between the WB/GS and Jordan.

There are of course in-between scenarios of territorial partition between Israel and Jordan (Allon Plan), statutory binational or pluralist state with full immigration rights for Jews and Palestinian, or Israeli annexation of the territories while granting the inhabitants Jordanian citizenship (which many already hold). While some of these variations have been considered above, there are too many possible permutations to fully treat all scenarios. In any event, most variations would fall in between the two "extreme" positions outlined here.

The economics and populations resulting from each of the two scenarios are significantly different. This is demonstrated in Table 8.4, where the results of separate development are compared to those of Greater Israel. In the Greater Israel model, net Jewish immigration to Israel (which has fallen considerably in recent years, approaching zero growth rate) would be slight, because potential immigrants would be dissuaded by the political and security ramifications of binational Israel. By 1997, over 40 percent of the population would be Arab, based on a (low) 1.5 percent growth rate per anum of the Jewish population and a (high) 3 percent growth rate for the Arab population. The separation scenario might instead result in a higher net Jewish emigration to Israel, since some population loss is attributed directly or indirectly to the unsettled questions of binationalism.[12] This option could involve a massive return of Palestinian expatriates, (possibly

TABLE 8.4
Alternative Economic Projections for Israel and West Bank/Gaza Strip 1985*-1997**

	1985*		1997 Greater Israel (GI)		1997 Separate Development (SD)		1997 Difference %	
	Israel	WB/GS	Israel	WB/GS	Israel	WB/GS	Israel	WB/GS
A. Population & Employment (thousand)								
1. Average Population	4,264	1,336	5,170	1,740	5,410	2,800	4.8	60.9
2. Average Jewish Population	3,516	(48)	4,090	(144)	4,460	$\overline{500}$	9.8	–
3. Employment (adjusted for 1985 Hours)	1,368	242	1,730	315	1,950	500	12.7	$\overline{58.7}$
B. Distribution of GNP & Resources ($ million)								
4. Gross National Product (GNP)	20,950	1,600	28,500	2,400	41,700	5,400	46.3	125
5. Defense Expenditure (G_o)	4,920	–	7,410	–	4,920	100	-33.6	–
6. Government Civilian Consumption (G_c)	2,400	160	3,140	$\overline{220}$	4,590	800	46.2	263.6
7. Private Consumption (P)	14,040	1,200	17,380	1,780	24,270	3,600	39.6	102.2
8. Investment (T)	4,030	320	6,270	500	12,090	1,900	92.8	280.0
9. Resources ($R = G_o + G_c + P + T$)	25,390	1,680	34,200	2,500	45,870	5,800	34.1	132.0
10. Import Surplus ($IS = GNP - R$)	4,440	80	5,700	100	4,170	1,000	-26.8	900.0
11. Gross Civilian Product ($GCP = GNP - G_o$)	16,030	1,600	21,090	2,400	36,780	5,300	74.4	120.0
C. Per Capita Indices ($)								
12. GNP/Capita	4,913	1,198	5,510	1,380	7,710	1,930	39.9	39.8
13. GNP/Employment	15,314	6,612	16,010	7,620	21,610	10,500	35.0	41.7
14. Defense/Capita	1,154	–	1,430	–	909	35	-36.4	–
15. Private Consumption/Capita	3,293	898	3,360	1,020	4,490	1,280	33.6	25.5
D. Twelve Year Growth ** Indices (% per annum)								
16. Population	2.1	2.1	1.6	2.2	2.0	6.4	0.4	4.2
17. Jewish Population	1.8	–	1.3	(9.8)	2.0	–	0.7	–
18. Employment	2.0	1.6	2.2	2.0	3.0	6.4	1.0	4.2
19. GNP	2.2	3.7	2.6	3.4	6.0	7.0	4.4	3.6
20. Defense Expenditure	-1.0	–	3.5	–	–	–	-3.5	–
21. Government Civilian Consumption	4.0	1.8	2.3	2.2	5.5	14.5	3.2	12.3
22. Private Consumption	3.0	3.5	1.8	3.3	4.6	9.8	2.8	6.5
23. Investment	-1.0	1.5	3.7	3.6	5.7	11.8	2.0	8.2

Sources: *Central Bureau of Statistics, Jerusalem; **Bahiri, S., "Peaceful Separation or Enforced Unity: Economic Consequences for Israel and West Bank/Gaza Area," International Center for Peace in the Middle East, Tel Aviv 1984.

up to 600,000), creating the problems of absorptive capacity, although this would be less of a problem for Israel than it would be for any future government of this area. Table 8.4 illustrates that while Israel's Jewish population may be nearly 10 percent greater, the territories' Arab population could be up to 60 percent greater in the event of separate development. Nonetheless, it is fair to assume that both the WB/GS and Israel would receive considerable economic assistance from Arab countries and the international community.

We should also look at the effect of separation on the GNP and budgetary expenditures. In the event of separation, the gross civilian product (GNP less defense) would, in 1997 be nearly three quarters greater for Israel. The GNP would be up to one and a half times as large. Investment under separate development would be nearly twice the level it would be under annexation, while defense costs would be nearly two-thirds less. The GNP would grow at a rate of 6 percent rather than 2.6 percent. In general, our analysis shows that the demographic and economic structure of Israel would be better off without the territories. This would in turn generate some interdependence between Israel and its neighbors, thus helping to strengthen a vested interest in peace.

In the Greater Israel scenario, the WB/GS would become increasingly integrated into the core country. The current level of WB/GS employment in Israel, shown in Table 8.1 to exceed 37 percent in 1985, would rise, imports would be overwhelmingly (90 percent) from Israel, and exports to Israel would continue at the rate of nearly 70 percent. Nevertheless, full economic integration would not be achieved. The realities of binationalism in Israel (different languages, religions and cultures), almost guarantee that the WB/GS economies would maintain their identities, with many products produced in the territories or consumed locally.

The political separation of WB/GS from Israel would result in the development of an autonomous economic entity, capable of economic cooperation with Israel. Due to comparative advantage, such a Palestinian entity might actually import more from Israel, but this would represent a smaller percentage of imports or of overall economic activity. In short, the relationship would change from one of increasing dependence of the periphery on the core to one of greater equality of unitary economies.

Conclusion

Our analysis of the relationship between Israel and the West Bank and the Gaza strip shows that the present binational economy is the result of a particular concentration of several factors. These include the prestate experience of economic "Jewish-Arab dualism," the period of separate economic development from 1948–1967, the ad hoc, gradual economic integration under the Labor government under dependent conditions, and the Likud and National Unity government policies of increased economic integration. Nevertheless, due to the nature of binationalism cited above, no significant change in the continuing integration is expected in the near future unless there is some political breakthrough regarding negotiations with the Palestinians and/or neighboring Arab states.

At present, most of the direct costs of military occupation and administration are transferred to the inhabitants of the occupied territories. In addition, the extra earnings of value added by low cost Palestinian migrant workers, exports to the territories, cheap imports from the territories, and land and water resources expropriated from the WB/GS by Israel all lead to an overall net gain for Israel and a loss for the inhabitants of the territories. Nonetheless, this gain to Israel is far smaller than could be earned in both economies if there was a peaceful separation of Israel and the WB/GS and increased economic cooperation among all countries of the region.

The two alternative senarios presented above are stark in their implications for future economic development of Israel. While the present trend of the last twenty years has been towards integration, the alternative option of repention is still possible, and even desirable, when the long range demographic and economic implications of Greater Israel are considered. An economic analysis of binationalism thus demonstrates that there is still time to choose between the two paths of the future.

Appendix A

The basic approach used is exploratory forecasting—i.e., leading from the present situation along probable lines of development for each scenario. The forecasting methods applied involved both "objective" and subjective (intuitive) approaches which were quantified.

In order to generate economic and national accounts data from 1985 to 1997 a modified Cobb-Douglas Production Function econometric model was used for Israel. This model assumed that the annual growth in the GNP, AGNP/GNP or E is a function of the net capital increase (NCI) as a proportion of capital stock (CS)— i.e., $K = NCI/CS$: the per annum growth rate in labor hours—L and a residual productivity factor R. Relative proportions were given to K and L and the basic Formula $E = 0.4K + 0.6L + R$ where R is 1 percent for the option of retaining the Territories—e.g., "Greater Israel" and 2 percent for the "separate development" of Israel and the territories: The difference in R stems from the additional opportunities generated within the framework of peaceful economic cooperation. The net capital increase was a function of new investment I less depreciation of capital stock (6 percent per annum). New investment in 1985 was just over 18 percent of GNP and was assumed to have risen to 22 percent (the average in recent years) gradually by 1997 for the territorial retention option. For the separate development option a gradual increase to 29 percent (less than the pre-occupation average) of GNP by 1997 was used. The labor factor allowed for greater net immigration and a smaller standing army in the separate development option, and an increase in labor hours due to a decrease in reserve duty. The labor hours generated in this case (separation) increased by an estimated 3 percent per annum, while under continued occupation the increase was only 2 percent. Defense spending for "Greater Israel" was assumed to slightly rise per annum from 1985 to 1997 to reach 26 percent of the GNP—the post-1967 average—and for "separation" no increase nor reduction in defense expenditure were assumed.

Similar methods were used for the WB/GS. Moreover, the structural changes expected because of a massive return of Palestine expatriates (600,000) and the return of labor employed in Israel required that the model be augmented by normative methods as well as by analogical and intuitive inputs. Normative methods included setting minimum development targets and allocating resources to them, analogous to Israel in its early years. Inputs also involved a high degree of intuitive judgement.

Notes

1. Jacob Metzer and Oded Kaplan, *Jointly but Severally Arab-Jewish Dualism and Economic Growth in Mandatory Palestine*, (Jerusalem: The Maurice Felt Institute for Economic Research in Israel, 1985).

2. Don Peretz, *The Middle East Today*, 4th ed., (New York: Praeger, 1983), p. 346.

3. Peter Gubser, *Jordan Crossroads of Middle Eastern Events*, (Boulder, CO: Westview 1983) p. 51.

4. Eliyau Kanovsky, *The Economic Impact of the Six Day War*, (New York: Praeger, 1970).

5. Hillel Frisch, *Stagnation and Frontier: Arab and Jewish Industry in the West Bank*, (Jerusalem: The West Bank Data Base Project, 1986).

6. Kanovsky, ibid.

7. Sara Roy, *The Gaza Strip Survey*, (Jerusalem: The West Bank Data Base Project, 1986).

8. Brian Van Arkadie, *Benefits and Burdens: A Report on the West Bank and Gaza Strip Economics Since 1967*, (New York: Carnegie Endowment for International Peace, 1977).

9. Meron Benvenisti, *1986 Demographic, Economic, Legal, Social and Political Development in the West Bank*, (Jerusalem: The West Bank Data Base Project, 1986).

10. Ibid.

11. Avi Temkin, "Territories Find Most Routes to Economic Growth Blocked," *The Jerusalem Post*, August 27, 1986.

12. Simcha Bahiri, *Peaceful Separation or Enforced Unit: The Economic Consequences for Israel and the West Bank/Gaza Strip*, (Tel Aviv: International Center for Peace in the Middle East, 1984).

PART 3

International Implications of a Binational Israel

9

Israel and the Arab States in the Binational Era

Don Peretz

A major theme of this volume is that the New Israel, which emerged since Begin's Second Republic, is becoming or has already become a binational state. The policies espoused by the Herut wing of Likud served to diminish the Jewish exclusivity of the country by assuring that Israel will be not only demographically, but culturally and ideologically binational. As a result, the Arab population, within and beyond the Green Line, has become more aggressive in pursuit of its national rights and more resistant to attempts by Zionist ideologues to deny Israel's binational character.

As experience in other binational or multinational situations has demonstrated, seemingly domestic matters such as the relations between ethnic majorities and minorities, often have foreign policy implications. Israel itself regards treatment of Jews in the Soviet Union, not as a Soviet domestic concern, but as a matter of international import.

Obviously, the situation of Israeli Arab citizens and Arabs in the occupied territories is no less important to the surrounding Arab states than the situation of Soviet Jews is for Israel. As Israeli government policies towards Arabs under its jurisdiction inevitably lead to intensified Arab or Palestinian Arab consciousness, surrounding Arab governments are likely to seek involvement as spokesmen for or protectors of Palestinian national rights. As long as a state of war prevails with these states, Israel will be free to ignore their intervention. If peaceful relations exist, the policies of the Israeli government towards their Arab citizens will no doubt be a major issue in the relations between Israel and the surrounding Arab states. In order to understand how binational tension may effect the future of Israeli-Arab relations an historical overview is in order.

Arab Perspectives on Binationalism in Palestine

The present position of the Arab states toward binationalism can be traced to Arab and Muslim concepts of nationalism and statehood, and how these evolved in response to colonialism and Zionism.

The traditional Arab concept of national group identity was based on the Ottoman millet system of rules in the Middle East. The recognized millets, Muslim, Greek Orthodox, Armenian Gregorian, Jewish, and later Catholic, had gained autonomy in religion, culture, education and law, resulting in a patchwork of communities living side by side. However, the Muslim Ottoman Empire favored the Muslim millet, particularly in legal disputes against the *dhimmi*, or non-Muslims. This fragmentation would eventually undermine the integrity of the empire, as European powers, particularly the French and Russians, proclaimed themselves protectors of various Christian communities, and sought favorable economic treatment for their charges. First the periphery, and eventually the heartland of the empire was rocked by these forces. Even before the Ottoman collapse during World War I, Arabs had clamored for self-determination. They regarded the mandate system as an unsatisfactory, divisive solution.[1]

The second component of group identity, Arab nationalism, thus emerged in an area of cultural homogeneity despite lack of religious homogeneity. Homogeneity was the product of a common language and similar historical experience, all of which in the face of Ottoman domination and European colonialism had contributed to what Nadav Safran and others have called the impulse towards unity. Arab nationalism was viewed as a means to knit together religious communities in a common nationhood.[2] Though complete political unity under Arab rulers had not existed for many centuries, the psychological pull of nationalism had a legitimizing potential which inspired many short lived attempts at union among the diverse states.

At the same time, there were numerous obstacles to unity, produced by geographical discontinuities, patterns of development in government and society, uneven distribution of resources and population, and external rule, particularly colonialism. The piecemeal, disjointed independence movement, spanning from a semiautonomous Transjordan in 1921 to the revolutionary separation of Algeria in 1962 and to the withdrawal of British forces from the Arabian peninsula at the end of the decade, had a profound effect on the ability of governments to successfully implement political unity. As Safran notes, once independence was achieved, there were strong vested interests in the existing state structures that worked against unity.[3] In addition, throughout the century, states and groups within states have sought to exercise control over the means and goals of Arab unity. The Baath rivalry between Syria and Iraq, Abdullah's push for Transjordanian control over Palestine, and Nasser's Arab nationalism all sought the dominion of their particular political vision over the Arab world.

The evolution of pan-Arabism was also affected by the formation of the state of Israel. Already during the Mandate period diverse ideological currents had divided the Arab states, some semi-sovereign and others still under colonial rule, but all using the growing Jewish presence in Palestine in an attempt to maximize their positions both within Palestine and in the region as a whole. The works of Lesch document the extent to which these divisions contrasted with the more unified Zionist movement.[4] The prospect of a Jewish state in Palestine, the juncture of the Arab East (Mashreq) and West (Maghreb) represented a direct threat to the vision of Arab unity. In addition, the symbolic importance of Jerusalem (al-Quds) as the third holiest city in Islam should be stressed as a factor motivating the Arab states' opposition to Zionism.

Last, the question of group identity was affected by the differential impact of the forces of modernization, urbanization, education and mass media, challenging traditional legitimacy patterns based on tribal loyalties and norms. The conflicts between conservative and radical states, so well described by Malcolm Kerr and others, were like a fault line beneath other dynamics, such as the Arab-Israeli conflict, and becoming manifest every few years in the tremors that shook the Arab world.[5]

The concepts unifying these diverse facets of group identity are best described by Noble in his discussion of the Arab system.[6] He distinguishes between the domestic setting of Arab states (where geography, population, social and political structure, and military and economic capabilities are important variables) and the Arab setting, produced by the transnational linkages of language, religion, migration, and common core concerns, such as Arab unity, the Palestinians, and Islam.

The domestic setting of different states has alternated between periods of instability and challenges to old and new regimes (frequently framed in ideological terms) and periods of stability and pragmatism, where ideology was less important than consideration of national interest. The Arab enviroment played an important role in influencing the domestic setting, because the common perception of Arab identity meant every Arab state, particularly the more powerful ones, felt it had the right to intervene in the domestic politics of its neighbors and did so through propaganda and subversion. Cross frontier alliances were facilitated by political parties, such as the Baath, or charismatic leaders, such as Nasser.

The Arab system has characteristic properties in "the basic structure and distribution of power, the sources and level of conflict, and the patterns of conflict and alignment."[7] From the 1950s to the 1980s patterns of behavior in the system have varied considerably. The system in the 1950s and 1960s was revisionist in that actors sought to change the orientation and position of other actors. In the early period, limited military and economic resources restricted the ability of Arab states to use traditional instruments of statecraft, but not such tools as subversion and external alliances. The system was dominated by Egypt, due to its superior material and cultural capabilities (manpower, communications and cultural institutions such as the university). There were several sources of conflict, especially issues relating to the orientation towards outside powers and ideological issues of the legitimate domestic, political, economic, and social order. Patterns of alignments basically pitted conservative, pro-Western states such as Saudi Arabia and Jordan against Egypt, Syria and Iraq vying for the leadership of the radical, republican camp. But all actors "through conviction or through fear of the political consequences"[8] were united in opposing recognition of Israel. Noble notes that there was competitive posturing as second rank states challenged Egypt to be tougher on Israel, as in the Suez War or during the Jordan Waters dispute in the early 1960s.

The pattern of power changed considerably in the 1970s for several reasons. The 1967 defeat, rapid population growth, the strains of a war economy, and the limitations of state socialism reduced Egypt's capabilities. Nasser's death had also reduced Egypt's tendency to apply unifying pressure on the system, resulting in political fragmentation and the establishment of local spheres of influence (Saudi Arabia in the Arabian peninsula; Syria in the Western Fertile Crescent, etc.) Directional issues of ideology and orientation towards Israel increased in importance due to the magnitude of the 1967 defeat, the Israeli occupation of the territories and the emergence of Palestinian nationalism. The turbulance generated by the 1967 war split the Arab countries. On the one hand, there was a moderate Arab coalition headed by Saudi Arabia, Jordan and Egypt which favored pressuring the U.S. to settle the Arab/Israeli conflict. They were opposed by a coalition of Iraq, Syria, Algeria, radical elements in the PLO and other lesser actors hostile to American influence. Egypt's eventual decision to recognize Israel and participate in the Camp David Summit weakened the moderate coalition while at the same time sharpening the debate about the most appropriate Arab response to the growing binationalism in Israel.

Arab Response to the Begin Revolution

Since 1977 Israel's policies towards West Bank Arabs have become a prime factor in relations with Egypt, Lebanon and Jordan. The dynamics established between Israeli occupation policies and Arab reactions has intensified considerably. Almost from the beginning of the negotiations between Israel and Egypt, they differed on the issue of the current and future status of the West Bank and Gaza Strip. The crux of the disagreement was that the Begin government desired to perpetuate the binational character of Israel created after 1967, whereas Egypt preferred to terminate Israel's jurisdiction over the occupied territories and the Palestinians.[9]

Begin's autonomy proposals presented to the Knesset in his 26 point "peace plan" in December 1977 foresaw the integration of the West Bank into Israel; autonomy would apply to the Arab inhabitants but not to the territory which would become an integral part of the Jewish state. The Green Line, Begin insisted, "no longer exists, it has vanished forever. There is no line anymore. We want to coexist with the Arabs in Eretz Israel . . . under the autonomy scheme they will run their own internal affairs and we will ensure security . . . Jews and Arabs will coexist in Judea and Samaria as they do in Jerusalem, Ramle, Jaffa and Haifa."[10] With the abolition of military government in the occupied areas, the Arab residents would receive "administrative autonomy," electing a council charged to manage local matters such as health, education, social welfare and the like. With erasure of the Green Line and integration of the territories into Israel, the Arab residents would be free to choose either Israeli or Jordanian citizenship; all inhabitants of the state, Jewish and Arab, would be free to move within the extended boundaries. In effect, the proposal would create a "New Israel," with a larger area and population, more demographically diverse than the pre-1967 state, and considerably less Jewish.

Egypt and Palestinian Arab nationalists in the occupied territories opposed Begin's binational scheme because it imposed autonomy without consulting the Arab inhabitants and excluded them from full participation in important aspects of policy such as foreign and security affairs. In fact, Begin's interpretation of autonomy amounted to recognition of Arab rights in much the same way that Jewish "personal autonomy" was recognized in pre-World War I Western Europe. Jews were then recognized as a national minority with cultural autonomy, elected to West European parliaments, and permitted to manage a number of communal institutions and affairs.[11]

Since Begin's autonomy was adamantly opposed by even the more moderate Arab states, binationalism soon vanished from the agenda for peace negotiations. Egypt and the moderate Arab states proposed that autonomy lead towards full self-government in the occupied territories, separate from Israel, and preferably in some arrangement involving Jordan. The radical Arab states and Palestinian Arab nationalists opposed any form of autonomy and pushed for immediate statehood.

As the Arab opposition to the Camp David autonomy proposals intensified, there was an increase of identification with the PLO and its leader, Yassir Arafat. Nearly all surveys as well as observations by Israel's Military Government authorities at that time, indicated that the vast majority of West Bank/Gaza Arabs considered the PLO their sole legitimate representative and Arafat as their principal leader.[12] Consequently, the Begin government perceived the PLO as the greatest obstacle to integrating the territories into "New Israel."

Israeli Policy and the Palestinians

In an attempt to undermine PLO influence in the West Bank the Likud government decided to implement the autonomy scheme unilaterally. In November 1981, Military Order 967 established a civilian administration to "look after the civilian affairs of the Israeli inhabitants."[13] Civilian matters were to be separated from military and security affairs and placed under a new Head of the Civilian Administration appointed by the IDF area commander. The new Civilian Administrator, Menachem Milson, was an IDF reserve colonel whose recommendations for dealing with the PLO had caught the attention of Defense Minister Ariel Sharon.[14]

The Civilian Administrator was a professor of Arabic language and literature at the Hebrew University and a well known "Arabist." In an article in the May 1981 issue of *Commentary* magazine, Milson argued that Israel's failure to "play by the rules" of Middle East Arab politics and the previous Labor government's "non-intervention" policies in the West Bank had enabled the PLO to achieve political domination over the Arab population in the occupied territories.[15] This success had "silenced" the peaceful majority which was really eager to negotiate with Israel and willing to accept the autonomy plan. Because of intimidation by the PLO, West Bank and Gaza politicians were reluctant to join the peace process or engage in the autonomy talks. This position resulted in a deadlock in the Israeli-Egyptian-American peace negotiations and deterioration in relations between Jerusalem and Cairo. Milson perceived the need for a totally new policy to eradicate PLO influence and encourage "moderates." His tactic was to exploit traditional inter-Arab rivalries like those between West Bank rural and urban notables. According to Milson the PLO was backed by the urban elites who won the 1976 local elections. To counteract their influence, a rural resurgence would be encouraged through organization by the Military Government of Village Leagues whose members were regarded by urbanites as backward "illiterates."

The "rule of the game" as seen by Milson included offers to those who collaborated with Israel of financial patronage, priorities in employment and housing, establishment of a Regional Development Fund to disburse largesse to the Village Leagues, as well as extending League authority in regions where the organization was located. While every "encouragement" would be extended to "cooperative" elements, pressure would be exerted on those unwilling to "play the game." To strengthen control of the Israeli military authorities, millions of dollars supplied by Saudi Arabia to PLO supporters were cut off; personalities and institutions through which PLO influence had been exercised were punished in increasingly harsh ways; more severe methods were applied to "pacify" militant nationalists such as students in the four West Bank Arab universities and publishers of PLO inclined Arabic newspapers. Within a few months most mayors in the largest West Bank were dismissed, the pace of expulsions was increased, curfews, demolition of houses, seizure of property, and imprisonment without trial were used with increasing frequency against disloyal elements.

Regional and International Repercussions

The policies of the new Civil Administration (intended to undermine separatist tendencies and strengthen Begin's binationalist autonomy scheme) stirred strong protest in the occupied territories, within Israel itself among both Jewish and Arab citizens, and in the international community. Israel was castigated at the United Nations, was the target of diplomatic attack by Arab and Third World countries, and by Egypt, which further cooled its relations with the Begin government. By the end of 1981 the growing number and intensity of protests in the West Bank was the harbinger of a full-scale civil insurrection. The number and severity of bloody encounters with Israeli armed forces was greater than at any period in the previous thirteen years of occupation. Against Milson's advice the army chief-of-staff, General Rafael Eitan, increased personal and collective punishments and extended the authority of Jewish West Bank settlers to combat the unrest.

It became increasingly obvious that Sharon's Civil Administration was not working. His tactics were criticized by Labor in the Knesset and by editorials in most major newspapers. The *Jerusalem Post* observed in an editorial: "It is hard to believe that anybody in his right mind expects the army's punitive measures to cause the Palestinians to warm up to the idea of autonomy."[16] Sharon's failure to excise the PLO from the West Bank was a major factor leading to his June 1982 invasion of Lebanon. As early as December 1981 he revealed to U.S. Ambassador Samuel W. Lewis that the proposed invasion would help "solve the problems of the West Bank and Gaza."[17] Indeed, destruction of PLO military bases and other infrastructure in Lebanon was one of the three principal objectives. The other two were to force Syrian troops from Lebanon and to establish a Lebanese government which would accommodate its policies to Sharon's larger regional schemes. All together, they were designed to force the moderate and radical Arab states to accept the Israeli binational vision.

Ironically, the outcome of the war had severely undermined Likud's ability to push for the binational idea. Although the PLO infrastructure was destroyed, the nationalist sentiments in the West Bank hardly diminished. Due to international and regional outrage over the war and incidents like the massacre at Sarba and Shatila, Likud's concepts of binationalism became even less acceptable to Egypt and inhibited any dialogue with Jordan. Worse, the political and human sacrifices of the war convinced the Israeli public that the cost of binationalism may be too high.

The political deadlock over binationalism became manifest in the Israeli National Unity Government (NUG) established in 1984.[18] While many in Labor would be willing to divest Israel of heavily inhabited Arab areas in the occupied territories, Likud has worked to diminish possibilities of separation between pre-1967 Israel and "New Israel." Whereas Labor members of the NUG have called for a slowdown or even cessation of Jewish settlement and of policies which would lead to economic and infrastructural integration of the territories, Likud and its supporters insist on more rapid integration and policies which would inevitably lead toward a binational state. The result has been an impasse with agreement to maintain the status quo that existed when the NUG assumed office. This impasse has also stymied the several initiatives of Shimon Peres to renew the peace process.

The schism within Israel made it more difficult for the Arab states to formulate new policies on binationalism. The moderates and especially Egypt and Jordan warmly responded to Shimon Peres' efforts to create an atmosphere of accomodation. By far the most promising move was the Peres initiative in his speech to the U.N. General Assembly during 1986. His proposals were novel in that they departed from previous Israeli opposition to conducting negotiations within an international forum including the Soviet Union and because they did not overtly attack the PLO, contrary to the usual Israeli procedure. Later interpretation of the Prime Minister's comments suggested that he would agree to talks that included Palestinian representatives who would agree to accept Israel's legitamacy. King Hussein welcomed the "spirit" of the Peres Plan proclaiming that it represented "the beginning of movement in the right direction" and also reflected "a personal concern for the fate of future generations and a determination to contribute towards the achievement of peace in our time," by "a man of vision." Egypt responded with steps to improve relations in the "cold peace."[19] Negotiations were renewed with Cairo over Taba, the tiny enclave held by Israel adjoining its Red Sea port Eilat, disputed since the 1979 peace treaty.

But the stringent opposition of Likud and the internal squabbles in Labor brought upon by Yitshak Rabin's hard line towards the PLO, deterred the Arab states from a more serious commitment. When the Israel Air Force bombed PLO headquarters in Tunis, in response to a terrorist attack on Israeli vacationers in Cyprus, the action was generally perceived as a victory for hardliners in the National Unity Cabinet and reinforced the Arab hardliners as well.

The raid was condemned by the U.N. Security Council; Egypt and Jordan, the Arab states most active in responding to the Peres iniatives, joined the condemnation. In Cairo thousands of demonstrators demanded that Egypt sever relations with both Israel and the U.S. and President Mubarak suspended the Taba talks in protest. The climate of accommodation was further disrupted by seizure of an Italian tourist ship, the Achille Lauro, off the coast of Alexandria, by a PLO faction. Although Israel was not involved, its close ties with the U.S. placed it in the line of fire by Arab nationalists protesting American responses to the ship hijacking.

Israeli withdrawal from Lebanon, though seemingly a step towards disengagement from Sharon's binational design, hardly allayed Arab agitation. Although Israel was no longer "officially" in Lebanon, its influence remained pervasive in the south and Israeli policies were held accountable by the Arab states and Palestinians for continued unrest in southern Lebanon. In the West Bank and Gaza and among Israeli Arab citizens in particular, Israeli involvement in Lebanon was perceived as a direct affront to Palestinian consciousness, identity and demand for self-determination. Coinciding with the continuous unrest in the occupied territories, these sentiments made it difficult for either Jordan or Egypt to pursue their preferred response to the Peres initiative.

To make things worse, a major schism over binationalism developed in the NUG between Peres and the Likud members who vowed that Israel would never give up the territories. These inconsistencies made it difficult for Egypt and Jordan to determine who was in charge: Peres with his accommodationist approach or the Shamir-Sharon-Arens binationalist camp. Was the moderate Ezer Weizman, charged with Israeli Arab affairs, the representative spokesman for Labor or the hardline Defense Minister Yitzhak Rabin?

These ambiguities increased the political in fighting and indecision within the PLO. During 1985 high hopes were raised that the pact signed between PLO leader Yassar Arafat and King Hussein would remove many obstacles to a settlement.[20] According to the pact both Jordan and the PLO agreed to participate in peace negotiations under auspices of an international conference in which the PLO, as part of a joint Jordanian-Palestinian delegation, would be recognized as the sole legitimate representative of the Palestinian people. Lack of response to the Hussein-Arafat accord by the U.S. and its denunciation by Likud strengthened the hand of the militant factions within the PLO. They were aided by the radical Arab countries who all along objected to any solution involving binational concepts.

As a result, early in 1986 King Hussein renounced the agreement, accusing Arafat of failure to accept U.N. Security Council resolution 242 and 338 as a basis for a settlement, and of dragging his feet. In a marked policy switch, the King now coordinated his policy in the occupied territories with Israel, where the NUG announced that it would seek to "improve the quality of life." This meant allowing for foreign (largely American) investments in the occupied areas, opening of some Arab banks in the territories and replacement of Israeli officials in municipal posts with West Bank residents sympathetic to the Jordanian monarchy. King Hussssein indicated his approval with a call for a five year, $1 billion economic aid plan.[21] As conceived by Labor, the cooperation with Jordan was designed to rebuild a pro-Hashamite constituency on the West Bank. Such a constituency could be used at a later stage for giving up the West Bank to Jordan.

Labor's cooperation with Jordan was criticized by Likud, since it could have undermined the plans to establish a binational state where Israeli authorities would be in full control. In the final analysis Likud had the upper hand: while the continuation of the status quo on which NUG agreement was based prevented Labor from using the West Bank and Gaza as bargaining chips, it did not prevent Likud from "thickening" the Jewish presence, expand the existing settlements' integration of the electricity grid, acquire additional land and water resources, and increase Jewish commercial investment.

Despite opposition from Likud and the approaching termination of Peres' tenure as prime minister, he attempted to keep the negotiation process alive. In July 1986 he secretly visited Morocco where he met with King Hassan for two days to discuss the Arab League's 1982 Fez peace plan. Although Peres radiated optimism at conclusion of the talks, King Hassan emphasized his failure to persuade Israel's prime minister to accept the PLO as a negotiating partner and to evacuate the occupied territories, two goals which were hardly realistic in light of Labor's association with Likud in the NUG.[22]

Arab reaction varied from overt Egyptian approval to frantic denunciations by hardliners. The militants seemed to win the day when Hassan resigned from his titular post as president of the Arab League and the 1984 Oujda treaty of union between Morocco and Libya was cancelled.

In spite of these setbacks, Peres, in his last months as Prime Minister, succeeded in improving Egyptian-Israeli relations. At the September 1986 summit meeting in Alexandria Peres and Egyptian President Mubarak agreed to place the Taba dispute before international arbitration and to renew further discussions on normalization of relations. The Alexandria Declaration marked "a new era in bilateral relations . . . as well as in the search for a just and comprehensive peace in the Middle East." The year 1987, they declared, was to be "a year of negotiations for peace" all parties to the conflict were called "to dedicate this year to intensive efforts to achieve the common and noble objective of a just, lasting and comprehensive peace."

As a token of its earnest intent, Egypt reappointed a new ambassador to Israel replacing the one withdrawn in 1982 to protest Israel's invasion of Lebanon. Differences still persisted, primarily over Egypt's insistence that the PLO be recognized as the legitimate representative of the Palestinians and a full-fledged partner in any peace negotiations.[23]

Likud at the Helm

The struggle over binationalism intensified when Shamir replaced Peres as the Prime Minister in the NUG. A key issue was Labor's initiative for an international peace conference charged with finding a comprehensive settlement of the Arab-Israeli dispute. Shamir and his associates opposed such a conference fearing it might apply pressure on Israel to return any of the occupied territories. Moderates in Likud were satisfied with the status quo in the occupied territories. They hoped that in time the West Bank and Gaza would become part of Israel, like the territories Israel acquired beyond the 1947 U.N. Partition Plan. If a sufficiently long period passed and discussion of the territories would be minimized in international debate, even the Arab states and the Palestinians would adjust to the "New Israel."

Precedent seemed to justify the analysis. Between 1948 and 1967 not only the Arab states, but the larger international community refused to accept Israel's armistice frontiers as *de jure*. Even the U.S. refused to transfer its embassy to the Jewish sector of Jerusalem lest the move signify American recognition of the armistice lines as definitive borders. Within twenty years preceeding the Six Day War several Western statesmen, including Anthony Eden and John Foster Dulles, have proposed border "compromise" that would have cut Israeli territory back to the original UN Partition Plan. Some Western leaders even proposed a settlement based on Israel's surrender of the Negev or Western Galilee.

Victory in the 1967 war changed all that. After the war, the 1949 armistice frontiers were generally accepted as legitimate. Although the U.S. refused to recognize annexation of Arab East Jerusalem, the Jewish sectors of the capital were informally accepted as part of the Jewish State. Most Arab leaders ceased their demands that Israel withdraw to the Partition borders and permit Arab refugees who lived within the armistice frontiers to return. Now pressure was exerted through the UN and the major powers to surrender territories acquired in June 1967: the West Bank, Gaza and the Golan Heights. Even PLO moderates discussed a two-state solution in which Israel would return to the pre-June 1967 borders, not to the UN Partition Plan.

Therefore, Likud moderates could argue that time played into Israel's hands. Continued occupation would eventually guarantee integration of the territories. On the other hand, any form of negotiations would stir up problems and undermine the long-term binational scheme. Militants and nationalists to the right of Likud were less patient. They too opposed any territorial concessions, but insisted that Israel announce immediately its decision not to return occupied land. Annexation would thus dispell any doubts about Israel's right to hold Judea and Samaria (West Bank), Gaza and the Golan Heights.

Both Likud moderates and militants were determined that Israel remain binationalist, notwithstanding the fact that it would entail a substantial Arab population within the pre-1967 frontiers, there was no reason why it could not deal with the larger Arab mass in Greater Israel. Few in the nationalist camp called for evacuation of Arabs from the state. Only a tiny minority supported Rabbi Meir Kahane's Kach Party in its demand for removal of all or most Arabs.

Given the sharp division of public opinion in Israel, neither the liberals nor the nationalists could prevail. While Peres might engage in summitry with Arab monarchs and presidents, there was little tangible he could offer in exchange for contractual peace agreements. These negotiaitons were not totally worthless—they served to create a less hostile enviroment and to defuse prospects for immediate renewal of war. Arab leaders who agree to engage Peres in a peace dialogue, i.e. Mubarak, Hassan and Hussein, could, it might be argued, strengthen the position of Israeli moderates. Those who persisted in maintaining the Arab diplomatic boycott only strengthened Israeli nationalists who opposed any compromise.

Until December of 1987, it was doubtful whether any Arab diplomacy, conciliatory or hostile, can at the moment swing enough of the Israeli public opinion to break the tie between moderates and nationalists. Because of the deep emotional issue of national and religious identity embodied in the territories, breaking the binational status quo is virtually impossible. Only the strongest external pressures or some unforseen internal disaster could have moved Israel from the territories.

The *Intifadeh* might have changed the firmly entrenched binational reality. The efforts of continuous subjugation of a large and militant minority, could give credence to the argument of Israeli moderates against enforced binationalism. The uprising has already increased the political standing of the Palestinians in the regional community. Syrian reconciliation with the PLO and the support of other Arab states are early indicators of a new trend. Whether violent or not, the *de facto* binational reality raises issues in Arab relations with Israel which have no parallel in their past experience. The nature of these relations can only be speculated upon as it involves many possible scenarios.

Conclusion: Looking at Regional Politics
in the Binational Era

Whether the conflict will continue in its present form or end in a peace treaty, Israel will certainly be more binational in the future than during its first two decades. If a settlement is not reached, binationalism would be built in by default. Yet, even if the map of Israel is drafted by the most accommodating political moderates, it will still include territory extending beyond the armistice lines and a significant number of Arabs.

In any event, relations with the surrounding Arab countries will be strongly affected by how future Israeli leaders deal with the binational reality of the country. If they continue repression of Palestinian national sentiment and consciousness, resistance to Jewish domination in the binational state will intensify, irredentism will become an increasingly troublesome problem, and meddling in the country's internal affairs by neighbors will be facilitated. Hostile minorities like the Druze in the Golan Heights and Palestinian nationalists in the West Bank and Gaza will become more threatening, leading to Belfastization of the entire country.

If, on the other hand, the Jewish majority agrees not only to extend the country's borders, but to peacefully integrate the population of newly acquired area, prospects for regional peace will improve.

Peaceful integration of Arabs does not necessitate diminishing Israel's Jewish or Zionist character. It would require broadening the ethnic base, recognizing that the country is Arab and Palestinian as well as Jewish and Zionist. The policies of Pierre Trudeau in dealing with ethnic strife in Canada might serve as an appropriate lesson, if not an exact model. Until Trudeau broadened the concept of Canadian identity to include both English and French the country was on the verge of civil war. Ethnic strife had reached the point where violence was common place, where civil authority in Quebec was threatened, where loyalty to the central government was questioned by a large part of the citizenry, and where cessation was threatened by one of the country's most populous and richest provinces.

Initially Canadian authorities thought to squash ethnic unrest and dissidence with usual methods: secret penetration of Quebec's nationalist front, police emergency measures including torture and imprisonment without trial, imposition of outside authority on rebellious students, etc. Many of the anti-dissident measures used by secutity authorities in Northern Ireland, Iraq, and by Israel in the West Bank, Gaza and the Golan Heights were tried in Canada, but none was as successful in defusing violence as granting French equal status with English, adopting a binational flag and giving Quebec authorities control over their own political, cultural, and economic affairs. None of the "concessions" granted by Trudeau diminished English culture or undermined national security, prestige or honor.

Can binational Israel learn from Canada? Would implementation of the UN Partition Resolution calling for equal status of Hebrew and Arabic undermine Hebrew culture? Would granting full citizenship to the million and a half Arabs under Israeli jurisdiction diminish Jewish rights? Would encouragement of Palestinian identity in any way subvert Jewish identity? Many in Israel feel threatened by the idea of broadening the ethnic base of their country, but most have not become fully aware of the threat of Belfastization.

At present the notion of fully recognizing and accommodating to the binational character of the "New Israel" seems rather outlandish to most Jews and Arabs. The concept of two fully equal nations in one land appears anachronistic, a relic of the pre-state era when idealistic romantics such as those in Hashomer Hatzair, or Ihud still had a small following. The concept of full binationalism is no longer conceivable even to those who once espoused it or to their spiritual heirs. Oddly, the idea was recently revived by a leading young West Bank nationalist identified as a PLO sympathizer, Professor Sari Nusseibeh of Beir Zeit University. The time may soon be at hand when growing integration of the territories will prompt a dramatic shift in Palestinian strategy, he advised. They may soon demand citizenship and voting rights within Israel as they shift instinctively from outright rejection to exploitation of Israel's social, economic and legal resources. How Israel's leaders adapt to this trend will probably determine whether or not it will have peace with its neighbors. For Israelis to adapt to the New Israel would require a totally different perspective of the Middle East situation. Until now most have argued that the fate of Israeli Arab citizens and those in the occupied territories depends on policies of the Arab states toward Israel. A new perception would require a different analysis in which the fate of Arabs under Israel's jurisdiction will determine Arab state policies toward Israel rather than vice versa.

Notes

1. Don Peretz, *The Middle East Today*, 4th ed. (New York: Praeger, 1982).

2. Nadav Safran, "Dimensions of the Middle East Problem," in Roy Macridis, ed., *Foreign Policy in World Politics*, 5th ed., (Englewood Cliffs, NJ: Prentice-Hall, 1985).

3. Ibid.

4. Ann Mosely Lesch, *Arab Politics in Palestine 1917–1939*, (Ithaca, NY: Cornell University Press, 1970).

5. Malcolm Kerr, *The Arab Cold War: A Study of Ideology in Politics*, 3rd ed. (New York: Oxford University Press, 1971).

6. Paul C. Noble, "The Arab System: Opportunities, Constraints and Pressures," in Baghat Korany and Ali Dessouki, ed., *The Foreign Policies of Arab States* (Boulder, Co: Westview, 1984).

7. Ibid., p. 50.

8. Ibid., pp. 60–61.

9. Aryeh Shalev, *The Autonomy: Problems and Possible Solutions*, paper No. 8, January 1980, Center for Strategic Studies, Tel-Aviv University.

10. *Jerusalem Post*, April 30, 1979.

11. Don Peretz, *The West Bank, History, Politics, Society, and Economy*, (Boulder, Co: Westview Press, 1986), p. 54.

12. *Al-Bayader Assiyasi*, Jerusalem, June 1983.

13. Michael Oren, "A Horseshow in the Glove: Milson's Year in the West Bank," in *Middle East Review*, Fall 1983, vol. xvi, no. 1, pp. 17–29.

14. Peretz, op. cit., pp. 83–86.

15. *Commentary Magazine*, May 1981.

16. *Jerusalem Post*, March 22, 1982.

17. *New York Times*, May 28, 1985.

18. Peretz, op. cit., p. 86.

19. Arthur S. Banks, ed., *Political Handbook of the World 1987*, p. 286.

20. See pact in *Survival*, International Institute of Strategic Studies, London, Nov/Dec. 1982, vol. no. 6.

21. *Jordan*, Fall/Winter 1986.

22. *Jerusalem Post Weekly*, 1343, week ending August 2, 1986.

23. *Jerusalem Post Weekly*, 1350, week ending September 20, 1986.

10

The United States and a Binational Israel

Linda B. Miller

Introduction

What difference would the emergence of a binational Israel make in the formulation and execution of American foreign policy toward the Jewish state? International relations scholars may be tempted to answer "little" or "none." Surely, this subject matter is better left to observers of comparative politics for whom the structure and processes of domestic politics are a central focus. Yet, if the line between domestic and foreign policy is blurred in the contemporary international system, as the conventional wisdom explains, then major demographic shifts in the Israeli policy may well affect the bilateral U.S.-Israel connection. Moreover, since U.S. policy toward Israel also reflects the many facets of the American Jewish community, the evolution of a binational Israel as it might shape those subnational interests could have an impact on the government-to-government relations that are a main concern of international relations specialists.

In order to delineate more precisely the probable or possible consequences of a binational Israel for the bilateral relationship between the United States and the Jewish state, it is important to assess the legacy of the Carter-Reagan era. It sets the stage for what any successor, Democrat or Republican, will confront in conceiving and implementing U.S. policies in the Middle East, especially if the next administration should decide to continue the peace process that culminated in the Israel-Egypt peace treaty in 1979, a process belatedly reactivated in the last year of the Reagan presidency.

Future American political leaders will have to consider the extent to which the two rationales for a close working relationship with Israel are still valid, namely, that the Jewish state is the only functioning democracy in the Middle East and is also a strategic asset. They must also evaluate changes within the United States, within Israel, and within the Arab world that make options other than a comprehensive regional solution to the Arab-Israeli conflict seem more attractive or realistic. Since these judgements flow from the experience of the recent past, this essay is divided into two parts. In Part 1, the Carter-Reagan record is assessed. In Part 2, the choices and constraints facing the next administration are weighed.

One assumption is that while the United States has been and will remain the most important external player in the region, its capacity to affect the overall political situation in the Middle East is subject to new challenges at home and abroad. A second assumption is that while tacit Israeli retention of the West Bank and Gaza might be tolerated, though not preferred, by American policymakers, outright annexation of the territories could create severe strains between Washington and Jerusalem with deleterious consequences for bilateral ties. But, as will be shown, this outcome is probably the least likely in the next decade because it is so divisive politically in Israel. Thus, while U.S. policymakers ought to consider it in terms of sound planning, they should be prepared to cope with less immediately threatening, yet no less serious, issues if the status quo persists.

The Carter-Reagan Record

Like their predecessors, Presidents Carter and Reagan employed the concepts of Israel as a natural, democratically and as a strategic asset to serve American interests. Used at different times by different U.S. policymakers, these two tenets have resonated in Israel and in the American Jewish community. In the interplay of American domestic politics, public opinion and bureaucratic politics, they have reinforced a definitively pro-Israel U.S. stance in some periods, for example, in the Lyndon Johnson administration. At other times, they have prevented the inevitable tensions in the bilateral relationship from escalating out of control, as in recent years. Neither Carter nor Reagan was forced by circumstances at home or within Israel to question the validity of these views, so long as neither one ignored the larger context in which the relationship with Israel develops, a context that acknowledges the importance of bilateral relations with key Arab countries, especially oil producers, and the East-West dimension of regional developments.

Both presidents discovered that while American and Israeli interests might converge in a way that would encourage intimacy between a superpower and a smaller ally, such interests could also diverge to the point of estranging the two countries. In this respect, American-Israeli relations resemble other bilateral ties. In other respects, the density of the connections between Washington and Jerusalem in the military, intelligence, economic and cultural spheres is unusual in the contemporary international system, if not unique.

Despite the similarities, it is the differences in style and substance between Carter and Reagan that have attracted more attention. President Carter presided over the Camp David accords and gave high priority to a Middle East peace process that required upgrading U.S. commitments to leading Arab countries, along with Israel. By contrast, President Reagan, apart from two efforts, downgraded the peace process and fostered unprecedented military, intelligence, and economic exchanges with Jerusalem that included elevating Israel to the status of a non-NATO ally, like Japan and Australia, and establishing a Free Trade area.

It would be misleading to conclude on the basis of this record that a close working relationship with Israel requires an American administration to reduce its interest in promoting diplomatic solutions to the Arab-Israeli conflict. Rather, it suggests that an American peacemaking effort depends first on preparing the political ground at home and second on formulating acceptable diplomatic frameworks. Equally important is the skill (or lack thereof) with which Washington plays Israel's domestic politics, as the coalition of the time develops its posture vis à vis its Arab neighbors and the Palestinians. Here, some of the similarities between the Carter and Reagan administrations are as striking as the obvious differences.

Although President Carter's initial world view favored reduced East-West tensions and President Reagan's outlook stressed the continued salience of cold war hostilities, both presidents and their entourages found balancing local, regional and global interests in the Middle East to be a frustrating experience. Both groups of U.S. policymakers tried to combine pragmatic and ideological considerations in dealing with Israel, Egypt, Jordan, Saudi Arabia, Syria, and other Arab states. Both understood the U.S. domestic value of apparent "even-handedness" in American declaratory policy in the Middle East, whatever its limits when applied in the region itself. Both discovered the hazards when the U.S. decides to act as mediator or conciliator. In such cases, local parties must be satisfied and American elites must be persuaded. Success abroad, always a tenuous prospect, does not ensure endorsement at home, or vice-versa. Both administrations realized that even if a delicate balance between external and internal prerequisites is achieved, the capacity of others to confuse U.S. objectives is large.

It is this sobering conclusion that events like civil strife in Lebanon, revolution in Iran, the Gulf war, hostage-taking and "state" terrorism have underscored. Moreover, as the Iran-contra fiasco so amply demonstrated, endemic squabbling in the American foreign policymaking establishment impedes any consistent U.S. course in bilateral or regional relationships in the Middle East. Thus, it is not surprising that the idea of Israel as both a functioning democracy and a strategic asset has appealed to American executive and legislative leaders seeking some measure of predictability in an otherwise chaotic geographical area. Some of the same unsettling developments, especially the merging of the the Gulf and Arab-Israeli conflicts, formerly kept separate by Washington, have placed the bilateral relationship under stress and raised questions about the vitality of the two guiding principles reinforced by the Carter and Reagan presidencies.

Both administrations found that, as in other parts of the world, the gap between American objectives and the instruments available to realize them is widening in the Middle East. Diplomacy, economic levers, arms sales and the threat of force are less successful in attaining U.S. aims than was the case twenty years ago. The addition of a newer American policy goal in the Carter-Reagan years—the prevention of the spread of Islamic fundamentalism beyond Iranian borders—has dramatized the dilemma. Indeed, this newer objective has exposed the internal inconsistencies of America's prior bedrock positions in the region, positions that have withstood a variety of upheavals. The goals of containing the Soviet Union, preserving the State of Israel and maintaining secure oil supplies are still the centerpiece of U.S. declaratory policy, however problematic they may be in the actual conduct of day-to-day relations in the region.

Worthy as these bedrock positions remain, they provide little concrete guidance when further American administrations will have to decide whether to promote a partial accommodation of competing interests in the Arab-Israeli conflict or to urge local parties to reach a general peace based on the resolution of all outstanding issues. Because President Carter was willing to pay an initial price for a highly visible role as peacemaker, he was able to force the conflict onto a regional agenda, at lease temporarily. Yet even Carter, who was personally and rhetorically committed to a regional approach to the area's future, as evidenced in the unfulfilled second part of the Camp David accords, eventually yielded to traditional U.S. geostrategic imperatives. The successful conclusion of a bilateral Israel-Egyptian peace treaty, no small achievement for any of the parties, resulted when Presidents Carter and Sadat and Prime Minister Begin transformed the Arab-Israeli conflict into a manageable interstate dispute susceptible to bargaining, rather than striving for something more—the much touted, perhaps unattainable, "comprehensive peace."

After the Iranian revolution and the invasion of Afghanistan near the end of his presidency, President Carter placed more emphasis on the Soviet threat and down played the Palestinian issue in favor of strengthening state-to-state relations with a number of Middle East countries. This latter approach characterized President Reagan's two terms. U.S. officials saw little advantage in criticizing the excesses of the Begin government when it articulated its historical or other claims to the occupied territories. Indeed, many observers, no doubt exaggerating American influence on Israel, believe that Washington's apparent indifference emboldened the Begin government to undertake the Lebanon invasion. This conclusion downgrades Israel's own political dynamic, one that was leading to a more agggressive posture toward the Lebanon strife, whatever Washington might advise. In any event, the Reagan world view, with its misguided emphasis on an anti-Soviet Middle East strategic consensus of Israel, Egypt, Jordan and Saudi Arabia, appeared to countenance Israel's claims to disputed lands, a posture that the Begin government used to its short-term advantage.

Not surprisingly, U.S. attempts to resolve the Arab-Israeli conflict from September 1982 onward proceeded to place a high value on better Israeli-Jordanian relations as the vehicle for peaceful change on the West Bank and Gaza. Although rejected by Jerusalem as "poorly timed," Reagan's peace plan, with its preference for the Jordanian option, eschewed any U.S. interest in a broader diplomatic framework emphasizing the Palestinian dimension of the conflict, and fostered the most elaborate U.S.-Israeli relationship achieved since the founding of the State in 1948.

With the perspective of a decade, it is easier to understand why, after Camp David, any subsequent efforts to move beyond an end to belligerency between Cairo and Jerusalem failed. The Begin and Shamir Likud governments were obdurate in refusing to make additional territorial concessions, while Arab governments continued to focus on their own, chiefly domestic, priorities. Neither the Carter nor Reagan policymakers found the appropriate mix of carrots and sticks necessary to prod King Hussein to enter the peace process, with or without some form of Palestinian participation. While the Carter group was slow to acknowledge that the Palestinian movement would remain internally fragmented and therefore incapable of mounting a sustained diplomatic-military position in the Middle East, the Reagan assemblage, was quicker to recognize that an Israel weakened economically, militarily, politically and psychologically, would be a heavier burden for the United States in the post-Vietnam era, and that a restatement of the Palestinian question was likely to cloud, but not really change, the basic issue of whether the Arab states would accept or reject a non-Muslim, Jewish state in the Middle East.

In keeping with its greater willingness to accept at face value prevailing Israeli government statements of Israel's security requirements, based on retaining part or all of the West Bank, until 1988, the Reagan administration was more willing to await the proper political atmosphere, perhaps a Labor majority in the coalition in 1988 or earlier, before discussing a "comprehensive," "final," settlement, covering withdrawal from occupied territories, a contractual peace, and border guarantees, at an international conference or elsewhere. The Republicans seemed to understand the extent to which both Arabs and Israelis might wonder who would guarantee the guarantor, if the U.S. did succeed in extracting territorial concessions from Israel on the basis of vague U.S. commitments.

Characteristically, when Secretary of State George Shultz tried to revive the peace process in the wake of the violent protests in Gaza and the West Bank in 1987–1988, his plan stressed the trade of territories for peace in a staged fashion under the aegis of the United States, essentially the position the Democrats embraced. No U.S. policymakers while in office have admitted publicly that the land for peace formula might have been overtaken by economic or political trends on the West Bank and Gaza.

Shultz's proposal for interlocking negotiations based on the formulas of an international conference, direct Israel-Jordan-Palestine talks and arrangements for the final status of the territories evoked Arab rejection of the Camp David scenario and Likud rejection of any efforts to move beyond bilateral Jerusalem-Amman accords. Predictably, and probably correctly under the circumstances, the U.S. refused to link acceptance of its rapidly cobbled-together proposals to the signing of a final memorandum of agreement that would institutionalize U.S.-Israeli military and strategic cooperation beyond the Reagan years.

As the Reagan administration drew to a close in the wake of the Iran-contra scandal, it bequeathed to its successor a number of persistent problems in U.S. Mideast policy, including: (1) Arab factionalism that is capable of undermining any settlement; (2) cyclical splitting and reforming of Palestinian political groups within the intricate Syria-Egypt-Saudi Arabia triangle; (3) virulent anti-Western and anti-American biases, fears and phobias that internally insecure Arab regimes displace onto Israel as a symbol of "colonialism" and "imperialism." Although any of these structural problems could discourage U.S. attempts to revive the peace process, an equally vital obstacle are persistent internal conflicts in Israel, pitting annexationists versus accommodationists on West Bank and Gaza issues.

The Carter-Reagan record is instructive in terms of how well or badly the two administrations played Israeli domestic politics to serve American interests while, simultaneously, Israeli leaders played America's domestic politics to their advantage. Although both Carter and Reagan exhibited maladroitness in dealing with the Rabin and Begin governments respectively, there were break throughs for Carter at Camp David, and for Reagan after Jerusalem's rejection of his 1982 peace plan. Reagan managed to speak to Labor's interest in a territorial compromise with Jordan and encouraged other Arab states to pursue a diplomatic solution with Israel. More important, the President was responding to the demands of American electoral politics by enhancing his own credibility at home though espousing the cause of peace. He wisely refused to reduce military or economic aid to Israel, a move that would have justified an even harder line in Jerusalem, and touched off alarm bells in Congress and Jewish community.

On balance, the Reagan experience in dealing with Israel is best described as erratic. As Barry Rubin observes:

American vacillation over bilateral relations affected Israel's political culture adversely. Since Israel was afraid of what the United States might do, it repeatedly acted quickly to grab any possible advantage during periods of apparent American support. The September 1981 strategic understanding was a good example of the effect of administration policy shifts, which inspired neither concessions nor restraint from Israel. As Shlomo Avineri, former Director-General of Israel's Foreign Ministry, wrote, "It just does not reflect seriousness of purpose when the United States hastily signs a strategic memorandum of understanding with Israel merely to placate the Israelis in the wake of the AWACS sale to Saudi Arabia and then, just as hastily, voids the understanding after Israel's de facto annexation of the Golan Heights."[1]

A similar lack of subtlety in Washington was noticeable in the scapegoating of Israel by some U.S. officials at various times during the protracted unraveling of the Iran-contra affair. This bungled effort compounded the bad judgement some American zealots had demonstrated in pushing arms sales to Iran in the first place, with or without Israel's encouragement to do so.

Of course, playing domestic politics is a two-way street. For every American attempt to shape the content of the bilateral relationship, there are corresponding Israeli efforts. Sometimes both sides miscalculate. The Jonathan Pollard spy affair is the most egregious recent example of such miscalculation on Israel's part. That the bilateral relationship may surmount these mistakes, albeit with difficulty, testifies to the mutual benefits each country derives, with leaders on both sides appreciating the resources each brings to the connection. Every U.S. administration, those of Carter and Reagan included, has sometimes underestimated Jerusalem's capacity to use its clout in Congress, in the American Jewish community, and in the media to maintain high levels of foreign aid and to resist pressures to withdraw to the 1967 lines on terms imposed by Washington. While some presidents, including Carter and Reagan, have found ways to exploit personal relationships between Israel's ambassadors and some American secretaries of state for U.S. goals, they do so with respect for the powerful, if latent, instruments Israel's leaders may employ in order to stave off unwelcome pressures from the Executive Branch or Congress.[2]

Within the fluid boundaries of friendship that characterize the bilateral relationship, ties have now intensified to include military and intelligence cooperation, joint planning, advanced weapons research, and anti-terrorism training. These tighter links have given the U.S. considerable, but narrow, leverage, principally on the pragmatically inclined Labor members of the Government of National Unity. Thus, after many months, Washington was able to put decisive pressure on the Israeli cabinet in order to get the Lavi fighter project dropped, when the projected expenses mounted. Washington is expected to help the coalition bear the costs by extending offset agreements for the purchase of U.S. arms and by increasing the amount of U.S. aid Israel may spend at home, a tradeoff deemed "unreasonable" by some U.S. bureaucrats and Congressmen, but one likely to obtain anyway.

This American influence in the defense and security realm does not necessarily carry over into the political realm. Indeed, by compartmentalizing the bilateral relationship more successfully than the Carter administration, the Reagan administration helped revive Israel's economy and later confined the damage caused by the Pollard spy case and Israel's role in the Iran-contra scandal. During a year of intricate manuevering when Israeli politicians worried about the implications of a Hussein-Arafat accord, the U.S. reluctantly embraced the idea of an international conference, while holding fast to its 1975 pledges not to deal directly with the PLO, unless or until it accepted Security Council Resolutions 242 and 338. Israel's Government of National unity could take considerable satisfaction in Washington's sympathetic support at the highest level, despite the fact that such support remained essentially untested on the thorny question of Jerusalem's annexation of the occupied territories.

The fact that the U.S. abstained rather than exercise its veto on a U.N. Security Council Resolution castigating Israel for its handling of the December uprising on the West Bank and Gaza produced predictable consternation in Jerusalem, as did Washington's support of a second resolution deploring Israel's planned deportation of protest leaders. These acts reflected unhappiness with the competing pressures placed on Washington, not a wholesale shift in the Reagan administration's priorities in the Middle East.

The Carter-Reagan record reveals that in the absence of a shooting war in the Middle East, American commitments could and would grow to Israel, Egypt and Saudi Arabi as the cost of preserving an uneasy status quo. Future American leaders will find the burden as heavy if not heavier, but still preferable to bearing the devastation of a shooting war. U.S. policymakers wanting to take a fresh look at the prospects for a comprehensive peace as a desirable alternative to such a prospect are likely to discover that the opportunity to press Israel's coalition is infrequent, whatever its particular composition. Both Carter and Reagan had to temper verbal attacks on Jerusalem during the Lebanon war and after Israel's strikes against the Iraqi nuclear reactor or the PLO camp in Tunisia. Both learned that threats to reduce foreign aid or to take other direct action against Israel could back fire in Congress. Instead, American leaders delayed arms shipments or technology transfers to get their message across.

Both administrations were slow to admit that the vast stores of American weaponry in Arab hands provided little U.S. influence on "moderate" Arab regimes. Both footdragged on the need to divorce the question of an Arab-

trapped in a civil war, would constitute a wild card in predicting future U.S. responses.

What these admittedly crude measures of opinion suggest is that after the Lebanon war, American expectations about Israel increasingly rest on the region's turmoil remaining within bounds that the local parties may manage themselves, without requiring American troops to keep the peace, and without embroiling the United States in conflicts with the Soviet Union. The peace with Egypt and the absence of Arab negotiating partners beyond Cairo have given Israel significant room to consolidate a closer tie with Washington. Insofar as that relationship is seen by the American public and its leaders to rest on trust, additional strains, like those caused by the Pollard and Iran-contra affairs, could be very damaging to Israel in both the American community at large and even more so in parts of the American Jewish comunity, which generally is accustomed to airing its criticisms of Israel's mistakes privately, but increasingly is willing to speak out publicly.

A consequential change in approach has been signalled by the announcement of the American Jewish Congress that it would support Shimon Peres' efforts to take Israel into an international conference with Jordan that could result interritorial concessions on the West Bank and Gaza. Notable in this unprecedented statement was the assertion that Israel would have to choose between remaining a Jewish state based on democratic value or becoming a non-Jewish, non-democratic state, if it retained the occupied territories in the face of a rising Arab population. Also remarkable, given the source, was the recognition that Israel and the territories have become a defacto binational state, with different laws and rules for Jews and Arabs,[8] a condition dramatized by the West Bank and Gaza riots and the sympathy strikes of Israeli Arabs. These sentiments, echoed by some Reform Jewish leaders of the Union of American Hebrew Congregations, are, in effect, a call for more effective leadership in both Israel and in the Palestinian community, leadership capable of dealing with fundamentalist threats to Arab-Jewish co-existence in Israel. Other parts of the American Jewish establishment have refused to go along with this break with official Jewish policy, citing the need for Israel to maintain sole responsibility for the security of the Jewish state and to make their decisions at their own ballot box.

Potentially more important and a sign of growing disenchantment with Likud's perceived obduracy was the publication of a letter signed by 30 U.S. Senators, including several prominent Jewish representatives, supporting Labor's willingness to go beyond the status quo toward territorial compromise. If nothing else, these American reactions, unofficial and official, may have the net effect of forcing the territorial question on the Israeli electoral agenda as soon as 1988.

However the American Jewish community handles the debate over retaining or annexing the territories in terms of Israel becoming a defacto binational state and thereby sacrificing both democratic values and its Jewish character, an issue of equal concern in the American policymaking debate will be the fate of the U.S.-Israeli strategic relationship. Signs of a willingness to re-examine the existing rationale are appearing. Those who worry that much myth making has accompanied the murky definition of mutual military cooperation point out the excessive dependence on Washington that Israel's receipt of massive foreign aid has engendered. Noting that some of this aid has been used to strengthen Israel's hold on the West Bank and Gaza, such critics accept Israel's security needs vis à vis Syria and Iraq, while remaining troubled by the assymetry of the obligations between the U.S. and Israel.

Arguing that Israel is unlikely to use its ground or even air forces to help the U.S. in the admittedly unlikely event of Soviet incursions in the the Gulf, they also doubt that Israel could repeat its role in the 1970 Jordanian civil war, should a similar situation arise. In their eyes, Israel is a burden for Washington rather than an asset and an obstacle to America's attempts to upgrade U. S. military links with Jordan and Saudi Arabia. While these attitudes are not necessarily widely shared, they do appear in forums where U.S. policy is debated actively.[9]

Significantly, there is also a parallel discussion in Israel that questions the utility of too great a dependence of Jerusalem upon Washington. That neither strategic cooperation nor the free trade area were debated in the Israeli Knesset is worrisome to those who believe that Israel needs to broaden its contacts with Western Europe and Japan, along with Black Africa and Eastern Europe. Although the American connection could play some role in the next Israel election campaign in 1988, any distancing of Israel from America on Israel's part is apt to be carefully measured if it occurs at all. Nevertheless, the questioning of the relationship is itself important.

Any U.S. administration interested in moving the Arab-Israeli conflict off dead center could find in these shifts of opinion a basis for readjusting its political and psychological commitments to Israel. Without another round of fighting between Israel and its Arab neighbors, no American president, particularly one newly in office, is likely to risk personal prestige in a peace making effort based on such permutations. Much more likely to occur is some reappraisal of the relative costs and benefits to the United States of assuming a cautious approach, allowing events to take their course, as opposed to assuming a higher profile, aimed at pushing ahead with an international conference or similar effort at a political settlement to the Arab-Israeli conflict.

The first approach will commend itself to U.S. policymakers who believe that the local parties, no matter how divided or adversarial, must take the lead in the peace process. The U.S. may then assist, or implement, as circumstances warrant. Those of this persuasion will stress that, in the five-year interval, during which the Camp David autonomy plan for the West Bank and Gaza remained a peace of paper, the Arab-Israeli conflict as an interstate conflict actually receded in ways that permitted the Palestinian issue to become more of an internal matter for the Israeli polity, like electoral reform or the internescine battles between religious and secular Jews. Israel's security requirements on the West Bank versus historical or religious claims to the land have been subjected to more careful scrutiny at home, though not yet to the direct decisions of the Israeli voters, an evolution that is logical.

From the American point of view, the fact that such scrutiny has resulted in further polarization of the Israeli electorate is itself sufficient reason for allowing the 1988 elections in Israel to shape the pace of U.S. peacemaking efforts. Should the outcome return a Likud-based coalition to power, with Labor in opposition, little is to be gained by forcing on Jerusalem American notions of territorial compromise. On the other hand, in the unlikely event that Labor will be able to form a narrow coalition, renewed talk of "time running out" should be expected in both Washington and Jerusalem. The need to pressure Hussein to reach accomodation before Jewish settlement or infra-structure proceeds (if it hasn't already) to the point of "irreversibility" on the West Bank will be voiced.[10] Should some variant of the 1984 Government of National Unity be returned to power, the advocates of caution would seem vindicated. Of course, continued stalemate would not enhance peace prospects, but the U.S. administration could focus whatever energy it chose to invest on improving Soviet-American relations as a necessary precondition of a distant, international conference, while at the same time endorsing the functional cooperation between Israel and Jordan that is developing on the West Bank.

In fact, a tacit accord rather than a formal treaty, could better serve American interests, if it allowed Hussein or the Palestinians to manage daily life while Israel controls security and the Jewish population. In due course, the possibilities of an independent Palestinian entity might fade, as local Palestinians devoted their political ambitions to securing recognition on an equal footing with Jews in Israeli political life, rather than in a separate state. The fact that this scenario presumes the premature demise of extremism on all sides is precisely what makes it attractive to American leaders, since they will find their preferences increasingly challenged by Jewish fundamentalism and Palestinian nationalism in the absence of a settlement.

Whatever its limitations, this cautious approach is one that would not rule out a bolder American role later on. In the interim, the internalization of the future of the territories within the Israeli polity should persuade at least some Israelis that maximalist demands must be abandoned and the psychological ground be prepared for mutual recognition of Jewish and Arab needs and aspirations.[11] This process should advance before the complex issues to be dealt with at a formal conference—borders and Jerusalem, for example, may be raised. There is always the danger that the absence of outside pressures, from Washington or the Arab states, will stimulate extremists on all sides. Israel, a pluralistic state, could become more xenophobic and subject to internal violence, paradoxically, just when additional Arab leaders or even local Palestinians may be willing to "accept" Israel—albeit grudgingly, silently, if the onerous parts of occupation are lifted. The cautious approach, giving fuller expression to local players, is not without its risks, since it appears to feed on both immobilism in Israeli coalition politics and radicalism in Gush Emunim or other fanatical annexationist groups on the Israeli right. But it may be the best of the available options, as binationalism becomes a fact rather than a potential threat.

As the Carter-Reagan record demonstrates, since peace proposals are good politics domestically, a future administration, if not preoccupied with crisis-coping elsewhere on the globe, might take a bolder approach than its predecessors, perhaps one that would acknowledge publicly the quasi-permanence of Israel's occupation, achieved through a combination of Israeli and Arab intransigence. American leaders could then throw their diplomatic support to Palestinian political demands for fuller participation in the Knesset and Israeli society generally. Since much of this scenario would be equally unpleasant for both Israel and the Palestinians, the old formula of land for peace as an alternative to a binational state might then look more attractive, and all parties would willingly go forward to an international conference where better U.S.-Soviet relations might encourage the appearance of superpower joint efforts to underwrite a political solution.

Of course, appearances are not reality, even in the Middle East. General Secretary Gorbachev, like his predecessors, is striving to limit Soviet collaboration with the United States to arms control rather than accept abroad agenda that includes co-managed regional settlements. On the other hand, Moscow is actively trying to maximize its influence in the Middle East with all players by taking a pragmatic rather than ideological approach.[12] Thus, the possibility of a joint superpower undertaking in the Middle East could seem less far fetched, if Israel is able to restore diplomatic relations, not only with key East European countries, but also with Moscow itself, as a prelude to increased Jewish emigration. Nevertheless, any future peacemaking efforts along these lines would have to recognize that a return to the Carter-Sadat-Begin leadership configuration that ultimately salvaged agreement from what also looked like an unpromising set of circumstances in the late 1970s is unlikely. Of course, advocates of a more active U.S. role maintain that the absence of visionary political leadership should not preclude bolder American efforts to bring the parties together now. The difficulty is that supporters of a more aggressive U.S. role in the formal peace process are unable to show that strictly American initiatives are needed to advance U.S. regional or global interests when other avenues are available. Quite the contrary.

Ironically, during the absence of forward movement in the formal peace process in recent years, U.S.-Iraqi relations were resumed, as were Jordan-Egyptian relations. A de facto Israeli-Syrian arrangement held in Lebanon. With Egypt's return to the Arab fold, after the 1987 Amman summit, symbolized by the restoration of full diplomatic relations with a host of other Arab countries on the basis of an anti-fundamentalist stance, a greater realism may develop vis à vis Israel and the presumed threat it poses to Arab states. In a parallel development, some Israel political figures are reassessing their own geopolitical strategy, one premised on aiding Iran. The old Ben-Gurion doctrine of anti-Arab alignments with Ethiopia, Turkey and Iran is correctly perceived by at least some Israeli Labor leaders, like Shimon Peres, as dated, despite the fact that the peace with Egypt they favored has fallen far short of Israeli expectations.

At this juncture, tacit informal contacts may be more effective techniques than formal diplomatic negotiations in the Arab-Israeli conflict, so long as deadlock prevails in Israeli domestic politics and intercommunal warfare is stressed rather than the ever-present, if somewhat dimished, external threat to Israel's existence. For intercommunal conflict is not necessarily susceptible to outside mediation, especially "when fundamental issues of identity and legitimacy are involved,"[13] as they are increasingly in Israel.

Conclusion

Clearly, the choices and constraints for the United States in the bilateral relationship with Israel are affected to a degree by the advent of a binational state in Israel, just as they are affected by U.S. relations with key Arab states and the Soviet Union. Binationalism is primarily an Israeli problem, not an international one demanding immediate American diplomatic or military intervention. Yet, because no Arab country will ever concede the West Bank to Israel and because this position is supported by a large number of third world and Communist countries in the U.N. and elsewhere, when outbreaks of violence in the territories and Israeli reprisals recur, they challenge the guiding precepts of U.S. policy that Presidents Carter and Reagan endorsed.

If Israel came to be seen in the United States as an unreliable ally or as a repressive society a fractious situation will arise in the U.S.-Israeli relationship. Nevertheless, given the inertia that marks U.S. foreign policy, it would take a more direct threat than binationalism in Israel to make severe shifts at the executive level in the bilateral relationship a reality. Rather, a gradual erosion of support for Israel in Congress, in the American Jewish community, is a more likely prospect, if binationalism is seen to undermine the foundations of Israel as a democratic, Jewish state. Here, too, Israel's traditional capacity to play American domestic politics should not be underestimated. An Israeli coalition willing to revisit "older" solutions, like Begin's autonomy plan for the West Bank and Gaza, might be enough to satisfy what ever American demands might ensue if worries about binationalism grow in Washington or elsewhere in the United States, especially in the Jewish community.

In the meantime, it behooves those American political figures cognizant of the dangers of political extremism to take opportunities to reinforce the democratic values both countries share in public speeches and in private conversations with Israeli leaders.[14] It also behooves Americans, in and out of government, Jewish and non-Jewish, to insist that the Arab-Israeli conflict is susceptible to bargaining, hence compromise, rather than the manifestation of a Manichean struggle. In concrete terms, if the timing is right, the agenda for the next administration should include support for the type of international conference that both Israel and Jordan could approve, one stressing direct talks, mutual recognition, and resolution of the Palestinian problem, without superpower vetoes. The agenda should also include support for other, less formal contacts that, over time, could help create the conditions under which a formal conference might succeed.

By definition, America will continue to play Israel's domestic politics, whether it wishes to or not, just as Israel will play America's. The question is whether a new administration will do so cleverly or haphazardly, advancing mutual interests or driving wedges between Washington and Jerusalem, as both countries try to sort out domestic priorities and international obligations. As events continue to demonstrate, the status quo is increasingly ugly and unsatisfactory for many key players in the Arab-Israeli conflict. Thus, without knowing the outcome of negotiations, the United States may do a service by rejuvenating the peace process in some guise. It would seem that

> when the communications between capitals ceased, when there were no more feelers, no more trial ballons in the poisoned air, no more high-level insistence on the imminence of developments, there was violence. For the Palestinians,

the absence of politics means continued misery and marginality. For the Israelis the absence of politics means a morally corroding occupation.[15]

Even if such U.S. gestures do nothing more than reveal once again the deep and abiding Arab hatred of Israel, the air will be cleared and the prospects for reconciliation or adjustments to newer conditions on the ground will beclarified.[16] At the same time, the consequences for Israel of basing its occupation of the territories on compromised standards of behavior it would not tolerate "at home" will be more starkly exposed, perhaps a precondition of a new realism in Jerusalem.

Notes

1. Barry Rubin, "The Reagan Administration and the Middle East," in Kenneth Oye, et al., eds. *Eagle Resurgent*, (Boston: Little, Brown and Company, 1987), p. 442.

2. For additional details, see Wolf Blitzer, *Between Washington and Jerusalem*, (New York: Oxford University Press, 1985), Chapters 2 and 10.

3. Examples of this vocabulary are found in op-ed "opinion" columns by David Smith and Douglas MacArthur II, in the *Christian Science Monitor*, editions of March 31, 1987, and September 16, 1987.

4. See Charles Mathias, Jr., "The Dangers of Disengagement," *Foreign Policy*, Summer, 1986,pp. 169–181.

5. This argument is advanced in Farid-el-Khazen, "The Middle East in Strategic Retreat," *Foreign Policy*, Fall, 1986, pp. 140–160.

6. Nimrod Novick, *The United States and Israel*, (Boulder: Westview Press, 1986), p. 138.

7. John Reilly, "America's State of Mind," *Foreign Policy*, Summer, 1987, pp. 39–56. See also Eytan Gilboa, *American Public Opinion toward Israel and the Arab-Israeli Conflict*, (Lexington, Mass: D.C.Heath, 1987).

8. *New York Times*, September 22, 1987, p. 9. For projected population figures and political implications, see *New York Times*, October 19, 1987, p. 1. Counterevidence that Israeli and Arab birthrates are remaining stable is given in Meron Benvenisti, *West Bank Data Project*, 1983.

9. See, for example, Harry J. Shaw, "Strategic Dissensus," *Foreign Policy*, Winter, 1985–86, pp.125–141.

10. On this controversial point, see Meron Benvenisti, *Conflicts and Contradictions*, (New York: Willard Books, 1986).

11. Such an approach is advocated by Mordechai Bar-On in "Peace Politics in Israel: From Sadat to Hussein," International Center for Peace in the Middle East, Discussion Paper No. 10, May 1986.

12. For an elaboration of this argument, see Galia Golan, "Gorbachev's Middle East Strategy," *Foreign Affairs*, Fall, 1987, pp.141–157.

13. Meron Benvenisti, "New Act, Old Tragedy," *The New York Times*, January 5, 1988.

14. A convincing case for this posture is presented in Ian Lustick, "Israel's Dangerous Fundamentalists," *Foreign Policy*, Fall, 1987, pp. 118–139.

15. "Delirious Palestinians, Sullen Israelis," *The New Republic*, January 18, 1988, p. 11.

16. See Ze'ev Schiff, "U.S. and Israel: Friendship Under Strain," *The National Interest*, Winter, 1987–1988, pp. 3–12.

11

Epilogue: The Future of Binational Israel—Beyond the Winter of Discontent

Ilan Peleg

Ten years ago a diplomatic revolution occurred in the Middle East: the most powerful Arab state, Egypt, signed a peace treaty with Israel and thus declared, in effect, that it would no longer be involved in future Arab-Israeli wars. Egypt kept its commitment despite the ascendance of a new president (Mubarak) and a series of Israeli actions perceived by many Egyptians as provocative (e.g. the destruction of Iraq's nuclear reactor and the invasion of Lebanon). Yet, a decade after the momentous Camp David Accords led to the first tangible results of the peace process—the return of a demilitarized Sinai to Egypt and the establishment of a full-fledged peace between Egypt and Israel—it does not seem as if the region is closer to a fundamental solution of its problems.

Egypt's withdrawal from active participation in the Arab-Israeli conflict did not signal an end to the dispute: it indicated merely a transformation in the *nature* of the conflict. The conflict between the Arab states (and their military organizations) and Israel has receded in intensity since Camp David: in fact, no total war has been fought between Israel and an Arab state since October of 1973, the Lebanese confrontation being mainly an Israeli-Palestinian clash accompanied by a partial collision between elements of the IDF and the Syrian army. Furthermore, the last decade has seen a decline in the number of attacks on Israel from Arab territory and, equally important, a growing Arab willingness to accept Israel as a political *fait acompli* in the region, if not to establish full-fledged peace with the Jewish state.

Interestingly enough, since the Lebanon war, even the intensity of the confrontation between Israel and the PLO has declined. As the clash between Israel and the Arab states, the collision between Israel and the

PLO has also resulted in an overwhelming military (although not political) Israeli victory. Israel's invasion of Lebanon led to the loss of a territorial base for the PLO, a base necessary for launching its attacks on Israel. The PLO-Israeli military conflict ceased to be the central fact defining the hostility between the parties, opening the stage for new forms of hostile relations.

As the interstate conflict between Israel and its Arab neighbors subsided, and as the effectiveness of the PLO challenge to Israel's power declined, a new form of confrontation emerged: a Palestinian-Israeli *intercommunal confrontation*. The intercommual clash, hidden and unrecognized for a long time, suddenly burst to the fore in December 1987, ushering in the winter of discontent.

The Palestinian Uprising

The state of Israel, emerging following a long-fought struggle, has been perceived by its citizens and leadership, and by most people in the world, as an entity fulfilling two roles. First, it appeared on the stage of history in order to serve as a safe haven for Jews, a role which the state of Israel took upon itself enthusiastically in 1950 when it adopted the Law of Return, making it possible for every Jew to immigrate and claim an Israeli citizenship with no delays or hardships. The "Jewish" role of Israel's mission was part and parcel of the original Zionist dream as formulated by Theodore Herzl in the first Zionist Congress (Basle, 1897).

The state of Israel, and the pre-state Jewish institutions, however, had another fundamental characteristic, a trait originally perceived as most compatible with the Jewish mission of the state. From its early days the Jewish state was perceived as truly committted to the ideals of democracy, equality, and civil and human rights. To the extent to which there were deviations from these ideals, these deviations resulted from an unauthorized action (as in the Etzel-Lechi assault on Deir Yassin about a month prior to the establishment of Israel), an action perceived as required by security considerations (as in the case of imposing military rule, until 1966, on large number of Arabs), or arrangements reflecting the unique character of the new state (as in the case of transferring jurisdiction in personal matters to religious courts). Futhermore, many Israelis (notably David Ben-Gurion and his labor camp) and others, subscribed to the idea that the Jews ought to build a model society in Eretz Israel, that modern Israel (as the ancient one) must become a light unto the nations, and that the Israeli society must strive for the highest ideals of the Hebrew prophets.[1] In brief, the Zionist revolution was begun, has sustained itself and flourished to a remarkable victory in 1948 by emphasizing the *duality* of its dream: national liberation was one side of the coin; a universal message of social justice, human equality and international peace was its other side.

The violent events begun in December 1987, Israel's winter of discontent, suddenly, although not quite unexpectedly, put the Zionist dream in jeopardy. The intifadeh, the uprising of the Arab masses in the occupied territories, focused the attention of the world on Israel's character as a democratic, liberal state; it also put a question mark on the long-term survival of Israel as a Jewish state. It is still unclear how Israel's national institutions, including the army (see Peri in this volume) would react to the new reality.

In and of itself, the uprising did not change the nature of Israel's dilemma; it merely brought the dilemma into a sharper focus. The nature of the dilemma is that by 1987, merely twenty years after its smashing victory in the Six-Day War, *the Israeli polity transformed itself from a mononational to a binational entity.* By late 1987, Western Palestine (Israel proper, the West Bank and the Gaza Strip) had a binational demographic reality in which roughly 3.6 million Jews were facing about 2.2 million Arabs.[2] More importantly, not only was the relative number of Arabs on the increase, and not only was it predicted that their number will continue to rise until it equals the number of Jews sometimes at the end of the first decade of the 21st century, but the political consciousness of the Arabs, according to all observers, was also on the rise. The Arab public has been radicalized.

The uprising reflected the refusal of the Arabs in the occupied territories to continue to live under Israeli control. Insofar as many in Israel believed that such control was possible, indeed necessary, the uprising constituted a challenge of major proportions to Israel's political system, and a new challenge at that: while in 1947 and 1967 Israel's existence was challenged by outside forces (mainly that of the neighboring Arab states), in 1987 the challenge was from within, thrown at the face of a government perceiving the territories as an integral part of Israel, presented to an Israeli public which became accustomed to view the territories as part of Israel's "cognitive map."

A New Reality

The uprising was only the symptom of a growingly difficult situation, a situation in which two nations—dramatically different in their history, values and aspirations, and viewing each other with outright hostility— reside sometimes side by side and often "within" each other, in a small geographical area between the Mediterranean Sea and the Jordan River. For quite a long time these two nations had refused to recognize not only each other's national aspirations but even the legitimacy of their very existence. Thus, many Palestinians have taken the view that Judaism was merely a religion and that, therefore, Jews were not entitled to a national state. Similarly, Israel's prime minister Golda Meir and others refused not only to recognize the national rights of the Palestinians—a fundamental tenet of the Revisionist movement—but even the existence of a Palestinian nationhood. The Palestinian uprising, and in a more general way Palestinian history over the last 30 years, has done to Palestinian consciousness what Zionism and the establishment of Israel has done to the Jews: it created a sense of nationhood focused on an unrelenting claim for an independent nation-state.

Although both nations, the Israeli Jews and the Palestinian Arabs, continue to have an inherently strong inclination to deny the other's very existence— believing that any recognition of the other's legitimacy is tantamount to the invalidation of one own's claim to the land—it cannot be convincingly denied that in Western Palestine or Greater Israel today two nations reside. The Israeli Jews and the Palestinian Arabs are two distinct nations whether one looks at them in objective terms (distinct language, religion, history, and so forth) or in terms of subjective consciousness (e.g. a sense of distinct nationhood). These national groups strive for dramatically different solutions of the Israeli-Palestinian dilemma as demonstrated by the article by Inbar and Yuchtman-Yaar.

The subjective element of Palestinian nationalism has been strengthened as a result of the Arab defeats of 1948 and 1967. It was greatly reinforced by the domination of large Palestinian communities—850,000 on the West Bank, more than 550,000 in Gaza, and 700,000 or more in Israel itself— by Israeli Jews. Israel's control over territories populated by a large number of Arabs has served as a painful, daily reminder to the Palestinians that their national aspirations have not yet been fulfilled.

The eradication of the Green Line, the armistice border between Israel and the Jordanian-controlled West Bank, aggrevated the situation. It generated an unprecedented level of interaction between Arabs and Jews, occupied and occupiers, intensifying the sense of frustration among the Palestinians. It also generated interaction between Israeli Arabs and West Bankers, radicalizing the former. The dymanics of these interactions could create in the long run a separatist movement of major proportions among Israeli Arabs, a traditionally loyal minority within the Jewish state. Although the Lustick article shows the growing involvement of the Israeli Arabs within Israel's political system, if the Arabs' demands remain unfulfilled, the separatist thrust might be strengthened.

The reality of a *de facto* Greater Israel is a recipe for further radicalization. It makes it inevitable. The existence of two large groups of Palestinians under Israeli military government, one on the West Bank and one in the Gaza Strip, deprived of citizenship and under seemingly unending occupation, ought to tip the balance within the volatile Israeli Arab public toward growing nationalism.

Thoughts About Solutions

The Palestinian-Israeli dispute is possibly the single most difficult international conflict of the 20th century. Its complexity is truly enormous, its emotionalism cannot be exaggerated, and the inability of both sides to empathize with the other is legendary. Even the most optimistic, courageous and insightful analyst would find himself dealing with a Promethian task when focusing on what looks like an inherently insoluble problem.

Nevertheless, the picture is not entirely bleak, nor is it completely beyond solution. The 1967 war brought Israeli Jews and Palestinian Arabs, for the first time, into close, daily contact with each other, the type of intensive contact that is a precondition for any dialogue. Futhermore, the intensity of the Palestinian uprising, its duration, and its impact on Israel's domestic and international reality demonstrated to many in Israel that the status quo, even if it were to be theortically desirable, is fundamentally unsustainable.

The Palestinian uprising ought to be assessed within the historical context of the modern era, and the lessons of this era are unmistakenable: a nation cannot oppress for a long time the national aspirations of another nation especially when (a) these aspirations are generally shared by the vast majority of the controlled group and are recognized as legitimate by most of the world, (b) when the controlling nation has a democratic regime, and (c) when there is no overwhelming demographic dominance in favor of the controlling nation. While the USSR has the capability of controlling Estonia due to her overwhelming demographic and military dominance, Canada could continue to control Quebec since most French Canadians desire to remain as part of the union, and Spain can maintain the Basques within its territory due to lack of international legitimacy for the Basque cause, the British experience in Palestine, the French experience in Algeria and even the American experience in Vietnam demonstrate the futility of a military effort designed to curtail what is generally considered a fundamental right of any people, their right for self-determination. The recent withdrawal of Soviet forces from Afghanistan is a case in point. The principle annunciated here, the predominance of self-determination in the contemporary world, is more valid today then in any other previous historical era.

A democratic system which rests on popular support at home and depends on public opinion abroad can ill-afford to ignore the consequences of establishing unilateral control over another people. Democratic regimes are highly vulnerable to the dangers generated by continuing internal rebellion of a subordinate group widely supported by the world. Such regimes may have to choose between maintaining control over the foreign people and maintaining their democratic form of government: they will quickly learn that control and democracy are incompatible.

In view of these realities, Israel's predicament is serious and even unique. A continuing Israeli control over the West Bank and Gaza Strip must result in the intensification of the uprising in the occupied territories and the unrest among Israeli Arabs, and a growing challenge to the policy of control on the part of liberal Israelis. A continued Israeli occupation would mean that Israel would become *the only democracy in the world maintaining a military control over an occupied territory inhabited by a large number of people who actively oppose that control.* Israel's claim for being the only working democracy in the Middle East—historically valid and politically important for Israel's diplomatic effort—could then be effectively challenged. While Israel's democratic character could somehow be maintained in a situation of transitory control, it is hard to see how it could survive the effects of long-term occupation.

The Israeli control over the occupied territories complicates the otherwise uneasy relations between Arabs and Jews in Israel. The occupation makes the success of any Israeli "Arab policy" virtually impossible, since such policy ought to be based on a measure of intercommunal (Arab-Jewish) trust, and such trust will not be present if the occupation were to continue. Israeli Arabs will continue to be torn between loyalty to the state of Israel and loyalty to their brethren on the West Bank and Gaza. In the absence of a move toward the withdrawal of the occupying forces, Israeli Arabs will almost surely choose in favor of loyalty to their brethren. The Arab minority and the Jewish state are on a collision course and the collision could be averted only by a decisive move toward a resolution of the present crisis. The Palestinization of the Israeli Arab is one of Israel's most serious dangers, both as a democratic society and as a Jewish polity.

The Future

If Israel remains a binational society without becoming a binational polity its future could be put in jeopardy. Inevitably there will be growing tension between a fastly shrinking Jewish majority and an equally fastly growing Arab minority, tension accompanied by ocassional terrorist attacks, flare-ups along the borders, and severe criticism of Israel from world public opinion. The binational reality would likely turn Israel into an increasingly conflict-ridden society, less liberal, tolerant and democratic.

Above all, binationalism could strengthen Israeli psychological complexes—along with Arab complexes—making a peaceful resolution of the conflict even less likely. Since continued Israeli control over the territories will necessarily result in harsh criticism from the rest of the world, it will reinforce the sense of many Israelis that Israel is once again alone in a hostile world. The Masada complex—the sense that Israel has to withstand the world's hostility and fight, if necessary, to the very bitter end—will be deepened. A dangerous psychological cycle will be created as an addendum to Israel's control over the rebellious territories. The particularist camp in Israel (to use Seliktar's classification) would be strengthened if the occupation continues. Coercive binationalism is a Gordian knot which ought to be cut in a painful operation; if the knot is not severed, it will become increasingly tight until it may choke everyone involved.

A future, Israeli binationalist state will probably be characterized by increasingly severe waves of internally generated violence, a protracted civil war of a sort with lows and ebbs, peaks and valleys, a low-intensity conflict where the front is nowhere and everywhere, where planned and spontaneous assaults (from both sides) are mixed. On the one side of the uncertain fence in this internal conflict will be a popular army, the IDF, traditionally respected as the main institution of integration within the Israeli society but now with an increasingly controversial role. In a future, protracted conflict with the civilian population on the West Bank and Gaza Strip soldiers and officers of the IDF will have more intense moral doubts, feelings that must filter into the Israeli society as a whole. On the other side of the fence there will be a growing number of radicalized, embittered, determined Palestinians, energized by the support of other Arabs, some Jews, almost the entire outside world, but above all by the sense of their own newly-found worth, nationalistic feelings, and religious faith.

If the Israeli political leadership will be determined to keep the control over the territories at any cost, it will have to adopt Draconian means. The internal security service (the Shin Bet), already found by a Israeli board of inquiry (the Landoi Committee) to have committed atrocities, will have to intensify its actions. In an effort to shield the Jewish population from the impact of controlling the territories, it may be decided to use heavily the Border Police, where the number of Druzes serving is unproportionately large. Yet, even the Druzification of the conflict is unlikely, in the long run, to shield the Israeli population from the events in the territories.

A long, protracted civil war of the type described here is likely to become not only an inter-ethnic struggle, but inter-generational as well. A generation of young Israelis, mostly in their 20's, many of them confused and bewildered, will face a generation of Palestinians, generally younger but significantly more certain of the just nature of their claim.

Many Israelis and Israel's supporters will tend to deny the internal nature of the evolving conflict; as a psychological mechanism, the term "civil war" will remain unacceptable.[3] In frustration, accusations will be aimed at the PLO, the internal and international media, and above all the "world" who refuses to understand the security imperatives imposed on Israel. These accusations would be accompanied by harsher neasures, mostly measures designed to impose collective punishment on the restive Palestinian population.

Since human capacity for self-delusion is endless,[4] those in Israel determined to maintain control over the territories at any price are likely to find numerous explanations, excuses, and rationales in order to convince others that the conflict is easily treatable. The growing violence would be described as "passing wave" *(gal cholef)*, committed by masses who have been incited by religious preachers or outside manipulators (PLO, Arab governments), assisted or even manufactured by internal traitors (the press, the "leftists," PLOnicks or Ashafists), and made possible by the incompetence of the leadership or the inefficiency of those whose responsibility is the security of the state. Few will deal with the genuine, fundamental cause of the increasing violence in binational Israel, the nature of the polity itself.

Israel's choice is a difficult one, and it emerges out of stark realities that are only likely to get worse. Enforced binationalism breeds violence and conflict, resentment and hate, fundamentalist belief-system and radicalization. Although some may see Israel's control over the occupied territories as a precondition for containing Palestinian revolutionary fervor, and in many ways it is, in reality Israel's military rule of the territories has become, without a doubt, the prime cause for the revolutionary spirit of the West Bankers and the Gazans.

The anxieties of the Israelis over the intentions of the Palestinians are not unreasonable. They have grown out of a long-drawn conflict between the two nations, a conflict in which the Palestinians often played a destructive role. Yet, it seems that the denial of Palestinian self-determination cannot alliviate but feed the anxieties of the Israelis. The challenge facing the international community is to find mechanisms for limiting the military dimension of Palestinian existence without negating the Palestinian right for self-determination.

Binationalism Revisited

This volume on the emergence of Binational Israel demonstrates two difficulties: (a) there is still no one, agreed-upon definition of binationalism; (b) it is not clear at all whether the Israeli society today is already binational or how soon it will become one. In brief, the topic of binationalism is a difficult one, both definitionally and empricallly.

For some analysts, binationalism is a state of affairs in which two nations, living within one polity, share in the governing of that polity, equally or unequally. Binationalism thus requires that each of the national groups be recognized explicitly or implicitly as entitled to participate, as a collective, in the government of the country. This definition of binationalism implies a formal, *de jure* arrangement of the type we have in countries like Belgium or Canada, or in Cyprus in the first years of that island's independence.

It is quite clear, however, that if this is to be the guiding definition of binationalism, Israel today is not a binational state, nor is it about to become one. Even a formal annexation of the West Bank and Gaza is unlikely to enhance the status of binationalism in Israel, a country which would remain a Jewish, Zionist entity. In fact, such an act (annexation) would make binationalism even more remote insofar as it would increase the political inequality between the two national groups, Arabs and Jews.

There is, however, an alternative way of defining binationalism. Binationalism could be described not as a formal-legal power-sharing arrangement but, rather, a sociological reality, a political condition or even a dominant perception. A society with a significant number of people with divergent national or ethnic identities is a multinational society, and if there are two such groups, the society is, in essence, binational. The legal structure of a political system may or may not be compatible with the social reality prevailing within a society; often, in fact, the two are quite incompatible. While in our nationalist era there is a strong preference for the distribution of power, goods and benefits in accordance with the social reality prevailing within a society, often this is not the case at all. In brief, a binational society–in which two national groups live side by side–is not necessarily a society in which political goods are equally shared by members of the two groups, let alone by the two groups as collectives. Yet, even when such is the case, binationalism prevails.

The binational reality of Israel is interesting, complicated and extremely significant. Israel is a Jewish state: it was declared as such at birth by both the United Nations and its own Provisional Government, and it reinforced itself as such by enacting the Law of Return. Yet, the State of Israel has always recognized the existence of an Arab minority, the status of its language, the uniqueness of its religious and educational institutions, etc. The tension between the dominant, fundamental nature of Israel as a Jewish state and the status of the Arab minority as a different national group within Israel has always been there. It has intensified since the 1967 war, and even more so over the last few years.

The problem of binationalism in general and that of Israel's Arab minority in particular is a problem of power-sharing, namely, the political arrangements under which the national group lives. Within the Israeli polity of 1948-1967 this problem has never been seriously addressed. In fact, as long as the Israeli Arabs constituted a relatively small minority within Israel, there was not even a pressing need to address the problem of power sharing. As a democratic state, Israel "owed" its Arab citizens equal treatment under its laws, not a recognition as a minority entitled to special rights under a well-defined and legally binding political settlement.

The situation, however, changed dramatically over the last two decades, a change providing the impetus for this volume. Not only did Israel find itself controlling the West Bank and the Gaza Strip on their Arab populations but due to a prolonged, seemingly unending occupation the situation has acquired the characteristics of a permanent political condition. Moreover, while the Israeli Arabs were given citizenship and as individuals treated equally under the law—despite discrimination in some areas—the population in the territories has been dealt with, legally and in reality, as an occupied population.

The *de facto* "acquisition" of the West Bank and Gaza by Israel raised, then, the question of binationalism on all of its problematical nature. On the one hand, a condition of binational reality was established on the ground, with an increasing Arab minority and a decreasing Jewish majority. On the other hand, a radical inequality in terms of the distribution of political power and legal rights has been established. The incompatibility between the two conditions is the essence of Israel's binational dilemma explored by the contributors to this volume.

The result of the most recent elections in Israel (November 1, 1988) reemphasized the trend toward binationalism in Israel, not binationalism by design but binationalism by default. The continuation of the *intifadeh* demonstrates the Belfastization of the conflict, an ongoing violent struggle between two communities living within one political entity.

The processes of binationalization and Belfastization are by no means static: important changes are likely in a situation which is extremely volatile. It is possible, for example, that the Belfastization of Israel would intensify, with an increasing level of inter-communal violence. By the same token, it is possible that Israeli Arabs may vote in future elections more and more as a bloc, as a community, creating an electoral binationalism in Israel.

Notes

1. See Shlomo Aronson, "Fragmentation and Polarization in Greater Israel: Political Behavior in Perpetual Crisis," Chapter 4 in this volume.

2. *New York Times*, Dec. 27, 1987, based on CIA estimates. Although some observers (notably Rolef in this volume) limit the concept of "binationalism" to a condition of *shared* government, this is not my position: binationalism can exist within a society without being reflected in equivalent governmental arrangements.

3. Thomas Freedman, "How Long can Israel deny its civil war?" *New York Times*, Dec. 25, 1987.

4. Irving L. Janis, *Groupthink*, 2nd edition (Boston: Houghton Mifflin, 1982), and Ole R. Holsti, "The Belief System and National Images: a case study," *The Journal of Conflict Resolution*, VI, 3, 1962, pp. 244–252.

About the Editors and Contributors

Shlomo Aronson is professor of political science at the Hebrew University, Jerusalem. Among his books are *Reinhard Heydrich and the Early History of the Gestapo and the S.D.* (1972) and *Conflict and Bargaining in the Middle East* (1978) as well as a forthcoming volume on *The Nuclear Dimension of the Arab-Israeli Conflict*.

Simcha Bahiri has traditionally worked on problems of management engineering (1960–80). Since then he has devoted himself to research in "peace-oriented economics," with such organizations as Tel-Aviv University, Columbia University, The Armand Hammer Fund for Middle East Cooperation, The West Bank Data Base Project, and the International Center for Peace in the Middle East.

Michael Inbar (Ph.D., Social Relations, Johns Hopkins) has been on the faculty of the Hebrew University of Jerusalem since 1968 where he is now professor of sociology and incumbent of the Barbara and Morton Mandel Chair in Cognitive Social-Psychology and Education. Since 1984 he has been the Dean of the Faculty of Social Sciences. Dr. Inbar's publications include *Simulation and Gaming in Social Science* (co-authored with C. Stoll), *The Vulnerable Age Phenomenon*, *Ethnic Integration in Israel* (co-authored with C. Adler), and *Routine Decision-Making: The Future of Bureaucracy*. Dr. Inbar has also contributed many articles to the professional literature.

Ian S. Lustick is professor of government at Dartmouth College. He is the author of *For the Land and the Lord: Jewish Fundamentalism in Israel* (1988); *State-Building Failure in British Ireland and French Algeria* (1985); and *Arabs in the Jewish State: Israel's Control of a National Minority* (1980). He is currently writing a book comparing the British-Irish, French-Algerian, and Israeli-Palestinian relationships.

Linda B. Miller is professor and chairperson, Department of Political Science at Wellesley College. She has held research fellowships from the Council on Foreign Relations, The Rockefeller Foundation, and NATO and served as a research associate at Harvard and Princeton Universities. Her writings include books, articles, and monographs on a variety of topics in international relations, including American foreign policy, the Middle

East, European politics, energy, and international organization. Currently she is the national vice-chairperson of American Professors for Peace in the Middle East.

Ilan Peleg is professor and head, Department of Government and Law at Lafayette College in Easton, PA. He is the author of *Begin's Foreign Policy, 1977–1983: Israel's Move to the Right* (1987) and is currently working on a book on *Camp David: Diplomacy as Drama* (with A. Paul Have and David Naveh) and another on *Civil and Human Rights on the West Bank and in Gaza*. Dr. Peleg has also written numerous articles on the Arab-Israeli conflict and on other aspects of international politics.

Don Peretz is professor of political science at SUNY-Binghamton, where he is also director of the Southwest Asian-North African Program. He is the author of 10 books on the Middle East, including *The West Bank History, Society, Politics and Economics* (Westview, 1986), *Middle East Foreign Policy* (1982, with McLaurin and Snider), and *The Middle East Today* (1988, 5th ed.) as well as numerous articles.

Yoram Peri is a research fellow at the Jaffe Center for Strategic Studies at Tel-Aviv University. He is also the author of *Between Battles and Ballots: Israeli Military in Politics* (1985) as well as numerous articles. Dr. Peri specializes in military-civilian relationships, especially in Israel.

Susan Hattis Rolef is the editor of the English language monthly of the Israel Labor Movement *Spectrum*, and a regular contributor to the *Jerusalem Post*. She is author of *The Bi-National Idea in Palestine During Mandatory Times* (1970) and *The Middle East Policy of the Federal Republic of Germany* (1985) and editor of *The Dilemma of Power Sharing* (1985), *The Dilemma of Religion and Politics* (1986), and *Political Dictionary of the State of Israel* (1987).

Ofira Seliktar is an associate scholar in the Foreign Policy Research Institute in Philadelphia. She is the author of *New Zionism and the Foreign-Policy System of Israel* (1986). She also wrote papers for, among others, the *Journal of Peace Research, Political Psychology, Plural Societies, Foreign Policy, The Middle East Journal,* and *The Journal of Conflict Resolution* as well as for many edited volumes. Her areas of expertise include methodology, political psychology, and decision-making.

Lilly Weissbrod is a lecturer in sociology at the Preparatory Program of Tel-Aviv University. Her publications deal mainly with Israeli politics as a function of Zionist ideology and they have appeared in *Middle Eastern Studies, The Middle East Journal, Theory and Society, Review of Religious Research, Political Anthropoly, The Jerusalem Quarterly,* and *The Journal of Social, and Political and Economic Studies.*

Ephraim Yuchtman-Yaar (Ph.D., Social Psychology, University of Michigan), has taught as a visiting professor at the University of Michigan, Columbia University, and the University of California at Riverside. Since 1967 he has been on the faculty of Tel-Aviv University, where he is a professor of sociology and the dean of the faculty of social sciences. His research interests include the study of organizations and occupations, social inequalities, social-psychology and Israeli society. He has published in these areas extensively.

Index